DRUG LORDS OF OAKLAND

Published by CreateSpace
Available in paperback and Kindle editions
on Amazon.com

FIRST EDITION 2018

Editor & Cover Design by Terri Harper
terristranscripts@gmail.com

ISBN-13: 978-1724791566
ISBN-10: 1724791567

Library of Congress Cataloguing-in-Publication Data:
Printed in the United States of America
Bank Band$ Entertainment
PO Box 4826, Antioch, CA 94509

CW01497432

DEDICATION

This book is dedicated to

Amanda

My Mother, My Love

and to

The Streets of Oakland

that raised me

IT AIN'T NOTHIN' LIKE THE TOWN

When I'm talkin' about Gangstas,

I ain't talkin' about gang bangers,

ordinary corner hangers.

I'm talkin' about Bird Slangas,

Seagram Gangstas,

and Playas.

ALBUM Souls on Ice

Drug Lords of Oakland

The untold stories of California's most notorious Drug Kingpins of the 1970s, 80s and 90s

by Titus Lee Barnes

SPECIAL ACKNOWLEDGEMENTS

First of all, I would like to pay homage to my big cousin, Paul-Factor P-Booker, for teaching me at the ripe age of ten the definition of Town Business. Since then, I could never be nothing but an authentic Oakland, California representative. We set trends, we don't follow them.

Next, I would like to give thanks to my circle, the individuals that helped me eat throughout the years.

Special thanks to Kevin "Cuzzo Kevin" Hunt for opening so many doors for me. I could not have done it without you. I mean, really.

To the first baller chick I ever knew, Nicole Hunt, thank you for treating me like family all these years. I love you for that.

To Ronnell "Fat Twin" Brooks, the only person I knew that didn't count his money, but it was always right. You taught me so much over the years, not just about the game but about life in general. Good lookin' out.

To the one and only Willie "Snow" Hudson, the original Rubberband Man. Thank you for not just telling me what the difference was between a real nigga and a fake nigga, and for never turning your back on me when the bullets were flying and when the money stopped flowing. It's like holding a sack of flour in one hand and a key of dope in the other; you are definitely a thousand grams of pure dope. We back on Pimp Skillet.

To the mothers of my children, the two of you gave me the best gifts a man could ask for. I send you a thousand thanks.

To my children, my legacy, never exclude yourselves from all the good things that life has to offer. Always challenge yourselves to be better every day. Daddy loves you.

Last but not least, to Cee-Cee, my dearly beloved sister and second mom. If you had a place, I always had a door to close behind me. You showed me the difference between family and relatives. Love ya, sister.

To the future generations of the Town of Oakland, always remember; if it's profitable, it ain't questionable. If it's beneficial, it ain't artificial. Like Yukmouth said, leave that gang bang shit to somebody else.

Titus Lee Barnes

REST IN PEACE

Jeanette Marie Pruitt, Lanier (Bubba) Pruitt, Lorainne Renee Pruitt, Freddy Pratt Jr., Tyrone "Ty-Ty" Pratt, Stevie "Cousin" Fobbs, Green-eyed Clarence, Derlin "D-Folks" Hines, Kevin Blackman, Grady "Bo" Edwards, Camille Keith, Derrick "Fila" Turner, Tracy, James Abrams, Abram Pringle, Mike Dupree, DeMarco "Rio" Martin, Kenwell, Fat Ran 9-6, Kenny Stalker, Kevin Survine, Kenneth "Butch" Revels, Byron "Ross" Revels, Grayland 3-7, Little Miller from Ghost Town, Rappin Ron 8-8, Eric Spencer, Twon from 50th, Juan Yo, Fonz, Dino from Ghost Town, Troy Garrison, Henry Scott (the chess player), Kim "Superhands" Booker, Shawn Pickford, "Boxhead" Ray Woolridge, Acorn Suge, Champ from 50th, Bink, Big Will Harris, Highway Orv, Quaylis, Ant Patterson, Ahmad Belton, Puncho, Sam Grey, Sam Delocious, Cadillac Chad, Jacque Bastone, J. Fields, Fat Cocoa, Dante Titus, Jamie Wallace, Michael Scrilla, Mike Culpepper, Fat O.J., Young Mansion from Ghost Town, Lamar Patton, and Vance Sr. (the man who created me).

You are gone, but not forgotten.

Titus Lee Barnes

TABLE OF CONTENTS

AUTHOR'S NOTES

They say that if you want to write a book, think about a book you want to read, then write it. That is what I did with *Drug Lords of Oakland*. I wrote about the legendary figures that I grew up with, associated with, watched, admired, and respected throughout my lifetime. These individuals made phenomenal power moves and rose up out of some of the most adverse circumstances at very young ages. Unlike so many others that I've heard about from other cities and states, these soldiers didn't roll over and throw their friends, family, and counterparts under the bus when they were sent to serve decades in prison. This is a story that needed to be told; therefore, who better than myself to present this to the world with the integrity it deserves.

For those that are familiar with this history and era, I hope and (in the back of my mind know) that they will appreciate it in its entirety.

Respectfully,

Titus Lee Barnes

INTRODUCTION

Oakland, California is known as the Town to its natives. This fifty-six-square-mile city in Northern California's Bay Area has been a mecca to black folks since World War II when thousands of African American soldiers were stationed at the Oakland/Alameda Army and Naval bases. The majority of these soldiers' families were housed in West Oakland's Naval housing projects that were built specifically for this purpose. The Town also experienced a mass migration of blue collar blacks that moved westward to work at the Port of Oakland.

Seventh Street was the center of all the activity that took place in Oakland at the time. All the entertainment, clubs and restaurants were lined up and down this long strip that stretched from the base through downtown Oakland. The soldiers, the hustlers, the gamblers, the pimps, the prostitutes and drug dealers all co-existed in the Town's epicenter to ply their trades or simply to hang out. According to my grandmother and my great aunts and uncles, who were around during this era, Oakland was a beautiful town with cherry trees lining every single street. All the black folks lived on the west side and all the white folks lived on the east side. This would all become a foregone conclusion by the time my parents came of age in the 1960s when Oakland would become a political catalyst in the civil rights movement, sparking the Black Panther Party and Symbionese Liberation Army and many protests associated with those organizations. The white folks would head for the hills and the suburbs surrounding the town.

In my generation the story begins with three particular crews that were active between 1980 and 1982; A-C Mob, Broadway Hustlers, and 9-0 Lovers.

The A-C Mob acquired their title due to the fact that their turf was an actual bus line that rode up and down Telegraph Avenue and Foothill Boulevard, the 40 and 43 buses. A-C stands for Alameda County, which owned the transit line that became their namesake. The A-C Mob became legendary because they turned this bus route into a virtual hustling ground and a party all in one ride. It was nothing to get on board and see several A-C Mobsters all the way in the back of the bus with perms, waves and Shirley Temple curls in their hair, wearing Levi's 501 jeans and alligator shirts, with school boy glasses and surfer tennis shoes. They all went by names such as Sir Den Fin, Sir Demon

Den, and Sir Break-A-Bitch, to name a few. They etched their names on every bus bench and window next to a crude drawing of a Playboy Bunny smoking a joint. A person could get on the bus and purchase a dollar joint, a stick of sherm, or mescaline, and lose their money playing Three Card Monte or Shoot the Pee all in one trip while jamming to the boom box the whole ride long.

The Broadway Hustlers hung out in downtown Oakland on Broadway at the Doggie Diner, the Roxy and the Lux Chinese Theater. Their mode of operations was doing smash-and-grabs at all the local department stores in the area like Emporium Capwell, Nordstrom, I. Magnum, Sears, and J.J. Newberry. They also sold their share of good Columbian gold weed and shrooms and were known for the occasional random beatdown of a passerby if they felt they just had it coming.

Finally, there were the 9-0 Lovers. Their territory was on a strip of Macarthur near Castlemont High. This stroll was lined with dirtbag motels for blocks. The 9-0 Lovers were more famous for their dress codes than anything else. They usually wore Pittsburgh Pirates baseball caps with stars and zodiac signs ironed on the sides, derby coats, Ken Rosewall tennis shoes, white painter gloves, and plastic clip-on name tags on their shirts. Eventually these dudes traded in the 50ls with sewed-in creases for army fatigues and black berets. They joined the Guardian Angels and attempted to become vigilante crime fighters. This didn't work out too well for them and their careers would be short-lived in every aspect of the word.

None of these crews lasted long at all, however, their names and legacies would pave the way for several notable turfs in the future. They will forever be solidified in the history of Oakland's street game for decades to come. Everybody who was anybody from the Town can attest to the fact that these were the guys that started it all.

The 69 Mob was the first big name to be spoken as far as the dope game was concerned in Oakland. This was the home of Big Fee and the infamous 69 Mob, which later gave birth to Lil D and the SNV. 69 Mob under Big Fee's reign controlled 69th Village. The 23rd Avenue Family became their worst enemy under leader Mick Mo's rule. These two factions would engage in a bloody drug war over Oakland's heroin trade in the early 1980s. Funktown USA was created by a 23rd Avenue offshoot named Big Harv. He left The Family and started his own vicious drug gang across 13th Avenue, a stone's throw away from his former boss's turf.

The 23rd Avenue area would undergo several name changes over the years. What started off as the 2-3 Family would transform into the Rollin' 20s, the Twomps, then finally become what is known to this day as the Murder Dubs, named after the worst serial killer to ever grace the streets of this neighborhood, P-Dub aka Pondo. The Murder Dubs was the biggest turf in the whole Town block for block.

The 69 Mob, the 23rd Avenue Family, and Funktown USA were the big three. They were the most notorious money making, million dollar movements that set the trends in the Town. The rest were as follows: 11-5 Sobrante Park, 9-8 Brookfield Jungle Boyz, Dag Village, Stone City, Dirt Road, the Alphabets (A,B,C,& D Streets), 99th Village, Columbia Gardens, Sunnyside, 9-6 Boss, Walnut, Pimpyville, the Rollin' 100s, 8-5 Village, 8-5 Tilts, the Mini Park, 8-Duece (MAC), Arroyo Park, 81st, 8-0, 83rd & Holly, 77th Greenside, 8-Duece (E. 14th), Rudsdale, 8-4 & Dowling, 7-6 Bandit Block, 7-Duece Lacey Street, Big Bruce Spot, the Red Fence, Favor Street, Weld Street skinny block, the Burn Outs, the Derty People, 7-1 Bammer Boyz, High Street Bank Boyz, 50th (Champ's spot), 5-0 Melrose, 4-8, 4-1 Suicide, Scursville, 38th Allendale, 38th Locos (can't forget about y'all), Jingle Town, Quince East 15th, Fruitvale Gangsters, 35th Peoples Incorporated, School Street & Plietner, Seminary and the Alvingroom and 3rd Avenue Regency Towers.

West Oakland were as follows: Ghost Town, 2-4 Village, Dogtown, 3-4 Chestnut, the Million Dollar Mill Milton St., Mead Street, the Acorns, the Hi-Rises, the Mohr Houses, Cypress Village, Campbell Village, Westwood Gardens 0-7, 14th & Peralta, Louis Lot, Isabella, Athens Street, 21st and West, Filbert Street, Linden n Myrtle Streets, 18th Street, and the Boonies, now known as the Low Bottoms.

West Oakland had the most housing projects in all of Oakland. New Side Oakland is how north Oakland was originally referred to. Bushrod 5900 was the oldest and most respected turf in the north side, then there was 63rd, Roachville, Goldenville, 45th Market, Keller Plaza, Short Shattuck, the Wild Wild Web, Apgar APG, 55th and Gaskill, Pearl Street, and Tray Seven.

These were all the original and reputable turfs in east, west and north Oakland. No Crips, no Bloods. Strictly Town Bizness. That's it. WELCOME TO OAKLAND.

CHAPTER 1 --BIG FEE

Big Fee was undisputedly the Godfather of Oakland, California. The town was predominately black at the time of his reign, giving the city the distinct title of the Black Mecca of California. If anything hit the black market, it undoubtedly had to go through the African American community or else it wouldn't happen. During the 1970s until the early 80s, Big Fee was The Man.

He grew up in the Acorn housing projects in West Oakland that covered a six block radius consisting of Market, Filbert, Linden, Myrtle, and Adeline Streets, bordered by 10th and 8th Streets. This was where an adolescent Fee was exposed to the elements that every major ghetto had to offer; dope fiends, drunks, pimps, whores, crooked cops, robbers and killas. The Cornfields was a hotbed for all of the above.

Big Fee was smart, though. He attended high school in Berkeley, affectionately called BizerkIey because of all the strange stuff that was allowed to go on there. It was an offshoot of the peace, love, and happiness movement that was going on in San Francisco at the time. It was also a college town. Cal Berkeley was just a hop, skip and a jump from the high school.

Uptown Berkeley was where everything went down. People's Park was an open air drug market and hippie hangout. Big Fee got his feet wet in the weed game at school by selling joints to his classmates. He kept his grades up and managed to graduate with his class.

Eventually his momma (Big Momma) moved him and his siblings to East Oakland to the San Antonio Villa, known as the 69th Village. These projects were in actual walking distance to the Oakland Coliseum and the Oracle Arena where the Raiders, the A's, and Warriors play. The Coliseum BART station separated the two locations with two rows of elevated track that looked down on San Leandro Boulevard.

Connecting the two is an overpass that connects the BART station to the coliseum complex. People from all over Northern California frequent this complex regularly to attend games. All nationalities. It didn't take long for these attendees to find out where the good stuff was at, right across the tracks in the Village. The drug of choice at the time was heroin, sometimes referred to as dog food, hooch, or hop.

Big Fee dabbled a little in pimpin', but quickly figured out that there was much more money to be made in the dope game. The nearest track to his projects was East 14th Street. The majority of all the hookers, pimps and tricks all used heroin. This shit had virtually turned into an epidemic. It didn't take a rocket scientist to figure out the get down. It all made sense to Big Fee. He could see the potential profits to be made from all the different types of individuals tip-toeing through the Village to get their fix of whatever their drug of choice was. There were doctors, lawyers, scientists, people of all occupations. Whites, Asians, Hispanics, and people from all walks of life. The Bay Area was one of the most drug promiscuous environments in the United States.

He already had the location at his disposal. Now all he had to do was get his game plan together and assemble his team. The good news was that 69th Village had a sister complex called Lockwood Gardens, or 65th Village. These two projects had ridden together as one since Kermit the Frog was a polliwog. Therefore, he had plenty of talent to choose from. Most of the youngstas in 65th Village were disenfranchised and eager for a way out.

Around 1973, when Big Fee got his entire crew of soldiers organized, he set up shop so viciously that both projects became like fortresses, with lookouts and gunmen on the rooftops, count houses for the money, processing units for the heroin, distribution centers for customers to receive their fix, and people directing traffic with walkie-talkies. The money and the drugs were never in the same location at the same time. Big Fee became the head of the snake, never touching anything.

The machine worked' like this. A customer would approach whoever was directing traffic and would be instructed where to go to pay for their fix. After that, they would proceed down an alleyway to a water hose. The water hose would be dropped down from an upper level window. Once the order was called in on the walkie-talkie, it would be spat down the water hose for them to retrieve. Hanging around or using on the premises was not allowed. Numerous intravenous drug users got beat down or even worse for violating this rule.

By the time Fee was in his early twenties he was a multi-millionaire. He had a crew that was the equivalent of an Italian mafia family with armed bodyguards, chauffeurs, and enforcers that acted on command. These guys meant business and would institute street justice at the very thought of somebody getting in the way of their activities.

Once Big Fee had the machine rolling smoothly, he decided to expand his horizons. He had already accumulated everything that life had to offer; several Rolls Royce Silver Shadows, Phantoms, and a red Ferrari like the one Tom Selleck drove in the popular *Magnum PI*. He bought a home in the quiet upscale neighborhood of Walnut Creek, California. He opened up a limousine service and a car wash in Oakland. The car wash was located in West Oakland on the corner of West Macarthur Boulevard and Grove Street. The limousine service was on 73rd and Macarthur Boulevard, next to Fun City Arcade.

Ironically, Big Fee wasn't physically imposing at all. He was a slim built brother just over six feet in height. He was dark skinned with a really short, close cropped afro. He stayed suited and booted, with a regular manicure and pedicure. His jewelry game was immaculate as well. He wore diamond encrusted eye glasses with monster pieces on his pinkie fingers. His most recognizable piece was a golden miniature spoon around his neck connected to a Cuban link chain. He used the spoon when he was in the company of other players and they were taking a toke of that powder cocaine. Cocaine was a rich man's high and anybody who could afford it on occasion would indulge.

The entire Mob drove four-door Chevy Impalas. Glass houses. They patrolled the neighborhood usually four deep to a vehicle, strapped to the teeth with semi-automatic weapons. Everybody usually had covatis style haircuts like Telly Savalis wore on *Kojak*. That was their signature look. Even the later generation of 69 Mob would carry on that tradition. That's what is called mobbin' in the Town to this day.

The Mob also set up shop in other areas of the city and beyond. One of their other heroin machines was in the lower bottom section at the Westwood Gardens projects, sometimes referred to as 0-7 because it sat on the corner of 7th Street and Cypress directly beneath the Cypress Freeway structure, which would later collapse during the Loma Prieta Earthquake.

The Mob also had another operation nearby in Campbell Village projects on 9th and Campbell Street. One of Fee's main squeezes by the name of Sheila oversaw the day-to-day operations. Her family was well known and respected around them parts so she didn't have to worry about getting robbed or questioned at all. The area was pretty political when it came to the game. The Black Guerilla Family had serious roots in the area and would put the pressure game down on any freelancers who attempted to get money down around there.

Sheila used to get chauffeured to Campbell Village in one of Fee's blacked out Cadillac limos driven by Big Fred. Her job was to drop off and pick up. She would parade around the Village in all black leather outfits with her handbag stuffed full of ten thousand dollars worth of heroin balloons. One thousand dimes to be exact. She would issue them out to the workers along with daily instructions from Big Fee himself.

Another faction of the Mob was the Berkeley crew. They operated on a section of Sacramento Street on the Oakland/Berkeley border. Their machine encompassed all of San Pablo Park and Oregon Street. The individual in charge of that squad was known as Number 9. He was one of Fee's classmates at Berkeley High. Fee was real tight with him and his brother Billy Ray too.

Fee had another chick by the name of Sheila too. This particular broad was an ex-hooker of his. She used to sock it to Fee's pockets. It just so happened that her and Big Fee stayed tight after all these years. She seen how he was putting it down and really wanted to solidify her position next to the kingpin. One day she casually mentioned to him that her sister was about to marry a major cat out of L.A. named Tootie. She told him that Tootie was making moves on a high tech scale too. Apparently word was that Tootie had connections to some Afghans that might be able to help Fee take his game to epic proportions. She told him when the wedding was and invited him to go with her so she could introduce the two and they could do some networking.

When the time came they got in one of Fee's double-Rs and took the six hour ride down to La La Land. After attending the wedding, Sheila kept her word and introduced them. The two men hit it off smoothly and a partnership was born. Tootie lived down the hill from the famed Jackson family. He had a line on that Afghan black heroin known to be some of the best heroin in the world.

As time progressed, Fee would go on to purchase the famous Hollywood mansion formerly owned by Clark Gable. It was located in the lush enclave of Beverly Hills. This would become his player palace when he was in Southern California. He also purchased a home in the nearby suburbs of the San Fernando Valley in Northridge for his children and their mother. That way they would be nearby but they would also be far removed from any drama related to his business in the Town.

When Fee did make an appearance in Oakland he would usually go down to the Village and shower the neighborhood children with gifts.

He would slide through in one of his limos and throw basketballs, baseballs and footballs out of the windows and the sunroof. Sometimes he even used to rent trucks and pull up and give away bicycles to all the youngsters. During the summer he used to have swimming pools set up so the kids could go swimming. He could relate to all these little kids because once upon a time that was him. So even though he was sponsoring all the corruption going on around there, he also gave back.

Fee and all his lieutenants used to go on exclusive vacations to Hawaii and the Caribbean, not to mention professional boxing matches in Las Vegas and Atlantic City. They enjoyed the best front row seats, reserved for celebrities, costing upwards of fifteen hundred dollars or better. They sat ringside at fights like Ali vs. Frazier, Sugar Ray vs. Roberto Duran, etc. Fee was famous for wearing mink coats and hats to match, especially at events of that magnitude. Players from all over the country would be attending. Major figures from New York, Detroit, Atlanta, Chicago, L.A., and D.C. all knew of and respected the Oakland mob boss. When Fee stepped in these places he always had his henchmen in tow. It wasn't unusual to see him with the singer Natalie Cole on his arm when he went to these events. Natalie was one of his many love interests.

Frank Lucas made reference to Big Fee in his autobiography. According to Frank, Fee contacted him about purchasing fifteen kilos of China White heroin at fifty-two thousand a key. That's seven hundred and eighty grand. This was in the early seventies. By all definitions Fee was a giant in the game.

Eventually other competitors would pop up on the scene and attempt to get a piece of the action. One of the most notable was Mick Mo. Mick ran a squad called The Family across town in the 20s. The 6-9 Mob and the 23rd Street Family would engage in one of the bloodiest drug wars in Oakland history, the drug war of 1980 to '83. It all started because one of Mick's minions made the mistake of trying to push The Family's dope in the Mob's territory of 65th Village. This major blunder would spark a trail of bloodshed that would shake the Town to the core.

The Oakland Hills and Lake Merritt became a virtual dumping ground for the bodies. The local funeral homes were literally being paid money and drugs to cremate people. One local funeral director came forward and revealed several instances in particular. His conscience had gotten the best of him. He was put into the federal witness

17

protection program to ensure his safety.

Unfortunately, several mistaken identity killings took place during these gunfights. Some of these individuals were women and children, none of which had anything to do with the drug war whatsoever, they just happened to be in the wrong place at the wrong time. One young lady of about fifteen years of age by the name of Kim Greene was caught up in the crossfire while out shopping with her mother.

The Walker family suffered the greatest. They were part of another more mediocre drug faction out of the Acorn housing projects. Their leader was a slick talking cat named Red Walker. They were known as the Acorn Mob. Their machine was pretty well-oiled too. Fee had a lot of respect for them in the beginning and didn't go out of his way to try to infiltrate their projects. He was okay with them doing their thang as long as they got their work from him. It was very seldom that he sold weight, but he made an exception for Red because he knew him from childhood. That all ended when Fee found out that Red was trying to play both sides of the fence.

Red Walker started sneaking behind Big Fee's back and copping China White from Mick Mo every now and then. This act was considered treason to the mob boss and definitely required corporal punishment. Fee gave his hitters the green light to take care of the situation. He decided to spare Red's life and just send him a message that would stay with him forever. He made a call and requested Red's presence down in L.A. Red was under the impression that this would be a business meeting.

The rest of the Walker family was residing in a condominium in Pinole, California. This hillside community was located about fifteen miles outside of the dangers that Oakland provides. That was until this night of terror that would go down in infamy.

The Mob's hitters slid up to the Walker residence in the dead of night. They took everybody in the house at gunpoint and loaded them into a late model panel van. This included two of Red's brothers, Rick and Roger, and a female in-law. These were not only Red's brothers but his lieutenants as well. They shot each one of them point blank in the back of the head. Then they lined the back of the van with plastic trash bags. They dismembered all the bodies using a hacksaw and placed them piece by piece inside of Glad trash bags. After that they drove the remains to the top of the Oakland Hills and dumped them. A jogger discovered them several days later on Skyline Boulevard and immediately notified the police.

Meanwhile, Red was down in Los Angeles enjoying the sunshine, shopping on Rodeo drive, eating at five star restaurants and living it up. Fee never mentioned to him at the sit-down that there was any bad blood between the two factions at all. As far as Red was concerned, it was business as usual. When news of the remains of his family being discovered hit the airwaves, he was devastated. This was the ultimate back door move of all time. Red would fall into a path of drug use that lasted decades. He and his crew were never able to recover or retaliate.

Huey Newton and the Black Panthers still had a little influence in Oakland. The heroin epidemic had hit hard and affected several of the Panther members greatly as well as many others in the Bay Area. Huey and company considered themselves to be completely against all the drug dealers and pimps in the community. They felt like they were a cancer growing inside the predominately black neighborhoods. Therefore, it was their duty, as far as they were concerned, to tax these individuals. They believed that since they couldn't completely stop it, they could at least make these individuals pay a percentage of their ill gotten gains. Big Fee not being an exception, since he was the biggest of the big.

Huey and his soldiers made contact with Fee at one of his businesses, his limo service in East Oakland. Fee sat them down and listened to what they had to say, which was if he wanted to stay in business, he had to pay them. Big Fee was diplomatic about the situation and told Huey to stop back by the next day. He instructed them that by that time he would have a definite answer for them.

He was well aware of the power and influence that the Panthers formerly held over Oakland and other major African American communities. Those days were over now and a new era was on the horizon. King heroin was overshadowing any and all efforts made by their organization in the previous years. In other words, Fee came to the conclusion that he wasn't giving them shit.

The next day Fee had his soldiers on standby for the Panther's arrival. He had to be prepared because he was well aware of what they were capable of. They were black militants in every aspect of the word and could not be taken lightly.

Around three o'clock that afternoon a mysterious van began circling the block. This was unusual based on it was the immediate area of Fee's limousine service. Everybody in the neighborhood feared and respected Fee and knew not to play him close like that. After the van circled the block three complete times, Fee began feeling a clear and present danger. He was under the impression that these were Panthers setting up their perimeter to further advance their shakedown.

At that point, Fee decided to dispatch his soldiers to go deal with the situation. Two of Fee's boys jumped in one of his mob cars and slid up next to the van and unloaded multiple rounds with a double barrel shotgun, killing all the occupants instantly.

The people occupying the van turned out to be in no way, form, or fashion associated with the Panthers at all. As a matter of fact, they were a family of out-of-towners coming to visit relatives in preparation for a wedding that was about to take place. This killing turned out to be one of the numerous mistaken identity killings of the Oakland drug wars.

When the Panthers stumbled onto the scene they immediately noticed the yellow tape. The county coroner's vehicle was tending to the scene. Huey instructed his comrades to keep going. After that the Panthers never made any more attempts to make contact with the kingpin. It was evident that he meant business in every aspect of the word. The truth of the matter was the Panthers weren't equipped to go to the extremes that the Mob was.

The Oakland Police Department was aware of who Fee was, but basically couldn't touch him. During a routine traffic stop Big Fee was quoted as telling the officers that he was untouchable. Due to his Robin Hood status in East Oakland, the OPD couldn't convince anybody to reveal info on him based on the fact that he fed so many people and for fear of death if they flipped.

There was one standout officer that made it his lifetime mission to catch Big Fee. Officer Gremminger was in charge of a unit of sleazy cops that had a reputation for being dirty. They were referred to as the Gremminger Boyz. The Gremminger Boyz used to do raids with Halloween masks on, pulling up with the doors already open, bouncing out and busting people, planting drugs and guns on whoever they felt like taking to jail that day. Sometimes they would allow the local news stations to do ride-alongs with them. The Gremminger Boyz were the first to institute marked money during stings.

Officer Gremminger hated Fee with a passion. However, for the time being he knew he couldn't touch him. Whenever his boys attempted to do a bust in the Village, the police cruisers would get shot at by the gunners on the rooftops, which made it impossible for the OPD, Oakland Housing Authority, or the Feds to serve warrants or make arrests in the Mob's neck of the woods.

Officer Gremminger knew that he would have to wait patiently to develop intel on the 69 Mob boss. Seeing Fee around town in his Rolls Royce, his Ferrari, or his chauffeured limousine only made matters worse. Here was a rich black man that grew up poor in the city's most notorious housing projects living the life of a godfather. Big Fee was making more money in one month than the police chief made in a year.

Once the town started heating up with all the funk that was going on along with the heat from the fuzz, the Mob decided to expand once again. This time they decided to take the machine to the state capitol, Sacramento, California. They set up shop in one of the most predominately black neighborhoods in Sac Town, an area called Oak Park. The police were notified immediately. Sacramento is the state capitol and has every type of law enforcement agency at their disposal, the Feds, the Sheriffs, to the State Police etc.

The local authorities weren't having it and were quoted telling one of the Mob lieutenants to take his crew and leave town. The 69 Mob's lieutenant responded by saying, *We are going to turn Sacramento out like we did in Oakland.*

That didn't happen, however, because the police shut their program down immediately. In Los Angeles Tootie was being singled out in an investigation. Unbeknownst to him, he was doing business with two undercover agents. The federal agents approached him as hustlers from the East Coast trying to get a line on some cocaine and heroin. They capitalized on the fact that the prices of both drugs were cheaper in California. Tootie started meeting up with these cats and discussing prices. Little did he know that he was being recorded.

On one occasion in particular he was recorded as saying that he was connected to the biggest heroin dealer in California who just so happened to be his brother-in-law, Big Fee from Oakland. He also mentioned his own personal connection with the Afghans. Tootie did several deals with these agents that eventually got him, his wife and his daughter in a boatload of trouble. On one deal he had his twenty-one-year-old daughter and his twelve-year-old son drop off a few ounces of heroin and powder coke in one of his Rolls Royce Corniches. They met up with the agents in a Los Angeles area gym parking lot. Tootie, his wife, and his daughter eventually got indicted and were sent to prison.

By this time cocaine was making its entrance. This was the very early 80s.

Heroin was still booming, however. Thanks to Richard Pryor, the comedian, freebasing was becoming popular among the young party goers. Setting himself on fire sparked nationwide recognition for the new style of using cocaine.

Heroin had ruined so many people's lives in Oakland and abroad that the U.S. government had to step in. The violence that the drug gangs were instituting in the urban inner cities had gotten out of hand.

The Feds launched an investigation on the 69 Mob and Big Fee in late 1982. They made contact with Detective Gremminger and he brought them up to speed on his investigation and the collection of information that he had obtained on the subjects. He provided them with the file he had as well as his personal insight on Big Fee. Officer Gremminger became a corresponding officer during the federal investigation and played a big part in it. The Feds were actually surprised to find out the level of organized crime they were dealing with.

The web of the 69 Mob's activities was woven so intricately into the landscape of the East Oakland hemisphere that it would take thousands of hours of the federal government's manpower and technology to trace everything back to Big Fee. The agents assigned to the investigation found out quickly that they were dealing with an organized crime figure that was highly intelligent. Big Fee lived like a god, between the sun and the earth, he didn't touch dirt nowhere.

Every single aspect of the Mob's machine was handled by someone else on the payroll that was assigned to handle those duties. His bodyguards, his drivers, the sifters, the spitters, the gunners on the rooftops, the money counters and the lookouts all got paid every Friday like clockwork. His enforcers made the most per hit, along with their weekly salary. The lookouts made the least at three hundred a week, most of whom were children and teenagers. Almost everybody who lived in 69th and 65th Villages were benefitting from the Mob's presence in some form. Even the garbage men were on the payroll. Their job was to pick up the trash bags full of money out of the dumpsters on a daily basis and to drop them off at a designated location along their route.

Big Fee and his army watched the television series *The*

Untouchables and based a lot of their functions on the strategies of the prohibition era mobsters like Al Capone. This frustrated the police immensely and they knew that without somebody on the inside, taking down the Mob would be almost impossible.

Big Fee knew this and lived by the code that dead men can't talk. He made sure that his enforcers tied up any loose ends immediately. If somebody in his crew ran their mouth, they usually got found stankin' in the Oakland Hills.

One of the Mob's high ranking members named Alvin found himself in Santa Rita County Jail surrounded by the same dope fiends that he had abused and mistreated on the streets. The jailhouse was their world and he wasn't in there a week before he was beaten to a pulp and stabbed with a shank. While he was in the infirmary recovering, he called home and told his sister Bridgett to have the Mob bail him out or else he was gonna tell the police everything he knew.

His sister drove through the Vill the next day and relayed the message to some of Fee's soldiers who were standing in the parking lot. Before they could respond she burned rubber up out of there.

Big Fee and some of his affiliates were out of town parlaying at the Fresno Relays. His driver, who was sitting in the limo, answered the car phone and received the message. He got out the car, went and located his boss and whispered the message in his ear. Big Fee went back to the car and got on the phone back to the Town. He told his hitters that whenever they seen Alvin to down him, then he hung up.

A couple of weeks later Alvin got released on an early kick-out from Rita. He was highly upset that his own folks didn't bail him out but he didn't go to the fuzz and reveal any info. He thought everything was cool and Fee would understand that he was just blowing off some steam when he sent that message. When he exited the cab in the Village in front of Building 4 he went to his usual post. Norb, a mob hitman, approached him and gave him a hug, then patted him down all in one motion. Before Alvin even knew what was happening, a gunman approached him from the back and put two shots in his head and one in his neck. He dropped were he stood. Everybody outside melted into different apartment buildings until the ambulance and police came and went.

Alvin must of had nine lives because once again he survived an attack on his life. When he recovered he contacted Fee personally and begged and pleaded to get back in his good graces. He told Big Fee that he would never make that mistake again no matter what. Big Fee put him back on the team based on the fact that he hadn't actually told any information.

More dissension occurred in the Mob's ranks when six pounds of heroin came up missing from Fee's baby momma's house. She had two brothers who worked for Fee and he immediately blamed the oldest one. When Big Fee called the oldest brother on it in the middle of the projects one day, the conversation got heated and the two of them got into a fistfight. Big Fee was no physical match for his brother-in-law and his bodyguards broke it up. This was a cardinal sin and Big Fee felt like his brother-in-law deserved corporal punishment. Once he called the shot, his brother in law would never be seen or heard from again.

This would prove to be a major oversight on Big fee's behalf because everybody knew what happened and his brother-in-law's younger brother was still a part of the Mob. He was one of Fee's youngest and most ruthless killas. After the incident he kept the younger brother close and even took him with him to L.A. along with his baby mama and son to spend time at the mansion. Although Big Fee was rich and powerful, he knew that one day his young brother-in-law could pose a serious threat. He had been around the Mob since it started and knew its inner workings from top to bottom. His family had major roots in the Village and knew Big Fee's family well. Fee knew that eventually the young hitter would have to be dealt with, and he thought he had just the guy to do it.

The young man was in fact waiting for the prime opportunity to avenge his older brother's death. The hatred he had for the 69 Mob's leader was deep and all he was waiting for was the right scenario to handle his business. This wasn't an easy task because Fee's bodyguards were around and heavily armed at all times. Norb, the Mob's top and most efficient killer, was given the hit to knock the young man off. Big Fee felt like the time had come. But Norb wasn't too happy about the first call on the youngster's older brother. He had watched both of them grow up and had a lot of love for both of them. When he was given the order, he knew that he wasn't gonna be able to go through with it. He also knew that if he disobeyed his boss's orders, his career with the Mob was over.

Norb located the youngster at a safehouse and told him that he was sent there to hit him. Norb told him to pack his shit and get the fuck outta town immediately. He let him know that he wasn't gonna be able to go through with it because their families had too much history in 6-9. At that very moment both of these men denounced their allegiance to Big Fee and put the Mob in their rearview mirrors. This would be the tide that turned the Mob's reign from sugar to shit. When they got apprehended by the Feds later on down the line, they both made executive decisions to separate themselves from the shit that was flowing downhill in Big Fee and the 69 Mob's direction. Their knowledge and insight would be pivotal in helping the Feds take down California's largest drug empire.

Meanwhile, across town another one of the 69 Mob's associates, Terrance aka T.B., got caught up with some of the Mob's dope. T.B. was from West Oakland and ran the Westwood Gardens. One of his safehouses was located in East Oakland on 24th Avenue in Family territory. T.B. was in the spot counting money when the doors came off the hinges. The police discovered a kilo of heroin, a few handguns, and upwards of twenty grand in cash. As soon as he got to the station, T.B. asked to speak to a detective so he could cut a deal. The OPD knew he was a Mob affiliate and got on the phone immediately with the alphabet boys.

By 1983 the Feds had accumulated enough information on Big Fee to come down with a multi-jurisdictional, multi-count indictment on him and his associates, with Fee at the helm. They executed several search warrants around Oakland and the entire Bay Area. Big Fee, however, wasn't present during any of these operations. He was in Southern California under close observation of the Alcohol Tobacco and Firearm agents chosen to watch him.

One of Fee's younger sons fell in the swimming pool at the San Fernando home. By the time other family members pulled the young child to safety he was almost brain dead. They called an ambulance and had him rushed to the nearest hospital. Once Fee was notified about the accident, he rushed to the hospital immediately.

The authorities already had a heads up about the whole scenario. They were following the boss closely in their unmarked cars as he pulled out of his mansion in his Rolls Royce. They dispatched units ahead to be at the hospital preparing for the takedown of California's largest kingpin. When Fee pulled up and got out, he was draped in a brown full length mink coat with a hat to match. The plan was to let the drug lord enter the hospital and not to make a scene during the takedown. The agents on the scene allowed Fee into the hospital. Once he was inside, they used an ice pick to flatten all the tires on his Double R. When he emerged hours later, the agents quietly converged on him and took him into custody without incident. His car was put on a tow truck and the police caravan radioed in that they were on their way to the federal holding facility.

In February of 1983, Big Fee was extradited back to San Francisco to be arraigned by a federal magistrate. The indictment was the United States of America vs. Felix Wayne Mitchell, Nathan Charles Lewis, Morris McClendon, Marcus Wayne Edmundson, Alvin Gay, Donald Grogans, Randy Brown, Billy Ray Brown, and Tony Louvell Burton. All defendants were hit with CCE (continuing a criminal enterprise) as well as the RICO Act (racketeer influence corrupt organization). The 69 Mob was California's first and most notorious black run organized crime family.

Once the capture of the Mob hit the media, it spread like wildfire. The trial was followed closely by the *San Francisco Chronicle, the Oakland Tribune, the L.A. Times, Ebony, Jet, Time Life, and California magazine.* Each one of these media outlets did their own layout on the drug organization's breakdown of the machine and how it was run, as well as the flamboyant lifestyle of its leader, Big Fee. *California Magazine* in particular did a spread with aerial views of the Village and the locations of all the mechanisms that made the drug network function so smoothly with circled numbers highlighting each point of production.

Prior to Big Fee's arrest, he and his constituents took a trip to Atlantic City, New Jersey. They were photographed by the Feds at a hotel restaurant during a Sugar Ray fight. Each high ranking member of the 6-9 Mob's inner circle was seated around the table with their champagne glasses held high. Each one had a number above their head on the page to designate their status on the totem pole with the number one over Fee and the number nine over Randy Brown. This was where Mr. Brown acquired the nickname Number Nine.

California Magazine, Ebony and Jet all ran editorials including the picture and dubbed it the Last Supper because of its resemblance to the painting of Jesus and his apostles. To those that knew him, loved him, and depended on him, that was how they viewed the Mob boss, as a god. The articles received nationwide recognition and were at newsstands in every ghetto in America. The 6-9 Mob's capture was monumental news.

Midway into the trial another twist took place. The Internal Revenue Service, IRS, decided to hit Big Fee personally with separate charges concerning his assets. Once they did their research into his legit business affairs, they realized that he had forgot one essential thing, to pay his taxes. So the Internal Revenue Service stepped in and seized all his businesses, property and automobiles. They even seized his red Ferrari which he had given to his attorney, Arlene West, for services rendered during his trial. Her integrity was even taken into question for receiving the car as payment. Big Fee was the first person in the United States to be hit with the federal asset forfeiture statute, known as the double jeopardy law.

With all the testimony from the Mob's three star witnesses, Big Fee and the rest of the people named in the indictment were found guilty on all charges. Fee was sentenced to life without parole for his role as the Mobfather before a federal magistrate in February of 1984. Several days later, he was shipped to the maximum security federal penitentiary in Leavenworth, Kansas. His attorneys would immediately file an appeal.

Two years into his sentence Big Fee was stabbed to death in his cell by another inmate. According to the administration at the institution, Fee was murdered due to a ten dollar drug debt that the ex-kingpin owed another inmate. Several accounts from other inmates said otherwise. A fellow inmate by the name of Millionaire Corn, who was a member of the D.C. Blacks, spoke out years later on a BET documentary. His account was entirely different than what the prison statement said. He made mention of the fact that it may have been some sort of conspiracy. Fee was scheduled to be granted an appeal hearing that may have turned his sentence around. He had already won his property back in his double jeopardy hearings. Word was that Big Fee might be getting out soon when he was mysteriously murdered.

Once his body was released to his family, preparations were made for his funeral, which would be an event of epic proportions that would go down in gangsterdom. On a bright Sunday morning in 1986, a glass encased horse drawn carriage containing Big Fee's body inside a bronze plated casket pulled up to 1615 Seminary Avenue in front of Big Momma's house. It was followed by as many as fifteen all white Rolls Royce Silver Shadows, Lincoln Continentals, and Cadillac limousines from his own personal fleet, occupied by all his immediate family members. As the procession began to take off, people started to line the streets to pay homage to the man that they all loved and cherished. This would be his last and final lap around the Town that he called home. Oakland, California came to a halt to mourn the city's first black don.

Several news stations and media outlets were present to witness the spectacle. The procession caravanned down East 14th Street all the way through downtown Oakland onto San Pablo Avenue. It came to a stop at Star Bethel Baptist Church. During the funeral the song Smooth Operator (by Sade) was played quietly in the background. Several celebrities as well as gangsters and players from all over were present to pay their respects. When the funeral let out, a bright red Ferrari owned by Fee but driven by a federal agent pulled up. The agent got out and made the sign of the cross on his chest. He jumped back in the car and zoomed off.

Big Fee was laid to rest in a mausoleum at Rolling Hills Memorial Lawn in Richmond, California, overlooking the entire Bay Area. His legend lives on in popular rap songs by Too Short, Richie Rich, E-40, and other hiphop artists.

CHAPTER 2 --MICK MO

Mick Mo was the youngest of five boys; Dave, June, Manuel, Eddie Ray, and then Mick. He was nicknamed Mickey after his love for the Disney cartoon character Mickey Mouse. He spent most of his formative years being raised in the Boondocks, an area of West Oakland located near the naval shipyards. His momma and daddy had a small Victorian at the corner of 14th Street and Peralta. They were both hardworking parents doing their best to make due and provide for their boys. Eventually they saved up enough money to move their entire clan to a suburb of East Oakland near Highland Hospital.

23rd Avenue was a far cry from the grimy ghetto streets they left behind. It was a burgeoning black working class neighborhood that was bustling with activity. It ran from Macarthur Boulevard all the way to San Leandro Boulevard and was a major connecting point for these two main thoroughfares. The most notorious street in the neighborhood was East 19th Street, commonly referred to as Junkie Hill.

Junkie Hill was centrally located in the middle of 23rd Avenue where there was a liquor store and a laundry mat that attracted a lot of foot traffic. This was where the Mo-Mo Family would make the transformation from a working class existence to become known as a major crime family of legendary Oakland status.

The oldest, Dave, was the first original baller of the boys. He was murdered in a set of circumstances that would remain unsolved. His brothers didn't hesitate to pick up the ball and keep on rollin'. They would soon start enlisting their cousins, nephews, uncles, aunts, and whoever else was closely associated with their family to work for them in the drug game. Everybody in the area was on the payroll.

Their turf expanded quickly. What began on 23rd Avenue eventually stretched all the way to 13th and back to Fruitvale. The Family's call to arms was 2-7, 2-6, 2-5, 2-4, 2-3 ... Family.

This area began as middle class. Most of the homes were built in the early 1900s, mainly based on the Victorian theme. With the exception of a few Housing Authority apartment buildings, there were no projects in the area at all, so the heroin epidemic affected all the working class people as well as the street people alike. Simply put, there was plenty of money to be made.

The baby boy, Mick, showed the most promise as a singer. He had musical talent and aspired to be like the Temptations. For the most part, his older siblings tried to promote his musical goals and keep him out of the streets. Their efforts would soon prove to be fruitless, because lil Mick had a natural knack for the hustle. He had carte blanche to do whatever he wanted to do in the neighborhood, and his talents would catapult him to the top of the family tree in the dope game.

Mick kept it slick in the beginning and just dabbled here and there in between gigs. He didn't attempt to push his weight around just because of who his family was. He was popular and respected in the neighborhood. His best friend was a fly little dude named Dru Piazza. Dru was a stone cold player at a young age and had all the chicks in the area wrapped around his finger. Mick stuck to Dru like glue and caught all the rejects that Dru didn't want. Mick was a pretty smooth character in his own right. The fact that he could sing and was well dressed was just a bonus.

Eventually Mick would start a group called the Numonics where he was the lead singer. He did a little dealing on the side just to keep a few dollars in his pockets. When he was in high school he was arrested for possession of a drug called Seconal, a recreational drug that was popular on the music scene. This was in December of 1970. Young Mick was getting his feet wet in the D Game. Little did the police officers that arrested him know that they had in their custody a future kingpin.

Mick spent a lot of time doing gigs with his group all over the Bay Area. He met a lot of people who were on the music scene. Some of these characters had their hand in all types of nefarious activities, such as drugs. It was on the music scene that Mick made the contacts that eventually opened the door for a line on China White heroin. Once Mick secured the hookup, he brought his brothers to the roundtable and laid down the law. The baby of the bunch had risen to the top of the food chain. None of his family members had a problem with it. Everybody just fell in position and backed his play.

23rd Avenue and East 14th street were booming. This was where the Mo-Mo Family would put down their ten dollar balloons. Nobody else in the Town (Big Fee included) had anything remotely close to the China White that they had. The Mo-Mos had the best dope in town hands down and dope fiends were overdosing left and right, which caused a frenzy with all the other users around town. They all wanted a taste of that killer shit. Whenever somebody got arrested for dealing the poison, the additional charge of Attempted Murder, 187 PC, was added to the original charge of Possession of Heroin for sale, 11500 PC.

There were basically three types of heroin. At the top was the most potent, China White. Hailing from the Asian continent , it was usually in a powdery form. Next was Afghan black, which comes from Afghanistan and usually travels through Africa before it arrives in the U.S. The most accessible type of heroin was called Mexican Mud and it comes from Mexico, of course. It had a dark brownish color and possessed a gummy like texture.

Once the hop arrives in America by the brick (kilo), it gets broke down into forty individual twenty-five-gram pieces. Then, depending on how strong it is, it can be stepped on, meaning it can be stretched by adding milk sugar or super lactose and baked in an oven. Most good heroin can take a three-hitter, so one piece turns into four twenty-five-gram pieces.

Shooters heroin remains in the black tar gummy state. Once purchased, the user then places a piece of it on a spoon with a drop of water and then heats the spoon with a lighter until it turns to liquid. Then they drop in a small wad of cotton and draw it up with a syringe and inject it. However, snorter heroin was sold in the powdery form. It's sifted in a blender with the lactose cut (Quinine) and mixed down to its finest compound. Then it's placed in tiny little piles on an album cover or table and scraped into a funnel with a balloon attached to the nipple. The balloon is then removed and double tied. They were then sold at the bargain basement price of ten dollars on the street.

The Mo-Mo Family had the best in the west. They had officially arrived. All of Mick's lieutenants were paid in full too. His closest confidants like Dru Piazza, Tricky Dick, Billy Tate, Pimpy-Do, Big-H, and Money all had it made. If a buyer drove up 23rd Avenue at any time of the day they would see one of Mick's two Bentleys, Dru's yellow drop-top Jaguar, and a fleet of Benzes, Cadillacs, Lincolns and Corvettes. It looked like ghetto heaven out there.

Mick Mo was known to wear some of the most flamboyant jewelry in Oakland history. King Shit, to say the least. He frequented a nearby jeweler named Rudy who owned a mom and pop shop called Spitz in the Fruitvale district. Rudy was becoming well known for making custom pieces specifically for D-boys. Mick Mo and his entire squad had several pieces made costing millions. One of his most notable purchases was a diamond filled hourglass medallion the size of a soda can. He also wore a Ram's head pinky ring that sat an inch off of his finger, complete with diamonds, rubies and emeralds encrusted in the Ram's head, horns and mouth. His cufflinks were solid gold with black onyx set inside, sitting perfectly at the end of his sleeve. Poking out of his tailor made suit was usually a diamond studded gold nugget Cartier watch.

Being a musician, entertainer and a hustler all in the same right, Mick went to extremes to look the part of The Man. His appearance meant everything to him. Unlike his arch nemesis (Big Fee), mink coats really weren't his thang, although he had a few and could afford them at will. He preferred the suit and tie look for him and his crew. Bright colors and unorthodox fabrics such as velvet, velour, leather and suede. His shoe game would rival a preacher's. Mick had his shoes custom made and shipped from places like Italy, Alaska, and New York. Materials like, gator, ostrich, penguin, otter, and snakeskin.

He decided to purchase some real estate since he had an overabundance of cash at his disposal. Mick purchased an apartment building on the corner of East 19th and 23rd. He moved most of his family members in as tenants. This location would act as a makeshift headquarters for the Mo-Mo Family. He rewarded his momma and daddy with a ranch in Clear Lake, California. Then, as a sort of coupe de grace, he bought himself a three story home in the Oakland Hills on Sunkist Boulevard equipped with closed circuit security cameras and a state of the art security system.

The view was amazing. From where the house sat on the top of 73rd Avenue you could see the Bay Bridge, Alcatraz, San Francisco, the Trans America Pyramid Building, and the vast expanse of water that makes the Bay Area famous. Life was good. Mick Mo was on top of the world.

It didn't take long for his underlings to start having internal disputes. Everybody was getting their fair share of the pie, but Big H started feeling like Mick was showing favoritism toward his family members. Big H, also known as Harv, felt he was the main one doing all the dirty work. When somebody was delinquent on a debt, Harv always went to handle it. Or if somebody just needed to be dealt with, that was Harv's department. Meanwhile, several other individuals weren't getting their hands dirty but were still reaping the benefits.

When Harv brought this issue up to Mick, the boss man wasn't trying to hear it, so Harv decided to exit The Family and start his own thang. He wasn't a Mo-Mo by birthright anyway, so truth be told, he would always be an outsider. Therefore, it's safe to say that Harv left The Family on bad terms. However, he had a plan, he just needed time to regroup. The Family would hear from him again, but as time would tell, he would be the least of their worries.

Mick and his band of brothers were riding high, travelling to movie premiers and to professional boxing matches, partying with celebrities like Jayne and Leon Kennedy, a famous movie couple from Penitentiary 1&2 fame.

The Numonics was still one of Mick's pet projects. They released an album with the band on the cover sitting on the bumper of his all white Bentley. The standout single was a song titled *Time Brings About Change*. The music was good and real players in the Town bumped it while they were in they rides sliding, checkin' their dough.

Shit started to hit the fan around 1980. The Family and the 69 Mob were the two most powerful organized crime factions in Oakland. Both crews were raking in millions of dollars annually. It was only a matter of time before these two empires clashed. 1980 would prove to be the beginning of what would be the bloodiest three years in Oakland history, known to the police and the media as the Oakland Drug Wars.

Mick sold a lot of weight along with the bundles of balloons he issued out to his workers, whereas Big Fee funneled all his product through his network machine. Fee didn't sell no weight for the most part. Mostly everything he distributed was broken down to the smallest compound, five to ten dollar balloons. Mick, on the other hand, didn't have the massive outlet and location like Big Fee and didn't have control over where his work would end up. This would eventually be the catalyst that would make these two behemoths bump heads.

One of Mick's minions had ties to 65th Village through his baby's momma. He decided to use this as a stepping stone to try to filter in some of The Family's hop into the area. The China White heroin immediately got noticed because the Mob didn't push that around there. When Fee got wind of it, he was infuriated. There was no doubt about the source. The Mob's soldiers had already located the source of the problem in the Village. Basically, they were just waiting for the word from up top.

Big Fee bumped into Mick at a function one day and made mention of the issue, just to see where Mick's head was at. They kept the conversation cordial, although this in fact was a serious accusation.

Mick vehemently denied that he had any knowledge of anybody holding Family dope in the Village. Apparently, Big Fee didn't like his attitude, because afterward he gave the word to his Mob underlings to shoot on site if any more Family dealers got caught dealing in the Village. One thing he didn't play about and that was his moolah.

On a bright sunny day in the Town, a 450 SEL Benz came to a stop on 64th Avenue near the Village. The car was being driven by the wife of one of Mick's lieutenants. One of Fee's enforcers noticed the vehicle and figured this was another one of The Family's attempts to set some of that China White down. The Mob lieutenant rounded up a couple more soldiers and convinced them to go around there and make an example out of whoever was inside the car. Armed with an AR-15 assault rifle, a 12 gauge shotgun and a AK-47, they unloaded on the Benz with reckless abandon. Nobody in the car survived. The funk was on.

The casualties on both sides started stacking up all over Oakland. The City of Oakland Parks and Recreation Department dredged Lake Merritt and discovered several corpses, some in cars that had just been driven into the lake and sunk to the bottom. Skyline Hills was also a popular dumping ground for The Family and the Mob. The majority of these homicide victims could be linked to one or the other of the two warring factions.

Senseless mistaken identity killings were often taking place. Everyday people were getting caught up in the crossfire, a number of whom were children. This enraged the public. The Oakland Police Department started receiving several anonymous tips from concerned citizens. Oakland residents were tired of the random violence that was taking place in their city. Oakland, California became the most dangerous city in America.

OAKLAND'S DRUG WAR RAGES ON was the headline on the front of the *Oakland Tribune*. The Family truthfully was no match for the 69 Mob. Big Fee's hitters were too vicious for Mick Mo and Company. Big Fee's international status made it almost impossible for The Family's enforcers to ever have a chance at taking a shot at him personally, he was simply too elusive. The Mob's enforcers had entirely too much firepower and were entirely too vicious to compete with. When Big Fee was in Oakland he was surrounded by more killas than the president of the United States.

The Family was still making money by the ton, though, plenty of it. About this time the FBI started to take notice. They had been receiving intel about Mick Mo and the Mo-Mo Family for a while. His name as well as several of his underlings had been implicated in multiple shootings and homicides, but Mick himself never got his hands dirty so they had to wait for somebody who was willing to come forward and testify about specific incidents.

For the most part, Mick and his brothers kept their business intact. From the outside, the leader of the 23rd Family appeared to be a musician, real estate owner and legitimate businessman, which was exactly how he carried himself.

He expanded his drug empire into the area where he was born, the Boondocks at 14th and Peralta in West Oakland. People from across the water in San Francisco could hop on the BART train, get off at 7th Street, get their fix and return back to the city in less than thirty minutes. The West Oakland BART station was perfectly located, everything was in walking distance.

In early 1984, a new drug was starting to rear its ugly head, a concentrated form of cocaine called crack. Aptly named because of the sound it made when it burned on a pipe while being smoked.

This same year Big Fee and the core members of his 69 Mob were arrested and indicted in a statewide roundup. This was good news to Mick Mo and The Family because that eliminated their biggest rivals. Mick was still rolling in the dough for a good while. The war with the Mob was officially over and business was running smoothly.

Then one day an old friend turned enemy re-emerged, Big H, now known as Funktown Harv, popped back up on the scene with a new crew of youngstas that were ready to do his bidding in the name of Funktown USA. Their turf was right next-door to The Family's across 13th Avenue. Suddenly, a new rivalry was born.

Mick started keeping coke around since heroin sales were on the decline. He just sold weight to the up and coming dealers that were placing all their stock in the crack game, but heroin was still his bread and butter.

Between the Feds being on his line and the competition with Harv and his crew, things were getting hectic. It would all come to a head when the Feds served a warrant on his hillside home. Mick was pulled over on his way to the house in his white Bentley and placed into handcuffs. They used his key to enter the residence. A search of the property would produce a few kilos of China White heroin, one key of

Peruvian Flake cocaine, several thousand dollars, and a semi-automatic weapon. The drug boss was taken into custody.

The arrest hit the front page the very next day. Mick lawyered up, but was denied bail. The federal magistrate was well aware of the fact that she was dealing with the head of a black organized crime family. His outward appearance didn't reveal that Mick Mo was a black don, a self-made multimillionaire with a large crew who operated on his orders alone. Mick would be transferred to a San Francisco federal holding facility to face trial on multiple charges including continuing a criminal enterprise.

Mick was eventually found guilty on all counts; drug possession, manufacturing with intent to distribute, with numerous enhancements. He was also implicated in several killings, however, none of them were proven. He was sentenced to twenty years in federal prison.

The Family would still carry on and keep the ball moving. For a long time Mick still ran his operation from behind the walls. Things wouldn't be airtight like they were when the head man was around. The Mo-Mos would still be a dominant force to reckon with in the 23rd Avenue area. Several of Mick's nephews and nieces would come off the porch and follow in his footsteps.

His son, Mick Jr., would eventually catch a life sentence for a kidnap/robbery gone bad at a local auto paint shop called Mico's. His brothers, June and Manuel, would continue to push weight in the form of cocaine. His favorite brother, Eddie-Ray, started smoking crack for a few years. He would eventually bounce back and open an auto detail shop called Feddie Eddie's on Fruitvale Avenue. Mick's daughter Dae-Dae would become the bottom chick to a rising star in the game by the name of Hollyrock. The Mick Mo legacy would live on for decades to come.

Mick Mo became a model prisoner during his stay in the Feds. He became an avid Christian and ultimately became an ordained minister through mail order bible school. His correspondence courses resulted in Mick receiving his associate degree in ministry. He also became the musical director at every institution he spent time in. He also penned his own autobiography chronicling his rise and fall in Oakland, California's dope game, aptly titled *The Man*.

Mick was released from federal prison in early 2000 after nearly twenty years. The Town was a completely different place by then. The youngsters weren't listening anymore and were doing more killing than hustling. Big Fee was dead and gone. The crack era came and went. The art of selling dope had basically petered off to a certain degree.

The BET Network approached him about being in a documentary about Big Fee, since he was Fee's arch enemy and closest nemesis. He played such an integral part in the whole storyline that it was only right to put him on to tell his side of the story. He agreed. The documentary was aired as part of the American Gangster series on BET.

He himself had changed. He wasn't just a jailhouse preacher. He no longer put material possessions on a higher plateau than his personal lord and savior. He opened a small storefront church right on the block where he had made millions of dollars in heroin sales decades before, right on the corner of 14th and Peralta. He also became a legitimate businessman and runs a small gospel music label. He now resides in a middle class community in Antioch, California.

Mick Mo, the leader of the Mo-Mo Family, survived the game. He was the second, and most flyest, in the long line of kingpins in Oakland, California history.

CHAPTER 3 --FUNKTOWN HARV

Little Harvey grew up in a small one story house on 11th Avenue in the Lake Merritt section of East Oakland. He went to Franklin Elementary School and Roosevelt Junior High. During junior high and high school he became friends with members of the Mo-Mo Family. They both shared the same school district even though they were from two bordering neighborhoods.

Roosevelt Junior High was extremely rowdy. Harv would prove to be big for his age and had major chunkems. The boys from the 23rd Avenue area had no choice but to respect him. He was known for knocking motherfuckers out before, during, and after school.

In high school Harv played football. He enjoyed the aggressiveness of the game and was good at it. In his freshman year he was already six-five and well over two hundred pounds. He would respectfully be referred to as Big Harv, or H for short. He became a high school football star and was in the newspaper frequently.

After high school he spent a lot of time on 23rd Avenue with Mick Mo. He started off doing a little enforcing for Mick, then making collections on unpaid drug debts. Harv was a beast. Most of the time people would just cash out instead of undergoing the beat down that Harv was known for. He wasn't afraid to bust that thang. Putting in work was his specialty.

Harv ended up parting ways with The Family and found himself back on 11th Avenue trying to put a crew together. He had managed to stack a little change from his days working with the Mo-Mos. Heroin was going out of style and the new drug of choice was crackola. A lot of crack spots were popping up all over the Town and generating a lot of revenue.

According to a physician who testified in 1979 before a U.S. Senate House Committee, crack was documented by UCLA researchers as early as 1974 in the San Francisco Bay Area. It didn't really become the drug of choice until early 1982 when the majority of users who freebased cocaine using ether started rocking it up with a combination of baking soda and hot water.

Initially the neighborhood Harv was living in wasn't popping at all as far as drugs were concerned. The area was primarily occupied by Asians. About two blocks to the south on East 12th Street was Korea Town. Downtown Oakland, Lake Merritt and Laney College were all in walking distance.

Harv assembled a squad of roughnecks from around the area as well as from West Oakland's 24th Village, all straight gangsters. His immediate circle consisted of dudes with names straight out of a bank vault like Master Charge, Big Visa, and Payroll. Then there was Merc Man, Killa Kev, and Fat Dave. All killas, Fat Dave being the worst of the worst. He was a short, fat, light skinned dude with the devil tatted on his back. Fat Dave was a monster that used to like to rob, kidnap, and fuck people in the ass. He was straight out of West Oakland, transplanted to the east to wreak havoc.

The young up and coming funkstas in Harv's army were Shawny-Bo, Criddy-Bo, Buck, Ant Lane, Black Ray Ray, Deddy-Bo, Angelo, And Davey-D, Harv's nephew. None of these cats gave a fuck about nothing but doing what Harv paid them to do, which was to mob up and take shit, taking what somebody else had and making it theirs. It didn't matter who you were or thought you was. If they crossed your path, you were in trouble.

In the beginning Harv couldn't put a name on the crew. Their headquarters was 11th Avenue, but they terrorized throughout East Oakland. They launched several hostile takeovers of known drug turfs. Their first (failed) attempt was Sobrante Park. They tried to slide through there and put the smash down, but the Sobrante Boyz held their own and ran them out of there. A couple of bodies dropped in the process and Harv and them kept it moving.

The next spot they hit was the Dirt Road on 99th and Plymouth, one block of unpaved portion of a dead-end street called the Big Rock, known for being Oakland's first and most profitable crack spot on record. Several major playas made their bones on this spot, like T.B., A.B., A.F., Burley Mo, Fat Craig, Jerrin (RIP), Jed, and Ki-Ki.

Once Harv and his boys got wind of all the money being made down there, he dispatched Fat Dave and a few others to slide thru there and let them thangs holla. When they did, several individuals got bodied up. Once the smoke cleared, the Dirt Road was theirs. From then on Harv and his crew were known as Funktown USA because the term "funk" meant drama or beef in the Town. The earth was their turf. They were the original spot smashers in the Town and they would funk with anybody. The name stuck and they ran with it.

To pledge allegiance to their turf they used to throw up their index and pinky fingers with the middle fingers held down by their thumb, which symbolized 11th Avenue, their home base. Their call to arms was "Funk or die."

Walnut Street was their next takeover, around the corner from the Dirt Road. Killa Kev would spearhead the takeover due to his relationship with a local dope fiend bitch named Gilda who had a house on the block. Walnut was a four block strip that ran from 98th Avenue to 102nd. The youngsters over there were stealing business from the Dirt Road and didn't really have no organizational structure. Funktown decided to stake claim. When the Funksters pulled up and bounced out, Fat Dave pulled out a joker gun, a .357 Long Nose, stepped up to the first nigga he seen and slapped him with it and pulled the trigger at the same time. The barrel exploded in the kid's ear. Fat Dave yelled out "Break yoself Bitch!." The rest of the crew were holding 12 gauge shotties on the crowd. They stripped everybody buck naked and took their dope, jewels, and money, then jumped back in their buckets and smashed off. Walnut was theirs now too.

Several other known dope spots would fall victim to Funktown's wrath. Each would become an extension, such as 51st Avenue, which started being known as 5-1 Funk. 82nd and Olive got taken over by an enterprising young funkster by the name of Deddy-Bo, who turned it into a million dollar heroin machine and renamed it the Burnout Block. A couple of spots in West Oakland conceded to the Funk and got taken over all in the name of the game with Harv at the apex.

Harv stayed around the corner from a Mexican family that owned a taco truck business. Harv's backyard was adjacent to theirs. The patriarch of the Mexican family knew Harv since he was a little boy and used to pay Harvey to mow his lawn. Now that Harv was all grown up and the leader of the neighborhood roughnecks, the padron decided to holler at him about a few things, mainly money. One day when Harv stopped at his taco truck on Fruitvale Avenue, the padron asked him to stop by the house later on that evening. When Harv arrived, he was greeted by the padron's vivacious daughter who escorted him into her father's study. When Harv entered the room, the padron was sitting behind a burl wood desk with ten bricks on top of it. Harv sat down and the old man let him know that he had been paying attention to all the moves he was making in the neighborhood and informed Harv that he was personally related to a member of the Mexican Cartel who could provide all the coke in the world to Harv. The ten bricks of coke on top of the desk were just a drop in the bucket. Harv agreed, and from that day forward Funktown was on.

About a week later, Harv, Fat Dave and Merc Man pulled up at the 13th Avenue Liquor Store. They was three deep with no sleep in Harv's white on white Jaguar. At the same time Mick Mo pulled up in his burgundy Bentley. Harv was the man now and still had a little animosity toward Mick because of how they had parted on bad terms. When Mick got out of his car, words were exchanged. Fat Dave hauled off and slapped the shit out of Mick like a bitch. Mick stumbled and jumped back in his car and burnt rubber up outta there. Harv and Merc Man was busting up laughing. Funktown and The Family was officially at war.

Funktown was getting money and opening up shop all over. The youngstas in the crew started going to all the major events in the Town, terrorizing concerts, carnivals, house parties, and sports events. Laney College was the location of a carnival every summer. Funktown was the nearest turf to Laney. The summer of 1985 was infamous.

On this particular sunny day at the Laney College Carnival, the 69 Mob, now with Lil D at the helm, just so happened to be at the carnival when they bumped heads with the Funktown crew and all hell broke loose. The Funktown Boyz tore the carnival up getting on them 69 Mob nigga's heads. They even chased Big Fee's son Lil Wayne down to nearby Lake Merritt and stomped him out before throwing him in the water.

The Mob had never experienced getting they asses handed to them like that. The next day, after most of them recuperated from the massive beatdowns they suffered, they regrouped. Lil D had a dopehead go rent the largest U-Haul truck he could find. Then they all piled in as deep as they could and went back down to the carnival to look for the Funksters but only found a few of them there. The damage was done, Funktown and the Mob became mortal enemies.

The Funktown Boyz was getting deeper and deeper every day. Solid individuals from everywhere was hooking up with Harv and them. Harv was passin' out bundles like candy. He opened up an auto shop on 13th Avenue that would double as his headquarters. He also invested in a paint and body shop that was formerly owned by Mick Mo called Estelle's. When Mick got wrapped up by the Feds he was out the way. The original owner, Carl, a crooked cop, was a childhood friend of Harv's and needed a little financial help. Harv came to the rescue.

Funk's home turf was massive and several splinter groups started getting a little notoriety. They were all under the same banner with extended names like Fila Funk, the Palm Trees (9th Ave.), Eleven-Twenty four (11th Ave., East 24th), the Regency Towers (3rd Ave.), and the Junk Yard (13th Ave., East 23rd).

The foothill buses that ran through Funktown were the 40 and the 43. One of the most dangerous stops was on 11th Avenue right smack in front of a small housing project where a lot of the young Funksters hung out. Sometimes they would be out there throwing up funk when the bus came to a halt. Every now and then some unsuspecting sucka would yell something back. The Funktown Boyz would commandeer the entire bus and put hands and feet on whoever was on there, including the driver. They was known to throw people out the back windows. The shit was serious and Funktown was for real.

Oakland High was their school. If somebody from Funktown got into it with another student, the rest of the Funk-A-Maniacs would team up and jump him or her. If that didn't work, more Funksters would come up to the school the next day. When school let out they would be waiting by the bus stop ten to fifteen deep, niggas with perms and braids, wearing burner gloves and packing pistols.

Juvenile Hall on 150th in San Leandro started filling up with delinquents from Funktown. Most of them were getting caught up in drug stings and robberies, selling rocks to decoys and getting caught with marked money, or doing drive-bys on other turfs they was trying to take over.

Criddy-Bo was the leader of the younger Funktown faction. Harv and Crid's older brother Buck were the only two people Crid answered to. He reigned supreme over all the other Funktown youths. Criddy-Bo hated the 69 Mob Boyz with a passion. He thought they was all cowards because they never fought anybody one on one. Plus, he just so happened to be one of the individuals that got caught up in the Laney College carnival smackdown when the Mob doubled back the next day. Every chance he got he would get on a Mob nigga's head if he caught 'em slippin'.

One day in the Town some Mob Boyz were congregating outside of a smoke shop on 65th and East 14th, one of which was Lil D's lieutenant by the name of Rick. Criddy-Bo and one of his cohorts were in a taxi cab strapped to the teeth with a 12 gauge and an Uzi when they spotted the group. They instructed the cab driver to pull up on the Mob

Boyz and then they started shooting. Nobody was hit and Criddy-Bo was apprehended by the police and eventually sent to juvenile hall.

When he got to the hall they housed him in D Unit with all the rest of the young hogs. The nigga that ran D Unit was a big cat named Big Pokey From the Village. Crid knew he had to bust a move to make his presence felt. The first morning when they let everybody out to wash up for breakfast, Crid slid up next to Big Pokey at the sink and faked like he was brushing his teeth. When Big Pokey bent down to spit the toothpaste out of his mouth, Crid got off on him with a cold right hook. Pokey was out, his jaw broken in three places. When the counselors on duty grabbed Crid and rushed him out the unit, he yelled "Fuck the Mob, this is Funk." His message was clear.

Meanwhile, back on the avenues, Harv was making big bucks. One of his rock spots on 13th Avenue was getting twenty thousand a day. His patna from the Mick Mo days named Pimpy Do defected from The Family and jumped on board with Harv and the Funk. He was a master cooker and could stretch one kilo into two. The padron from the taco truck connection was dropping the bricks off by the wheel barrel. Shit was booming.

Harv bought himself a Corvette Stingray that was his pride and joy. All the young Funksters had Falcons, Cougars, and Mustangs. They used to caravan up and down Foothill Boulevard with the music bumpin' throwing up funk out the windows, trying to get at all the little bitches that were on foot patrol and smashing on anybody who looked like they deserved some funk.

Fat Dave was terrorizing the Town. Whenever Harv had his sights set on a spot he wanted to take over, he would dispatch Fat Dave to make it happen. Dave was a certified beast on the streets. He was also one of the best drivers the Town had ever seen. He used to do donuts in his drop Cougar backward with no hands on the steering wheel, bracing it with his stomach, throwing up funk with one hand and shooting his pistol with the other.

The Santa Rita County Jail was full of niggas from all over Oakland. Most of them where there because of drug and gun cases and rival organization members would commonly bump into each other. The jailhouse was a whole different monster. Dope fiends ran the joint. Big Grey Stone and Lil Grey Stone were vicious. Lil Grey Stone was situated like army barracks with no police supervision whatsoever. Once you were in the dorms, you were on your own.

Fat Dave was in there serving a year on a gun charge in the mid 80s when one of Funktown's worst enemies happened to show up in the dorm. Dave immediately jumped on his head like an African drum. Bruh started fighting back like the soldier he thought he was, but he was no match. He had size on Dave and caught him with a few good ones. That's when two other niggas in the dorm from Funk jumped in and overpowered the nigga and stomped him out. Fat Dave woke him back up by putting his dick in his ass and fucking him senseless. When he finally came to, they made him suck the shit off Fat Dave's dick at knife point.

Funktown Harv's power and reach was clear. If you crossed him, he could have you touched on the streets or in lockup. It didn't matter, he would have you touched in a town business minute. However, he did have one particular weakness. Harv liked fresh, young bitches, especially the pretty light-skinned ones.

One day Harv was sliding in his four-door Jag with the sunroof open when he decided to stop at Kwik Way Burgers for their infamous five dollar chicken and fries. Kwik Way was a landmark and a notorious drop spot for dealers. While he was there, a beautiful high yellow chick got started complimenting his car. Harv started poppin' back at her and got her number. The bitch was light skinned with long golden brown hair to the middle of her back. She had pretty white teeth that looked like piano keys. Her ass was fat enough to put a champagne glass on without it falling off. Harv was hooked. He had to have this fly young thang.

Over the next few months Harv and this young lady were inseparable. He would take her with him on pick-ups and drop-offs. They would stop at his safehouses where he kept hundreds of thousands of dollars and multiple kilos of cocaine. She was impressed. She would spend intimate nights at Harv's high rise condominium in San Francisco fucking the shit out of him and sucking his balls dry. Harv would return the favor by giving her a virtual tongue bath, sucking everything from her toes to her nose. He basically put her on a diet of Grade A gangsta dick from the time they met until the time they parted ways.

Unbeknownst to Harv, this pretty young thang was actually a federal agent who had gone beyond the call of duty and gave a gangsta some booty. When he finally figured out what was happening, it was too late. The doors came off the hinges and Funktown Harv got took down by the Feds. They hit him with the RICO Act and seized some of his assets, mostly cars. Harv was a true gangsta and a thug, so he didn't wear much jewelry or dress flamboyant and most of his property was in other people's names.

In court it would be revealed that the bitch had put bugs all around his condo, his safehouses and in his vehicles. Harv's lawyers tried to put the bitch on blast by revealing her sexual exploits with the drug lord. She herself got on the stand and admitted that she had done whatever was necessary to take down the Funktown boss. She also admitted that she had developed feelings for Harv. She was in too deep, so to speak.

After all was said and done, Harv was convicted and sent off to federal prison for fifteen years. The press had a field day with the drama, sex, money and drugs. The story read like a movie.

While Harv was down, Funk lost a lot of its steam. The majority of the hitters started smoking their product and became raving lunatics that would kill for nothing. Jacking and robbing became their thang. Fat Dave was gunned down on a freeway off-ramp. Criddy-Bo is still around putting in work for another major crew in East Oakland called The Firm that was financed by a millionaire NBA player.

Harvey was eventually released around 1998. When he touched down he worked at Carriage Trade Liquors on East 18th Street. He got in real tight with the Arabs who owned several businesses in the area, including a ranch in Patterson, California that bred world class beef and distributed it all over the Bay Area. Big Harv was back, Funktown lived on, however, never again the dominating force they enjoyed in the glory days. Funk or Die.

CHAPTER 4 --BIG RUDY

The game started for Rudy on Berkeley's waterfront in a neighborhood near the marina called H^2O. The waterfront was a melting pot inhabited by Blacks, Whites, Asians, East Indians and Jamaicans.

Rudy was athletic growing up with a penchant for weightlifting. He also had a fixation for hot rod vehicles. One of his bodybuilding buddies named Big Willie taught him how to hotwire cars and they eventually started stealing them as a means to make money.

His family eventually moved to North Oakland's Bushrod neighborhood where Rudy played basketball, football and baseball at the nearby recreation center and park. The center was situated on 59th and Shattuck behind Washington Elementary School. Former Oakland A's shortstop Rickey Henderson also grew up honing his skills at the center. Rickey and Rudy knew each other well.

Rudy started showing promise on the bodybuilding scene, winning several local competitions. Lifting weights was something that he was good at and enjoyed doing. Rudy was five-eight and all muscle. The streets were calling him. Cars were his first love. Rudy and his buddies started buying, stealing and fixing up '68 Chevy Camaros. They hooked up with an auto shop owner and began chopping the cars down and tagging them with false VIN numbers. Ironically, what began as a hobby among friends became an extremely profitable endeavor.

Rudy reached back to his old neighborhood in Berkeley and started recruiting some of his childhood friends and eventually started a Camaro club. All of the cars were souped up with Corvette rally wheels, custom paint jobs, and GT Qualifier racing tires. On a hot summer day they would caravan around Berkeley and Oakland with Rudy leading the pack with the top down and wearing a wife beater shirt, wearing sunglasses and sporting a short afro with pork chop sideburns.

The Feds eventually got tipped off and caught up to Rudy and his sidekicks. They broke up the entire auto theft ring. Rudy was pegged by one of his associates as the ringleader. Shortly thereafter, he was shipped off to federal prison for a short period of three years. The time Rudy spent away in prison would turn out to be life changing.

While Rudy was in the pen he would become extremely health conscious, exercising daily. Having a lot of spare time along with unlimited access to Olympic style weights would play right into his wheelhouse. The fact that he had a semi-professional body building background would make him extremely popular with other inmates that were trying to get into shape. They would constantly come to Rudy for advice and exercise tips.

One inmate in particular would prove to be the best thing that ever happened to Rudy. He was a Columbian drug trafficker from the Medellin Cartel who had landed in the pen for a short period of time. Rudy and the Columbian became really good friends and spent a lot of time working out together. Rudy shared his story with the Columbian and the Columbian shared his story in return. The one thing that they had in common was that they both liked money. Ironically, they were both scheduled to be released around the same time.

Rudy wasn't necessarily a drug dealer prior to his prison term, however, he knew that with the correct connect along with the recent crack epidemic, there was potential for much money to be made. His Columbian friend was the real deal and let Rudy know that whatever he needed, he had him covered. One of the Columbian's favorite sayings was "In my country no poquito, just tons." The big fella had dollar signs in his eyes.

For the rest of their stay Big Rudy put his arms around the Columbian and made sure nobody messed with him whatsoever. The Columbian stuck to him like glue. Not only were they workout buddies but they were best friends, all the while planning their takeover of the Oakland drug trade.

Rudy was the first to parole. He went about doing his homework on how he was going to lay his program down. He got together with a few neighborhood ballers and laced they bootstraps about what was about to come. Then he got everything laid out for when the Columbo touched down, making sure all the hotel accommodations were reserved for his arrival. He stayed in close contact with his buddy and gave him a number to call while he was still in jail.

Rudy used his sister's address on 55th Street in North Oakland as his parole address. This was where he would lay his head for the time being until he got things up and running. He would also conduct the majority of all his business transactions there, located right around the corner from the Bushrod neighborhood where he was raised.

Bushrod was a bustling working class black neighborhood that sat on the upper Berkeley border. The nearest main street was Shattuck

Avenue. This area had a rich athletic tradition, mainly because Bushrod Park and Recreation Center on 59th had produced so many professional sports stars. Numerous hustlers, players, con artists, drug dealers and pimps also hung out at the center, smoking weed, shooting dice, showing off their cars, or just hollering at the neighborhood hotties.

Big Rudy was already well known in the area and he didn't waste no time putting the word out that he had some things about to be coming down the pipeline real soon. Rudy knew he wasn't going to have to do any street level dealing because of the caliber of individual his connect was. He was gonna jump straight to brick status. All high quality product, he was sure.

The Columbian touched down on schedule and immediately got in touch with Rudy. They sat down over breakfast and got the paper route in order. The bottom line was the Columbian was a man of his word and saw to it that high quality Grade A coke was delivered straight to Rudy's doorstep courtesy of the Ochoa Family, leaders of the Medellin Cartel.

Rudy started boomin'. He instantly put some of his younger protégés in the game. Cats like Hillbilly, Phil Moe, RC Cola, Joe Broughtnax, P.B., and several other notable characters, most of whom were still teenage celebrities at Oakland Tech. This school is famous for the movie *The Principal* being filmed there. Lined up outside the school was a fleet of Mercedes Benz 450SLs, 280 SL convertibles, and many more exotic cars. Their dress code was usually v-neck sweaters, Izod Lacoste shirts and Panama Hats. Oakland Tech was also known as Bushrod High (hoe or die).

Big Rudy was also serving a high school D-boy out of East Oakland by the name of Lil D. Rudy had keys galore. Heroin was no longer a factor in the dope game, coke was it. Crack had kicked in full blast and Rudy was flooding the Town.

When he finally officially moved out of his sister's house, he purchased a sprawling new mansion in Napa Valley's wine country. Rudy decorated the spot with modern décor, leather sectionals, mahogany and oak dining tables, granite and marble everywhere. He also equipped it with an Olympic style weightlifting gym. The garages where full of his collection of classic hot rods.

Once again Rudy began participating in weightlifting tournaments. He was in tip-top condition physically. The time he spent in prison served him well. He was exceptionally well preserved for a guy his age.

Rudy was crowned as Mr. Oakland when he won a local competition. His accomplishment would be on the front page of the *Oakland Tribune* along with a picture of him flexing his twenty-one inch biceps and wearing speedos with a Mr. Oakland banner slung over his shoulders.

He continued training all over the state and was a regular on Venice Beach during the time of Arnold Schwarzenegger and Tookie Williams, avid bodybuilders themselves. Venice Beach soon became known as muscle beach because of all the movies that were filmed there about body builders.

Rudy rubbed shoulders with celebrities and athletes. The baseball player Reggie Jackson was a real good friend of his. They shared the same obsession for classic cars and stored their collections together in an air conditioned warehouse in Redwood City where they owned over fifty flawless automobiles. The collection was worth millions of dollars and was open for public viewing. A freak accident burned the entire warehouse down to the ground one night and every automobile inside. When the news broke, Rudy was fortunate that his name was not mentioned, only Reggie's. Rumors circulated that the fire may have been an inside insurance job.

Thanks to Rudy, the Town was flooded with cocaine. Kilos on the street were 14.5 per. If you bought more than one they could be as low as ten a key. One kilo could be turned into one and a half with the proper cooking methods, especially the Columbian grade coke that Big Rudy had.

Rudy set some of his closest buddies up with businesses. He bought into a liquor store called Ezelle's in East Oakland on 48th Avenue and Foothill Boulevard. Ezelle, the owner, was a buddy of his that developed a coke habit of his own and had gotten too deep in debt to pull himself out of the hole. Rudy had used the store as a work reference in the past and thought it would be a good idea to have his name associated with the store, so he invested.

The break in their relationship came when Rudy's federal parole officer came to the store to do a check of his work reference. Ezelle wasn't aware of who the person was that was inquiring about Rudy's employment status and told the PO that Rudy was not an employee there. This mistake would be the cause of Rudy being violated on his parole and sent back to the pen for a few months. Big Rudy was furious.

During his absence, his sister stepped up to the plate and kept his business affairs in order, proving herself to be quite the businesswoman. Using her 55th Street home as her central headquarters, she took the ball and ran with it. She also started to expand his network by plugging in the husbands and boyfriends of some of her clients from her beauty salon. It wasn't long before 55th Street would be bustling with traffic. Luxury car after luxury car would be seen pulling up to her house, picking up and dropping off. All her neighbors turned a blind eye to her activities because of who her brother was.

When Rudy came back he had a few scores to settle. A couple of cats had taken his absence for granted and defaulted on several payments owed to him and his sister. Ezelle, (the store owner), being at the top of the list.

On a hot sunny day Big Rudy met up with Ezelle at an auto detail shop located on West Macarthur and Market Streets. As Ezelle was attempting to plead his case with the muscle bound brute, a car slid up and Rudy stepped to the side as shots went off. Everybody ducked for cover, including Rudy. When the smoke cleared, Ezelle was lying on the ground in a pool of blood, his eyes wide open, staring straight up at the bright sun.

After Ezelle's death, his store would be left unattended. Rudy didn't have the time or the business knowledge to keep the liquor store running so it was eventually boarded up with the inventory inside. Soon the neighborhood kids pried the boards off the side entrance and commenced to looting the store on a daily and nightly basis

Another cat by the name of Tone was running around fat-mouthing about how he had got some work from Rudy and never paid him for it. Tone was one of Rudy's runners from back in the auto theft ring days. He had started smoking base rock cavies and was an excellent getaway driver. Rudy liked having him around. His mouth, however, would prove to be his undoing.

Rudy got wind of Tone dragging his name thru the mud and playing him like he was a sucka. He put the word out that if anybody dealt with Tone, he would cash them out, clarifying that he didn't want Tone dead, just roughed up a lil bit.

Tone was up in one of the neighborhood smoke shacks getting his smoke on when the goons finally caught up with him. The lady of the house always kept toss-ups in there to attract the young D-boys. She also rented out rooms for dope fiends who just wanted to sit in the house and smoke crack all day.

On this particular day some young Bushrod Boyz had dropped by to serve some knocks some cream. While they was there, they decided to hang around and get they dicks sucked by a lil hooker bitch. They had a video camera to film the little episode with the chick. They were interrupted when Tone came out the bedroom door running off at the mouth. All the little young gangstas in the room eyes lit up with dollar signs. Next thing you know, one of them pulled a pistol and pointed it at Tone. They explained that Big Rudy had put a bounty out on him, and Tone started begging for his life.

One of the Bushrod Boyz got the bright idea to go in the backyard and get the lady of the house's German shepherd. Then they got a spatula and slathered peanut butter and jelly all over the dog's genitals. They told Tone that if he wanted to live he had to suck all the peanut butter and jelly off the dog's dick. Tone got on his hands and knees and licked off every bit while the youngsters filmed it to show Rudy. Once the footage got out, everybody in North Oakland saw it and Tone's name was shit in the area.

Rudy exacted his revenge on all those that had took him lightly. He pumped the fear of God into all those that knew him. This became evident to even the FBI. Mr. Oakland, as Rudy was referred to by the authorities, had come under the scrutiny of a federal drug taskforce. They began surveilling the big guy and developing a dossier on him. All this, combined with his previous stints in the federal joints, made it even easier for them to stay on his heels without him knowing.

In 1986 the Feds obtained a wiretap warrant and began trailing Big Rue everywhere he went. They also had the kingpin's sister under the microscope. On one occasion while listening in on Rudy's cell phone, they picked up a conversation between him and the Columbian. Apparently there was a discrepancy concerning the delivery of a hundred thousand dollars, the money was not included in Rudy's latest drop. Rudy seemed to be annoyed that the Columbian kept calling him about the slight mishap. It was evident that the Columbian feared Rudy. Rudy literally scolded him like a child for repeatedly sweating him about what he considered to be little shit.

Rudy gave the Columbian the runaround for several days while the Columbian was staying in a five star hotel downtown Oakland. When Rudy finally got around to dropping off the hundred thousand, the Feds had a front row seat of the drop. What they witnessed was incredible, according to their reports. Rudy arrived wearing a cotton Gold's Gym sweatsuit, carrying a gym bag. He had the desk summon the Columbian down to the lobby. When the Columbian arrived, he was shaking like a pair of dice. The agents could not understand how a Columbian drug dealer would be scared of a black man from the ghetto, unless the black man was really powerful.

Shortly afterward, the DEA received an anonymous tip that there was a beat-up Chevy Nova parked on 55th street near Rudy's sister's house. The tipster went on to explain how the vehicle was loaded to the gills with kilos on top of kilos of cocaine. This was the break the alphabet boys needed. They immediately started watching the vehicle from sunrise to sunset. Rudy was photographed on numerous occasions accessing the Nova's trunk. Once the DEA could directly connect Big Rudy to the vehicle, they knew their case would stick. When they finally secured the vehicle and thoroughly searched it, they discovered forty neatly wrapped kilograms of Columbian cocaine. They processed the coke into evidence immediately, then proceeded to serve warrants at Rudy's sister's house and on his mansion in Napa Valley.

Rudy's sister was apprehended quietly. Rudy was tracked to the Gold's Gym on Grand Avenue near Lake Merritt and taken into custody. He and his sister were booked into the Oakland City Jail with federal holds. They both lawyered up instantaneously. Rudy retained the infamous defense attorney Penny Cooper. She worked wonders with previous high level drug offenders. Penny just so happened to be the niece of an Alameda County superior court judge. His sister retained Larry Ward.

Rudy was charged with several drug trafficking and manufacturing charges with multiple weight clauses for possessing such a large quantity. The *Oakland Tribune* did a fantastic write-up on the apprehension of Big Rudy, complete with an organizational chart with him at the top of it. The chart also had photos of Hillbilly and a fledgling high school dope boy by the name of Lil D.

Rudy was eventually transferred to the San Francisco Federal Holding Facility where he would remain for a period of two years. Meanwhile, Miss Cooper would be filing motions and waiving time on his behalf. During the trial period Miss Cooper tried every trick in the book to exact the best results for the drug king. The evidence along with the government witness's testimony was just too overwhelming. The big fella was sentenced to a term of twenty-five years in the federal penitentiary. Penny Cooper filed his appeal motion immediately upon his sentencing.

The appeal took about six years before it was actually heard. Rudy was brought back from the big house and housed in the Frisco County jail at 850 Bryant Street. While Rudy was there he received several visits. One of his visitors was the son of one of his weightlifting cronies from back in the day, Big Willie. His son Little Willie had grown up and started a little crew of his own. He needed Rue to slide him a multitude of them keys so he could beat the streets up.

Willie was a young savvy street dealer off of 37th Street in North Oakland. He had been wounded in a street shooting that left him paralyzed from the waist down, so he was often referred to as Wheelchair Will. He had a saucy little drug team of his own on 37th Street that was known for selling fat ass thirty pops, big, fat, thirty dollar rocks that the drug addicts could break down, smoke a little, sell a little, then come back and buy more. He also pushed weight from Oakland to Pittsburg, California.

During the visit, Rudy and Willie discussed the terms of the business at hand, in code of course, and came to an agreement. The truth of the matter was that Rudy needed money to keep his lawyers paid. Once Rudy gave his lines the go ahead, all Willie had to do was go to the pickup location. Waiting for him was ten kilos of primo cocaine complete in the plaster casts.

Will got his hands on the ten bricks and got over the stove immediately. It took him almost a whole day to cook them all up, break them down and get them packaged for street distribution. He put what he called the gypsy twist on them. All thirty dollar rocks. He saved all the crumbs and put them in the freezer to give away on Tuesdays for free. This gimmick was what he called Tuesday Night Meltdowns. Soon 37th Street was jukin' at least ten thousand a day.

While Rudy was awaiting his appeal, his mansion in Napa Valley's wine country was auctioned off by the Feds for a measly six hundred thousand dollars. The local government officials, including Oakland's Mayor Jerry Brown, made a spectacle out of selling the property. There was actually a press conference held complete with a giant sized check for the amount the home was sold for. All the area news stations were on location to film the ceremony and the captions read *Local Drug Kingpin's Mansion Sold to the Highest Bidder*. The proceeds allegedly were to be donated to charity. The mansion had been vacant since the time of Rudy's incarceration. It needed major remodeling and had been the refuge for rattlesnakes and opossums for quite some time now.

Rudy finally got his sentence modified in the year 2000. He was released to a federal halfway house on Macarthur Boulevard on lifetime parole. After spending six months in the halfway house, he returned to the North Oakland area that he once lorded over and took up residence on 59th and Market Streets behind a fancy auto detail shop where he was a silent partner.

Times had changed since he left. With federal parole hovering over his head for the rest of his natural life, he couldn't move like he used to. He began making a living by going to car auctions and buying and selling used cars. He staged his cars at the auto detail spot. His brother was the manager and ran the day to day operations. He aptly named his new business venture Rudy's Beautys and placed paper plates on each vehicle with the business name emblazoned on them.

High grade marijuana was the fastest selling drug on the market at the time, so he dabbled in that on the side. One of his connects was a major weed man by the name of Fat Twin, who owned a hamburger joint on Piedmont Avenue and moved hundreds of pounds of weed on a monthly basis. Rudy came in as an investor, which allowed him to keep his hands clean. Basically, he was just funding the purchases and received a percentage on the back end.

Rudy's oldest son and his namesake came into the mix as a runner. He unfortunately did some side deals that would eventually cost him his life when a multi-pound marijuana deal went bad in East Oakland on 71st Avenue. The police found him slumped over the steering wheel of one his father's vehicles, a late model Lexus LS 400. Big Rudy was devastated.

Almost a year to the day after Rudy Jr. was murdered, Rudy Sr. would also be gunned down in a similar fashion, while sitting behind the wheel of a vehicle outside a famous soul food restaurant owned by the Hawkins family of gospel music fame, Lois the Pie Queen. Rumor was that Rudy was gunned down in a dispute over a beautiful young waitress that worked there. Also shot in the car with him was the baseball player Rickey Henderson's crackhead brother, who managed to survive.

Big Rudy's family members held a modest funeral at the Faith Tabernacle on 73rd Avenue and International Boulevard. It was attended by several notable players such as Berkeley Pierre, the Pimp, and his brother Rodney. Everybody came and went quietly to pay their respects to the fallen king.

CHAPTER 5 -- LARRY P

The Acorn housing projects, aka Cornfields, were a massive stretch of former naval housing. After Oakland/Alameda's closures of the naval hospital and bases, these single family units were rezoned for low income residents, also known as Section 8.

These projects would eventually give birth to several generations of drug kingpins. In the second generation of the Acorn movement a young man by the name of Larry P rose up out of the concrete. He wasn't the first kingpin to rise up out of the poverty stricken Cornfields by any aspect of the word. However, his organizational skills, cunning, and street smarts would rank second only to the Acorn Mob's founder, the legendary Red Walker.

Around 1984, Larry P would become infamous for his resurrection of what was called the Machine. He didn't invent it, but he was instrumental in implementing it and perfecting it in the Acorns as well as the Mohr Houses, Hi Rizes, Cypress Village, and 24th Village. The Acorn Mob was the biggest game in town after Big Fee fell.

The way that a machine was ran and functioned was a well oiled process that other dealers in other cities like Richmond and San Francisco or L.A. were never able to quite figure out and implement in their neighborhood distribution rings. The Machine was what made Oakland's drug rings stand out from the rest, not only in Northern California, but Southern Cali as well.

The Machine functioned as follows: a) everything was broken down to the lowest common denominator for street sales; b) the weight was packaged up in a designated apartment within the projects by individuals whose job was to do that and that only; c) everybody had a shift (the day shift or the all nighter); d) the field marshals dropped off the bundles and collected the money, e) The spitters stashed the bundles and handed out the product to the customers when they approached; f) the gunners stayed close to the grinders with their guns out as protection; g) The shooters were usually on the rooftops or balconies with hi-powered rifles or shotguns prepared to shoot at anybody that encroached upon the cheese line; h) the lookouts were strategically placed on corners or patrolling on bicycles with walkie-talkies, ready to notify the grinders when trouble was around. For example; "Rollers comin' down Filbert Street," was a common warning.

The boss was virtually the head of the snake. His job was to provide the major weight it took to supply the Machine and the artillery it took to protect it, as well as pay everybody their weekly salary to keep everything flowing smoothly.

Once the eagle landed, the boss would secure it at one of his tuck spots and notify his lieutenants of its arrival. The boss didn't touch anything but money. He only discussed prices with his line (connection) and his line only. Usually a Columbian or a Paisa (Mexican immigrant).

Larry P usually had his bundles issued out in ten-grand bundles. That's one thousand ten-dollar balloons of powder heroin or five hundred twenty-dollar rocks of crackola. Hundreds of these bundles would be passed out on a daily basis. Larry P singlehandedly managed to direct the traffic of a million dollar operation into the confines of one city block. When one block or parking lot got too hot, he would relocate the Machine to the next one over. He had three whole city blocks to choose from.

Larry P was a slick talkin', fly young nigga, bald headed, medium height, and outspoken. Another one of his strengths was the fact that he brought his entire immediate family in on his money making exploits from his momma and daddy on down.

His little brothers, K.K. and Rodgee, did whatever Larry P needed them to do. They were rewarded with the latest sportswear and they got picked up and dropped off at school in all of Larry's flamboyant automobiles. Their pockets would be stuffed with one dollar bills that Larry kept in a drawer for them as lunch money.

Larry's daddy, Will Moe, was an OG from back in the days of Red Walker. He would act as overseer and collect the money from the grinders at the end of their shifts. His moms didn't have to lift a finger. She barely had to show her face in the Acorns. Larry put her up in a luxury apartment in the suburbs of East Oakland.

His younger brother K.K. would eventually become his most trusted aide. All the other youngsters in the Cornfields rallied around K.K. because he had all the toys that they all wanted. He could drive any of his brother's cars whenever he wanted, plus he had all the jewelry and fly gear that the game had to offer. This was available to him all before he got out of middle school at Lowell Junior High.

Larry P's top tier soldiers and lieutenants kept his machine rolling smoothly. At the top of the totem pole was E.T., Dario, Kisu,

Stack-A-Dolla, Michael Dupree, Tiptoe, Roaster, Curdy-Bo, Black Martin, Fat Bo Bo, Steel Will, Darrel, Surrel, June Bug, Pigg, and D.B. These were the most reputable cats that made up the second generation of the Acorn Mob. These young teenagers made up the most sophisticated and organized drug distribution ring in all of Oakland at the time of their reign. No other group around during 1985 had a grand total of twelve entire housing project buildings under their control, including the 2-4 Village fourteen blocks away.

The Federal Building was just completed right over the 980 freeway ramp. The Twin Towers were menacing in the distance. Federal agents could be seen buzzing around Oakland in burgundy, gray or dark blue Dodge Aries K Cars. They were boxy little four-door economy cars with starfish symbols on the trunks.

To escape detection as well as to make a mockery of the Federal agents, Larry P purchased a fleet of the exact same cars, all paid for by the Mob. These cars would be company cars accessible to everybody within the ranks of his organization. When the Mob travelled outside of their territory they could be seen riding back, to back, to back in these K cars, four deep in each one. Mobbed out.

Larry P was ballin'. He stuck to the script and funneled every grunion of his product thru the streets. He didn't sell no weight. He broke everything down to the final compound. Two's, fews, plentys, manys, lumps and chunks. Better known as the Trifecta. Nickel bags of weed in one parking lot, dimes of heroin in another, and dub rocks of crack in the other.

Larry kept apartments and cars all over the Town. He was the proud owner of Mercedes Benzes, Fleetwood Cadillacs, and a Corvette. His favorite car in all of his fleet was his Lincoln Mark IV. This car was custom inside and out with starburst blue candy paint, with a peanut butter vinyl top and interior, equipped with opera lights and a Cartier clock, sittin' on gold Daytons and Vogues. When Larry painted the town in this vehicle, it was lights, camera, action. He paraded around with an Uzi on his lap and one of his soldiers in the passenger seat. They would both be draped in gold.

Larry took a liking to another up and coming baby kingpin out of East Oakland by the name of Lil D. Lil D took over the reins of the 6-9 Mob from Big Fee. Larry was older than D so he acted as his mentor and laced him to a few thangs he needed to know about running a crew. Their alliance was frowned upon by the older niggas from both of their projects. Big Fee, who was in federal custody in San Francisco, summoned Lil D to notify him of his disdain about the situation. According to him, there would always be bad blood between the two factions due to the bloody history that Big Fee and Red Walker had.

Lil D and Larry P continued their association and a new era was born never before witnessed in the Town. The presence of these two crews was unmatched in all of the Bay Area. They would attend local functions surrounded by an entourage of nearly a thousand youngstas, all ready to live and die for the cause.

The Acorn Mob was notorious for playing with they noses. Snorting cocaine and heroin was a daily routine for Larry P and his boys. This was another tradition that was passed on from the first generation hustlas from the area. Their perspective on this type of recreational drug use would be further validated by the portrayal of Al Pacino in the movie *Scarface*. When heroin and coke was snorted together it was referred to as a Belushi because that's how John Belushi died.

Unfortunately, Larry P's reign would be short lived. He would be gunned down in an ambush while exiting one of his many East Oakland apartments in February 1987. His presence in the Acorns would be greatly missed. His younger brother K.K. was rightfully the natural heir to his throne and the recipient of all his possessions. However, maintaining loyalty within the ranks would prove to be his biggest challenge.

Everybody in West Oakland loved and respected K.K. when Larry was alive. Now that Larry was gone, his little brother's gangsta would be tested. Several up and coming killas knew that the respect people had for him was more out of love than fear. His territory raked in millions of dollars annually and there were a number of players that wanted his spot as leader.

K.K. liked playing with his toys more than handling business. He still managed to keep the Machine together with the help of his pops, Will Moe. That would play out when it was discovered that OG Will Moe had started chippin'. Will was having trouble recovering from the loss of Larry. He felt like he had let his oldest boy down because he was in North County Jail when Larry got murdered. He was allowed to go to the funeral escorted by deputies. But when he got out of jail permanently, he fell in love with the pipe and stopped caring about the business.

With Larry P gone, Will Moe smoking, and K.K. just wanting to party, the Acorn Mob was falling off. Several other fledgling roughnecks started to rise up and challenge the Acorn prince. As a result, there would be several attempts on K.K's life. K.K. would prove to have more lives than a cheshire cat and survived every one of them.

On one occasion the Oakland drug taskforce raided one of the Acorn's parking lot dope spots. A shootout ensued and K.K took off on foot armed with a pistol. The officers gave chase and shot K.K. while he was jumping over a fence, severing part of his ear in the process. No weapon was ever found and K.K. was treated and released from Highland Hospital.

It was business as usual and K.K. was up to his old tricks again playing the crowned prince of the ghetto, riding around in all of his flashy cars, wearing all of his jewelry, huffing his own product over a C-note.

One afternoon he was riding up 10th street with D-Rell in his candy brandy wine '84 Caddie Brougham. As he approached the light on Market, a nondescript minivan rounded the corner and pointed an AK47 out of the sliding door. The assailants Swiss cheesed the car, hitting K.K. and D-Rell several times in the head. Both of them had to receive emergency surgery at Highland Hospital. D-Rell had to have a metal plate installed in his brain. They both lived.

K.K.'s nonchalant attitude concerning the assassination attempt would make it evident to his brethren that he was more of a prince than a general. Another lower tier soldier in the Acorn rankings would capitalize on this opportunity to seize the reigns of the Acorn Mob. His name was Derrick, aka E.T., nicknamed such due to his resemblance to the movie alien. He would allow K.K. to remain as the figurehead for the Mob and de facto leader. Meanwhile, he would call all the shots from behind the scenes. His love and respect for K.K. wouldn't allow him to turn his back on him or attempt to dethrone him. Even though several events would occur that would affect the Mob's solidarity greatly, E.T. kept it solid with K.K. and even went so far as to seek vengeance on all his enemies.

A large family of Louisiana transplants migrated to the Acorns from New Orleans. When they got to Oakland they realized the dope traffic in the part of the Corns that they lived in could be lucrative, so the younger teenage family members started to go outside and hustle, calling themselves the Bayou Boyz. This caused friction with the Acorn

Boyz and a civil war broke out between them. The Bayou Boyz had killer in they blood and refused to back down. They didn't have no problems bustin' a few heads; that's all they knew back home. Several casualties took place on both sides and the Bayou Boyz were on the brink of taking over the Acorns. This was until the Acorn Mob stepped up and let it be known that everybody could get it on the New Orleans side, women and children included. The Bayou Boyz packed it up and relocated to the Regency Towers on 3rd Avenue in Funktown, never again returning to the Corns.

The Oakland Housing Authority got fed up with all the complaints they were receiving from anonymous callers that resided within the projects. They decided to subcontract a group of armed security guards on location twenty-four hours a day in the first, second, and third Acorns. They would have an actual office as their headquarters. They were all big burly Samoans. Their approach was by the book, but sometimes roguish. When they caught anybody buying, selling or using any type of drugs on the property, they would beat that person within an inch of their life, then arrest them and hold them in their office until the ambulance or the OPD came to pick them up.

One day a young Corn nut named Sorrel was in the second Acorn serving a knock. When he was approached by the guards, he attempted to resist and they put hands and feet on him. He managed to wriggle himself free and run to a nearby unit where he kept a strap at. When he returned, he shot up the guard shack with an AK47 and killed one of the guards. The guard had 57 total 7.62 caliber holes in him. Sorrel fled the scene but was later apprehended, tried, convicted, and sentenced to Y/A. He wouldn't be eligible for parole until he was twenty-five. The Housing Authority suspended the security contract immediately and removed the guards from the location.

The Acorn Mob was fully entrenched in an all out drug war. 2-4 Village had decided it was time that they break away from the Acorn umbrella. K.K.'s younger brother Rodgee was the field general for the 2-4 projects. On a bright sunny day in 1990 Rodgee would fall victim to one of the worst triple crosses in Oakland history. One of the Acorns own workers named Legs would call him and inform him that their spot on 10th Street was out of dope. Rodgee said he would bring him a G-bundle to keep the spot warm until they re-upped. When Rodgee pulled up to the house, he told his passenger D-Wayne to stay in the car. Rodgee got out of the brown Toyota Supra as Legs was exiting the house. He popped the gas tank cover at the back of the car and went to hand Legs the bundle. Just then a white Hyundai pulled up with a light skinned nigga hangin' out the window wearing a beanie with a Jheri curl wig. The nigga yelled Rodgee's name, and when Rodgee turned around the nigga started whopping at him with an Uzi. Rodgee caught all the hot slugs in his head and torso and dropped to the ground where he lay floppin' like a fish. The car containing the shooter commenced to drive off, then all of a sudden came to a complete stop. The shooter started yelling at the driver *Back up, back up, he still movin'*. The driver slammed the car in reverse and skidded Back. The shooter jumped out and instituted the kill shot. Boom. When the Hyundai finally drove off a dark blue Fleetwood Brougham followed behind it and pointed choppers out the windows as it drove by. All the neighbors flooded out they houses devastated as they looked at Rodgee's lifeless body. His head looked as if it was a watermelon that had been dropped from a ten story building. An old lady came out with glad trash bags to cover his head up so the children didn't have to see this atrocity. The wind kept blowing it off as everybody stood silently looking at his blood and brains oozing out of his dome piece.

The next body to drop would be a female Acorn Mob member named Rhonda Red. She was West Oakland's first queenpin and ran the third Acorn with her brothers Mark, John John, Maurice and Lil Nate. Rhonda Red was found outta bounds with a bullet lodged in her skull behind the wheel of a rent-a-car that was still running.

E.T would be the last in the lineage of generals to keep the Mob on tap. He would become rich and prove himself to be a worthy adversary to any and all who stood against the Acorn movement.

K.K. would withstand several storms in the game and live to father over a dozen children in Oakland, Berkeley and Richmond by some of the baddest bitches in the Bay Area. The West Oakland legend lived well into his forties until he was gunned down in a mistaken identity killing while sitting on a side street in the car with his cousin in Berkeley California. OG Will Moe would outlive all three of his sons.

The Oakland Housing Authority launched a major redevelopment and tore down the original third Acorn and replaced them with beautiful single family homes. The Acorn Mob fizzled out but would re-emerge under an entirely new banner later on in the 33rd.

The Acorn housing projects have a rich history in the producing of mastermind drug lords like Red Walker, Larry P, K.K. and E.T.

Drug Lords of Oakland

CHAPTER 6 -- LIL D

Lockwood Elementary and Havenscourt Junior High were strategically located on 66th Avenue between two of Oakland's most notorious and historical housing projects, 65th and 69th Villages. They were also the training ground for Northern California's youngest, richest, and most prolific cocaine kingpin, Little D.

Little D (pronounced LiI D), came of age during the 1980s, an era most infamous for the Reagan Administration and the Oliver North/ Iran Contra Guns for Drugs scandal. The U.S. Government and the CIA were responsible for tons of cocaine being flooded into America's urban inner cities.

LiI D is the nephew of Oakland's first godfather, Big Fee. He was raised on Seminary Avenue about ten city blocks from 69th Village. His mother's family was one of the largest families in the Village. Two of his uncles worked for Big Fee during the Mob's reign, and his aunt was one of Big Fee's baby mommas. She was the actual link that tied Big Fee and Lil D's families together.

D spent a lot of time in the Village at his grandmother's house right in the heart of the Village. This was where he was first exposed to the Mob's business practices. He got to see how they moved from the time he was old enough to walk.

69th and 65th Village was a tight knit community. The people that lived there broke bread or starved together, shared good times, bad times, lived and died together. No matter what, they stuck together through thick and thin. It was only natural for the youngsters who came up in these projects to ride as one from the very first time they played with each other in the sandbox. East Oakland was a virtual battleground during the 1980s. The Village youngsters stuck together like glue. If you got into it with one of them, you got into it with all of them. From elementary on up to high school, the Village Boyz moved as one.

Little D became the center of attention during his Lockwood Elementary School years, mainly because of his uncle Big Fee and where he was from. He was also very athletic and played baseball and basketball for the youth leagues around town. A number of these sports events would end with the players and spectators fighting. Little D not only had hands, but he also had plenty of people to back him up. If you crossed paths with him at one of these games, he was usually in the company of twenty to thirty Village niggas that would stomp a person out on call. The Village even had a female faction that went by the name of the 69th Angels. They were quick to put in work on bitches that needed they asses beat.

You could always tell who the Village Boyz were because they usually all rode beach cruiser bicycles with white walls. Three deep to a bike, one rider, one person on the handlebars and another person on the pegs. Ten or fifteen bikes in a row. One of the beach cruisers would even be a double man bicycle.

Their dress code was Levi 501 jeans, cotton hoodies and beanie hats. The beanies would be boxed on top or left hanging like the Smurfs wore on the cartoon. Much like their predecessors, their signature hairstyle was straight bald heads.

These were little project kids that played a grown man's game in the streets. The sons and nephews of killas and gangstas from the original 6-9 Mob, they had been indoctrinated at an early age to the ways of the cutthroat ghetto they lived in. From the first time most of them looked out their windows as infants, they witnessed the mayhem that took place in plain view. Mob shit was the norm. Seeing bodies drop wasn't nothing unusual to them.

Not too far away from the two housing projects was the Rainbow Center on Seminary and East 14th Streets, a youth recreation center and park. Rainbow Center was the home for most of the sports programs that the area youths participated in. It also doubled as a hangout after school and during the summer months.

The original cast of characters that rallied around Lil D were Fat Hub, Kenny Wayne, Black, Scarfarce Sylvester, Da-Da, Wayne Gordon, Marvell, Candy Man, Lil Pat, Gary Tillery, Benny Mays; Green-eyed Floyd, Rick, Shawn, Pooh Man, Lil Jerry, Dudda, Duke, James Magnum, Seagram, Stone, Yogi, Fat Gene, Rab, Chauncey, Dion, Tim, D.H., and Lil Wayne, Big Fee's son, just to name a few.

Lil D was the glue that connected Seminary to the Village, and Rainbow Center was the meeting ground for this future team of natural born killas. Seminary itself was a vicious strip of drug dens, speakeasys, liquor stores, and alleyways. So many murders occurred on Seminary that it was sometimes referred to as the cemetery. By the time Lil D was in junior high school, Seminary and the Village were one clan, respectfully known as SNV. This vicious group of youngsters encompassed a territory that spanned two entire housing projects and at least twenty city blocks that surrounded them. They put emphasis on the phrase that strength comes in numbers.

Mojo's skating rink on 71st and East 14th was a popular hangout. Anybody who wasn't from the Village would run the risk of getting whupped, slapped and stomped by going there to skate. They would be asked where they were from, and if their response was anything other than the Village, their ass was good as done. They'd be lucky to get up out of there with a mere concussion.

The universal fight song at that time was the Tom Tom Club's *Genius of Love.* Once that song came over the speakers, everybody would go into a frenzy and be ready to fight. Only a few rival turfs attempted to go skating at Mojo's. They would always get the short end of the stick when the funk went down because the ViII was close by and reinforcements were just a hop, skip, and a jump away.

There were a couple other well known skating rinks, like Foothill Square and San Leandro's Roller Garden. Whenever the Village Boyz ventured out to these other venues they usually travelled fifty to sixty deep. Their uniforms were cotton sweatsuits with SNV ironed on their beanies, t-shirts, jackets, and pants legs.

They bumped heads with other turfs at carnivals, concerts, arcades, and malls. Places like the Malibu Grand Prix go-cart track, the Eastmont Mall, Four Star Movie Theater, and the Castle Video Arcade. The famed rap star LL Cool J got a slight taste of Town business after a concert at the Oakland Coliseum. He and his entourage decided to go to the Castle Arcade after the concert. Lil D was there with his squad. One of the younger Village Boyz asked LL for his autograph and LL got smart and told him "Hell no." Lil D stepped up to LL and slapped him like a bitch and said "Nigga, do you know who the fuck I am? I'm Lil D from SNV." The rest of the Village jumped in and whooped LL's D.J., Cut Creator, and his bodyguard. After this experience, LL wrote the song *I'm going back to Cali.* Uh-uh, I don't think so.

Lil D got his first crack at the game when his old school patna put him on selling weed on Elizabeth Street. Elizabeth was a cross street right off of Seminary Avenue. The spot was in the middle of the block in some white apartments. A person could walk up, drive up, or ride a bicycle up and purchase a nickel bag on up to a zipper of that Columbian Gold weed. Liz, as it was called, was one of the original weed spots in East Oakland. At the time it made pretty good money, a couple thousand dollars daily. All of D's folks used to go on Liz and take shifts grindin' for him whenever they needed a few chippers in their pockets.

Lil D implemented a payment plan that basically enabled his workers to pay themselves. He would give them twenty-four nickel bags worth a total of a hundred-twenty dollars, but he only wanted a hundred from it and they could keep the rest.

Liz was rollin'. It wasn't nothing for a cat to run thru a solid G bundle on a good day. On any given day there was like ten to twenty young grinders on Liz. To the young cats out of the Village and off of Seminary, Lil D was a godsend. Most of their mommas and daddies were drug addicts or on welfare, so the fact that they could go on the turf with nothing and come home with a couple of hundos was lovely, especially at fourteen or fifteen years of age.

Lil D used to get rode around on the handlebars of one of his patna's beach cruisers. He was still a young tyke himself, surrounded by an entourage of young Villsters that worshipped the ground he walked on. He wasn't flashy at all when he first started getting money, he was just a basic turf nigga with a plan.

By the time Lil D entered high school at Fremont High, he was already well known. Fremont High was basically dominated by the High Street Bank Boyz, a nearby turf. Fremont was located right on the corner of High Street and Foothill Boulevard. The Bank Boyz were a reputable old school turf that was run by a youthful knockout artist by the name of Big Wee Wee.

All of this changed in the fall of 1983 when Lil D began attending classes there. Fremont High became a 69th Village meeting ground from the time the gates opened in the morning until the final bell rang in the afternoon. Village niggas from every other school in East Oakland used to take shifts picking Lil D up and dropping him off safely. Tony's Pizza Parlor, across the street from Fremont High, became their headquarters Monday thru Friday.

When the Village and the High Street Bank Boyz bumped heads, it was usually after hours at the Fremont dances or the Fremont swimming pool. High Street wasn't deep enough to fend the Village Boyz off. After months of getting caught out of pocket and getting jumped by the Village Boyz, High Street had to throw in the towel. Fremont High School belonged to Lil D and the Village.

D was a good student and had perfect attendance. Fremont was right on the Foothill strip so it was a combination car show, fashion show, weed spot, and hangout all in one. Some of his classmates included the legendary rapper Too Short and his homey Freddie B. His best friend was another rising star by the name of Fat Hub. Hub used to drive Dee to school in a black Chevy El Camino on Starwire rims and Vogue tires. They were so tight that everybody thought they were brothers because they had a striking resemblance to each other. Hub came from a big family on Seminary that ran East 16th with an iron fist. His spot was known as the Block.

Lil D started coming out of his shell in high school when he started stepping up his clothing game. His favorite store in the Eastmont Mall was called Mr. Zee's. That's where he took all his workers to shop. The owner was an Arab cat who used to lock the store down when the Village Boyz came in there. Lil D used to get ushered to the back of the store to get first dibs on all the exclusives that weren't on the shelves yet. Mr. Zee's favorite pitch line was "Don't worry about the price, my friend, I hook you up." If you spent enough money, he would give you a flat rate on everything. Mr. Zee's was famous for all the popular name brands like Le Coq Sportif, Diadora, T.I, Fila, Troop, Bally, Nike, Reebok, Adidas. Lil D had a wardrobe like a rap star. Every shoe that came out, he had to be the first to have it.

He finally decided to get himself a car in the eleventh grade. All of his older patnas already had cars. It was only fitting that he paid homage to his older predecessors, so he flipped a 1971 four-door Chevy Impala. He had it painted smoke gray with a burgundy felt top and matching interior. Him and his schoolmate Byron from 7-7 Greenside used to ride back to back. Byron had a turquoise blue four door Chevy sitting on Vogues and color key hubcaps. When D pulled up, all you heard was the song *Aqua Boogie* by Parliament, his favorite song.

The weed game was fairly lucrative but it was getting old. Another hustle was on the horizon. His best friend Rick started dropping hints about how they should look into diversifying their game plan. Rick started lacing him on the new thang called crack. Rick's momma stayed on Ritchie and Macarthur Boulevard in some Housing Authority apartments. These apartments had a lot of foot traffic by dope fiends looking for crack cocaine. Lil D slid thru there to check out the movement himself. Shit was boomin'. By the end of the day he was convinced that this was the thang to do. He instantly rounded up his most loyal workers from Liz and redirected them to the apartments. He briefed them on the new get-down and put them to work.

Rick initially had all the hook-ups on the cola, so he went and snatched up a measly quarter ounce (7 grams) of hard. Basically it was just a starter package to see what it did. They bust it down in all twenty dollar dub rocks. That shit was gone in fifteen minutes. A couple neighborhood roughnecks had to get whooped in the process. Apparently they weren't too happy about them Village niggas just popping up and getting money. Once they figured out who and what they were dealing with, they fell back. Ritchie and Macarthur was officially 69 Mob territory.

Lil D applied his previous payment strategy from the weed spot on Liz to the new spot on Mac. Twenty on the hundred was the standard. It worked like a charm. The crack thang was moving a whole lot faster than the bammer weed. He pitted his workers against each other and kept them volleying for the employee of the month slot. The bonus was usually an old school Chevy, all original. The flip side was if one of the workers fucked up a bundle or started smoking gremies (rocks crushed in weed), then the other workers would have to whup him. This kept them in line for the most part.

Lil D never roamed alone. He was always in the presence of several head busters and wig splitters, all willing to give their life for this miniature phenomenon who stood only five-four. They started calling themselves LDI, Little Darryl Incorporated. They were the immediate branch of Seminary and the Village niggas that surrounded Lil D on a daily basis, his own personal secret service.

Several other squads associated with D all fell under his umbrella. The most notable was Peoples Incorporated on 35th Avenue. His childhood friend Stone was the field general for that area. People from everywhere starting claiming the Village. Then of course every major click had its share of wanna bees, people that aren't really part of the squad but claim it. D put them to work too.

Lil D was the consummate businessman. Everybody had a part to play in the scheme of things. If you came correct and were about your cheddar, he would work with you. If you were a sucker and he knew it, he would front you a kilo on consignment, then send the wolves to double back and rob you. After that you would owe him twice. Fuck that up and the LDI hittas were comin'.

Papa Joe's auto detail shop was just a stone's throw from the apartments that D and Rick had sewed up. It was a popular meeting ground for neighborhood superstars who came there to network, get they cars washed, and shoot dice. One hot, sunny day, D was up there getting his girlfriend Bernadette's candy apple red box Chevy buttered. Meanwhile, he was standing there hollering at T.B. from Dirt Road, another major coke boy. Little did he know that he would be the target of an assassination attempt this early in his career. An older loose cannon in the neighborhood was unhappy about how the Village Boyz had just took over the area. As D and T.B. were standing there discussing coke prices, shots rang out. One of Lil D's protégés jumped in front of him and yelled "Fuck tha World, I love Lil Darryl." He took two bullets in his side as he tackled Lil D to safety. D wasn't hit but T.B. caught a slewy to the spine. He would never walk again.

The fat ass individual that called the hit on Lil D would soon find out the hard way that this young man meant business. Lil D and his people wasn't no joke. He was laced by the original 6-9 Mob members and had several hittas on the payroll. His response was swift and effective. After this incident, everybody in the Town knew not to fuck with Lil D and the Village. That's if they didn't already know.

After that episode, Lil D started networking on a hi tech scale. The operation was moving so fast that his crew basically outgrew the apartments on Ritchie and Mac. He was playing with kilos now and was ready to spread his wings, all while he was still a junior in high school.

He was a regular around town and a standout among the older D-boys in the entire Bay Area. His squadron was unmatched in violence and moneymaking. The first real merger he made was with Larry P from the Acorn Mob. Larry was the general of the second generation Acorn Housing Projects. A beast, to say the least. This connection was frowned upon directly by Lil D's uncle Big Fee, who was being housed in the Federal Holding Facility in San Francisco at the time. D was a visionary though and was looking toward the future instead of the past. Larry P had a well organized machine of his own that made hundreds of thousands weekly. The two of them together consolidated the East and the West sides of Oakland and created a powerhouse never seen before in Town history.

Not long after that, another major factor by the name of Big Rudy got rolled up by the Feds. Lil D unwittingly inherited the bulk of his clientele. Lil D and Hillbilly were already cool because of Lil D's sister, who introduced them previously at a party. Hillbilly was one of Rudy's number one movers and shakers. He was a major dealer out of North Oakland's Bushrod neighborhood. LiI D and Hillbilly became thicker than thieves. Lil D's acquisition of this new money stream would catapult him to multi-million dollar status.

Lil D also took a liking to another high school D-boy by the name of E.B. from the Keller Plaza housing projects on 51st and Telegraph Avenue. D started flooding the Keller Plaza with weight and practically gave E.B. his blue drop 450 SL Mercedes Benz, a toy D got from Daddy G, his mentor.

Lil D had outgrown his initial coke line in the Town and had hooked up with some L.A. boys who couldn't keep up with his flow of things either. He was moving too much weight too quickly. It wasn't until he met up with a fellow Bay Area baller named J.B. that he would really take it to the next level. D met J.B. on Macarthur one day and they became boys immediately. They started pooling their money together and fucking with J.B.'s Columbian connection.

With the exception of a rival key boy named A-F from 99th and Plymouth, LiI D had the Town sewed up from the east to the west to the north. He expanded to Berkeley and had a cat named Luvell from the waterfront (H^{2}0) running that entire area. Then he met a real slick nigga out of Richmond's Kennedy Manor named Sonny for the Money whom he collaborated with on several levels from cocaine distribution to a favor for a favor in the streets. If Sonny needed somebody dealt with, he would use Lil D's soldiers, and if D needed somebody dealt with, he would use Sonny's soldiers. This worked out perfect. They had South Side Richmond on lock until Sonny got killed by another notorious Richmond hitter.

LiI D was Northern California's King Tut. By the time he graduated from Fremont High School, he was the boss of a multi-million dollar drug ring with connections to the Columbian Cartel. Rick was his lieutenant, Black was in charge of all day to day operations, Yogi was the lord high executioner, and Lil Jerry was the chick magnet.

Whenever a new car hit the market, these five cats went and bought a fleet of them. Not just one, but at least five of the same vehicles, all different colors. From the droptop BMW 325i, to the drop Corvette, drop Benz, Saab Turbos, Grand Nationals, to the convertible Maseratis. They could be seen campaigning past the Eastmont Mall with their arms hanging out the windows of their Maseratis all wearing blue face Rolex watches. This was phenomenal for the rest of the inner city youths to witness.

Lil D had become an Oakland don. When he and his associates made appearances at functions, it was like a celebrity sighting. Crowds parted at events like Moses parted the Red Sea when they saw Lil D and the Village come thru.

In 1987, the legendary Compton rap group NWA headlined a concert at the Oakland Auditorium. Several L.A. Crips followed the tour and made the six-hour drive to the Town for the concert. They stood out like sore thumbs in their gray and blue Pendleton shirts and Jheri curl hairstyles and driving lowrider cars. Those styles were played out in Oakland and nobody but Mexicans wore Pendletons and drove lowriders. The whole Town was there but the 69th Village was the deepest. With Lil D leading the pack, they came thru the joint like gangbusters wearing thousand dollar leather Bally sweatsuits with gigantic Bs on the back. The Crips mistook them for Bloods and got theirselves in a world of shit by making derogatory comments toward one of the Village niggas. All hell broke loose. Lil D and them mopped the floor with them Jheri curl wearing jerks. Security couldn't save them. Everybody ran for the exits and the Village Boyz went to they Chevys and popped the trunks. It was all bad for the rest of the Crip Boyz that they caught up with outside. The next day the *Oakland Tribune* headline went as follows, *L.A. CRIP GANG MEMBERS GET SHOT UP AT NWA RAP CONCERT AT THE OAKLAND AUDITORIUM.*

Lil D Incorporated moved like a mob. Nobody in any crew in Northern California could strike a match to their regime. They enjoyed box seats at the World Series, front row seats at a Sugar Ray Leonard boxing match only a few rows behind Donald Trump.

He also had his irons in the fire on several legitimate levels. The majority of his empire, however, was drug fueled. He purchased a couple homes in the Oakland and San Leandro Hills. He invested in record production and put out a single by his right hand man Rick titled *Livin' in a Cracktown*. The song described the impact that the drug had on the community. And then he invested into the upstart of rapper M.C. Hammer's career.

As a teenager Lil D ascended to a level of power previously unheard of. He started dressing differently, wearing casual slacks and button-up designer shirts with diamond cufflinks. He traded in his tennis shoes for designer flats with tassels. He began being revered in the streets as the most feared gangster in the Town.

Lil D preferred being driven around than driving himself. He was notorious for sitting in the passenger seat of his latest new vehicle while one of his boys was behind the wheel. He could barely be spotted sitting real low with his hat flipped up like a white boy. Usually he would be holding onto an Uzi or a Mac 10.

In November of 1988 his twentieth birthday was approaching. He wanted to celebrate his birthday in a fashion that no other D-boy in his age range had before, so he started planning a black tie affair. Mr. Zee from the clothing store would be the front man for the party cash wise. He rented out the Turf Club at Golden Gate Fields horseracing track. This would be a party of epic proportions.

On the night of the party, at the front entrance to the gala was a burgundy slant nose Porsche 930 Carrera with a ribbon on it. This was Lil D's birthday gift to himself. All the boys and LDI members wore black tuxedos with royal blue cummerbunds from Selix on Broadway. Lil D, the birthday boy, wore a white tux with a black shirt and no cummerbund. Gangstas from Detroit, Los Angeles, San Francisco, Richmond, and EPA were all in attendance. His closest business partner, J.B. from San Francisco, showed up in his black Rolls Royce droptop. M.C. Hammer and En Vogue performed their hits. Several NBA players were there to pay homage to the street king, Gary Payton and B. Shaw, just to name a few.

The party went off without a hitch for the most part. A few windows got broke when a few unruly ballers started high siding and throwing bottles at bitches. Golden Gate Fields just chalked it up to the thirty grand that D gave Mr. Zee to pay for the shindig. After the party, Lil D was escorted to his new Porsche by his boys with their Mac 10s out in true Scarface style. J.B. threw him the keys and he hit the Bay Bridge for a night of playing at the strip clubs.

Unbeknownst to D, the Feds had been trailing him for some months now. They had narrowed their mission down to an apartment building in Lake Merritt's Adams Point. This was where D and Black kept a bachelor pad and a safehouse. Coincidently, one of the Federales already had a unit right above theirs. On several occasions the Feds had been in the elevator with Lil D and made small talk with him about sports and stuff. They couldn't believe how young this man was.

Ten days after his legendary party, the Feds decided to move in. They could smell the cocaine cooking from below. They also claimed they could hear several loud chopping noises. They already had the warrant and the keys to the apartment. When they opened the door in their DEA flak jackets, guns drawn, Lil D was literally caught with his hand in the cookie jar. All he could say was "Y'all finally got me."

Lil D, the most feared drug dealer in Oakland, was booked into custody and charged with cooking and manufacturing fourteen kilos of crack cocaine, possession of seven kilos of powder cocaine, a semi-automatic pistol, and ten grand in cash. On his way to the station one of the arresting agents asked Lil D off the record not to harm his family, based on the fact that he knew Lil D had once dated his daughter.

Once the Feds had D in the holding tank, the officers and agents started celebrating. They all took turns peeking thru the two-way glass at the teen kingpin that ran the cold streets of Oakland with so much power and authority.

Lil D lawyered up immediately. He fought his case for about two years and lost. He was sentenced to thirty-five years in federal prison. He still held the strings to his organization for a while. He was allegedly recorded hooking his lieutenant Black up with one hundred kilos over the phone. He was also reportedly responsible for several contract killings that were never proven by the authorities.

During his prison stint he wrote a book chronicling his meteoric rise and fall in the dope game. He was also featured in the popular Prison Hip/Hop Magazine, Don Diva, as Oakland's Young Don.

In 2016 President Barack Obama commuted Lil D's sentence along with six thousand other federal drug offenders, and just like that Lil D was back.

Lil D was the youngest and most feared of all the drug lords that came up out of Oakland's inner city ghetto.

Drug Lords of Oakland

CHAPTER 7 -- BLACK

After Lil D fell, his field marshal took over. His name was Tim, but everybody called him Black. He acquired the nickname early on in life due to his pitch dark complexion. Black was left with the reins to a two hundred and fifty kilo-a-month operation. This was what Black had been groomed for his entire life. He took on his role with the seriousness of a third world dictator, only Oakland, California was his kingdom.

Black was raised in the 69th Village. His family was the biggest family in the Village hands down with sixteen children with him the youngest boy. He was the quintessential representation of the old saying that the dog at the end of the litter always had to fight for its food. From the time he was old enough to walk, his brothers and sisters made him scrap for his issue.

Two of his older brothers, Norb and Clyde, were enforcers for the original 69 Mob directly under Big Fee, Norb being one of the worst killers in Oakland history. Norb was given a license to kill by the FBI in exchange for his testimony against Big Fee during the Godfather's trial. Black worshipped his older brothers and watched their every move. His family name carried weight in the Village. Black learned at an early age that there wasn't no love outside of his household, so he tailored his attitude to be cold and calculated from day one. His older sisters were rough too. They took up for him just as much as his brothers did and they would hold they own in a scrap against any average nigga in the area.

At first glance, a person could tell that Black didn't take no shit. His eyes were darker than a coil snakes. He kept his mean mug on, and when a person crossed his path, it was usually all bad. Coming in contact with him was similar to running into a panther in the wild. His whole persona exuded danger and his cold stare alone was enough to send chills down the devil's spine.

Black went to Havenscourt Junior High with the rest of his Village brethren. He managed to keep a low profile due to his softspoken demeanor. It wasn't until he hooked up with Lil D that his name started ringing bells around the Town.

Initially, Lil D's best friend Rick had the right hand man slot before Lil D fell. Black played his position as second fiddle. He was solid and game tight. His business practices were immaculate and he executed his version of street justice with precision. Eventually, Rick started slacking and laying up with too many women to handle his business. Black stepped up to the plate and took over his spot.

Lil D didn't have no problem giving Black more responsibilities plus action at all the keyz he needed. For one, Black used to babysit him as a child. Secondly, he was older than D. Black was diplomatic and still had luv for Rick because they all was eatin' regardless. Even though Rick wasn't originally from the Village, Black never treated him differently.

Black's specialty was handling blood work. He loved getting greasy in the streets and busting that chop suey. He was bloodthirsty as hell to say the least. His brothers had instilled in him the code of the streets at an early age. As the years progressed, he grew to be a master practitioner in the art of war.

Black was a few years older than Lil D. He always acted as the voice of reason in Lil D's ears. All D had to do was give the nod and Black would put the smash down. He also started his own network of rock spots that he had to launch hostile takeovers to acquire, Bromely Street being the first.

The niggas that was already getting money on Bromley felt like they didn't have to lift up because Bromley was located in the same neighborhood as Seminary and the Village. Black went and rounded up as many wanna bees as he could and armed them with baseball bats, sticks and pistols. Then he dispatched them to slide thru there and whup, slap, stomp or shoot anybody out there who wasn't on his team. That's exactly what they did.

After that, Black forged an alliance with some other major cats on 77th and Rudsdale. They were more than happy to fall up under the Village umbrella. The main niggas getting money over there was Indian Tone, Ant Wash, Les Wash, Black Leon, Squeeze, Long Tone, Ty-Ty, Hashi and Dame (RIP).

One of Black's hangouts was a tiny little barber shop on Seminary called Yours and Mine. It was owned by an OG playa named Sonny. Sonny was game orientated and let Black, Rick and Yogi basically use the back of his shop as an office. The back of the shop was connected to a hole in the wall club called the Vintage Inn. When it got dark and the club started cracking, Black and his squad would suddenly appear in the joint deep as shit with their guns tucked.

In 1988 when Lil D fell, Black was the best man in line for the job, no questions asked. The stage was already set. He stepped up to the plate, took the ball and ran with it. The rest of Lil D's soldiers fell right in with Black. Rickey Cheater even played his position knowing deep down inside that the slot Black had should have been his.

They immediately started putting their foot down in the Town. In situations where Lil D would've showed diplomacy, Black chose force. In truth, Black was more violence prone than his young mentor was. He reinvented his network. Not only was Black's team a major presence in Oakland, but he built alliances with other individuals that spanned all the way to Houston, Texas. He developed a major bond with the heavyweight rap mogul J. Prince from Rap-A-Lot Records, home to the legendary rap trio, the Geto Boyz.

Black paved the way for record deals for his younger patnas from the Village, Seagram Miller, Gangsta Pat, and Yukmouth. The Rap-a-Lot family would become regular visitors to the East Oakland 69th Village housing projects. Scarface, Bushwick Bill and Willie D could all be seen making cameos in Seagrams video *The Vill, The Vill, The Goddamn Vill.* Speculation would have it that J. Prince and Black had a lot more going on behind the scenes in the distribution department aside from music.

Everything Black drove was the color of his name from his Buick Grand National to the Saab 900 Turbo he owned. Black was all business behind the wheel with his thousand dollar Motorola brick phone planted to his ear, usually being trailed by one or two carloads full of his hitters. This was their way of putting security on him.

Although he loved and respected Lil D for passing him the torch, he had his own way of doing things. D and Black still collaborated on issues via the prison phone, sometimes even having arguments. They were recorded orchestrating a hundred kilo deal in code by the federal correctional officers monitoring the phones. Black was also overheard telling D, "I'm runnin' this shit now."

Black was a cutthroat to say the least. He considered himself the judge, the jury and the executioner. In the streets he was the law. His primary goal was to take over the Town completely. There were only two major factors standing in his way, A.F., leader of the A Team, and Manuel, A.F.'s silent partner.

Every year Fat Hub and Too Short gave an annual picnic for their birthday. They both shared the same birthday, so it was only right that they invited the whole town out to enjoy it with them. In 1989 the picnic was held at Fruitvale's Diamond Park. All the gangstas, D-boys, local singers, rappers and top notch chicks showed up to partake in the food, drinks and booty shaking contests.

This was the golden age of hiphop. Richie Rich, Dangerous Dame, MC Ant, Pooh Man, MC Hammer, Digital Underground, the Conscious Daughters, Paris, the Gov, and the Geto Boyz were all there. Black was there with the Village squad too. A.F. and the A-Team showed up to support the Gov from Handle Bar Records, who just so happened to be his brother Joe-Joe. One of Black's headbusters named Squeeze, from 77th, had words with A.F. and they started chunken 'em. A.F. couldn't hang with Squeeze from the shoulders and he tried to run to his drop Mustang to grab his pistol. Fat Hub and his East 16th Block Boyz calmed him down and told him to let that shit go, so he jumped in his drop and bounced.

This incident would start a mini war among the two competing drug teams. Black already had hittas, but A.F. enlisted a young monsta off 85th named Dirty Red. The night after the picnic, A.F. had Dirty Red slide down 77th looking for Squeeze on a Kawasaki Ninja. When he pulled up, he let off on the crowd with two Glock 9 millimeters. Then he holstered the guns and popped the clutch on the Ninja and did a wheelie up outta there. Several people were hit in the fray, including an old lady.

Black had major love for Squeeze and had his killas bring out the heavy artillery for this special occasion, AK-47s, Tommy Guns, and 50 calibers on tripods. The streets was on fire. Handguns were obsolete, they were given to their baby mommas to put in their purses at the nail shop.

Due to the latest war, the Town got broke down in sections. Each turf was forced to take sides depending on which team was feeding them, 69 Mob or the A-Team. Black had everything from 77th to 48th Avenue sewed up in the east. On the west his allies were Campbell Village and the Acorns. In the north he had Bushrod.

The A-Team had the 100s, the 90s, the 80s and the Rollin' 20s. His counterpart Manuel was related to a cat named Hollyrock in West Oakland who ran Ghost Town. That consolidated their ties to the west.

Black himself was furious about the whole situation. For one, he had been hearing rumors about the A-Team having cheaper prices on the kilos than him. On that note alone he decided to release the hounds.

Yogi was Black's lead enforcer, however, he didn't mind puttin' in work himself. After all, his older brother Norb was a real live hitman for the original 6-9 Mob, so he was laced to the murder game. He also paid Norb to act as an overseer toward his muscle. The rest of his henchman would consult with Norb about how to pull off hits and get away with them.

Black ran a tight ship. When somebody within his ranks fucked up, he would bring them up on charges. His courtroom was inside an unfurnished single family home in East Oakland. The back room was lined in plastic and there was a single chair in the middle of the room. The plastic was used to catch any blood spatter and body parts in case it got ugly. Sometimes individuals had to be beaten, tortured or even disposed of piece by piece.

Black decided to bring heroin back in the Village. The new and improved machine that he was implementing sold five-dollar balloons of powder snorter's dope to the fiends. This would be an extra added revenue stream on top of the kilos of coke he was slanging on a day to day basis.

Black from the Village was the head nigga in charge in Oakland, California from 1988 till 1991. Wasn't no secret. Word on the street was that he was on a real live power trip. On one occasion him and a couple of his wanna bees were shopping in West Oakland's M/B Mall at Oxford Street when all of a sudden in walks Hollyrock, West Oakland's flyest hustla. Rock just so happened to be Manuel's cousin, one of Black's sworn enemies. Words were exchanged and Black put hands on Hollyrock, then slapped the bitch he was with. Rock swore on a stack of bibles that he was gonna kill Black from that day forward. This was a promise he never made good on.

All of this friction would kick off Oakland's second and bloodiest drug war. The violence and bloodshed would surpass what took place during the early '80s between The Family and the 69 Mob. Black and the Village already had a long line of hittas on the payroll. His muscle was all inhouse. A.F., however, had to import his gunmen from other parts of the city. He employed Dirty Red and L.G. from 85th. Manuel had P-Dub and Lock-Lock from School Street running with the A-Team as well. These were all certified killas.

L.G. got caught slippin' one day in the 65th Village. One of Black's vans fulla killas slid up, the door to the van slid open, the guns came out and shots went off. L.G. got hit several times. An Oakland PD cruiser just so happened to stumble onto the scene. The van took off and a hi-speed chase ensued. The van raced out of the ViII and ended up flying up Seminary Avenue with the police hot on its tail. The van ignored all the stop lights in its path. The officer attempted the same thing and wound up T-boning a vehicle that was crossing the four way intersection on East 16th. The driver of the vehicle died later at the hospital. The original shooting victim L.G. survived.

Days went by and the driver and occupants of the van were apprehended. Rick, Norb, and Squeeze were found to be the culprits. They were all booked into custody and charged with Attempted Murder, 187 PC, for the shooting of L.G. and Murder for the driver in the car that died.

The war raged on. On May 7th of 1990, a 69 Mob representative named Terry Cooper was at M.S. Market on Seminary to meet up with his baby mama to give her some money. As he entered the store, three men followed behind him armed to the teeth. One of the men bumped into his kid's mom while she was holding her baby in her arms and gave her a deadly menacing stare. Once inside the store, they unloaded on Terry with a Dae Woo 223 machine pistol and a Glock 9. Terry was rushed to the hospital but died of his wounds later.

His son's mother got a good look at all three shooters and identified them as A.F., A.B., and Lock-Lock. Terry was one of Black's crew and this was a major act of disrespect toward his organization. Several other incidents would occur during the course of the next few days that would send the Town into a frenzy. People started dropping like flies. Black started seeking retribution on the East Side of Oakland as well as the West.

Black had a saying that he repeated to his soldiers daily. He called it Funnin' and Gunnin'. The drama and funk in the streets was all part of the game as far as he was concerned. He preached this gospel to his hitters every morning. When he got to his headquarters every morning, he would brief his hit squad on who was next on the list of people that were in the Mob's crosshairs. The relationship with the Mob and the Acorns began to sour like Big Fee predicted. Big Fee's nephew Lil D's efforts to repair the decades long rift between the two factions would soon fizzle out and become null and void. When Black inherited Lil D's empire in 1988, he also got the entire 69 Mob's legacy of bad blood and mayhem. Black held the fuse to a virtual powder keg just waiting to explode, and as far as he was concerned, it was his destiny to light it. Mobbing was par for the course . He was born and bred for this.

A multitude of events would occur that would further divide the Acorn Mob from the 69 Mob, causing a complete separation in the on-again/off-again love affair they shared, and none of which the 69 Mob's leader, Black, or the Acorn's Leader at the time, E.T., had anything to do with initially. These incidents were just part of the tragic history that dated back generations before them. The bloodshed was just too far beyond repair to ever forget. Lives had been lost and once again the funk would be reborn.

In February 1987, Larry P, an Acorn general, was ambushed on the front porch of his momma's apartment. In January of 1990, his successor, Darren Banks, got blown away while exiting the freeway near Lake Merritt in his Saab turbo. There was much speculation about who was responsible for these acts, but no substantial proof.

The next general in the Acorn Mob's lineage was a vicious young street thug called E.T. who took over with a vengeance. He didn't know who to trust or who to blame for these Mafia style hits, so he took it upon himself to declare war against the Mob, the biggest shark in the pond.

One of A. F.'s underlings was driving along in a drop Chevy Impala on the back streets of the 80s when all of a sudden a wood paneled station wagon passed him by. Once the wagon was in front of him, he noticed a large caliber rifle on a tripod in the back with bullets being fed thru a belt and a man wearing a Freddie Krueger mask behind the trigger. But it was too late. Over one hundred shots rang out. He lost control of his vehicle and crashed into one of the buildings at East Side High School. When he bailed out of the car and ran, another masked gunman jumped out of the wagon and chased him on foot, shooting at him the whole way. He fled over a fence and dropped dead immediately. He was Dirty Red's best friend, Stan the Man.

The ultimate act of disrespect took place in front of Yours and Mine Barbershop on Seminary when Big Yogi was caught in a hail of bullets while he was waiting for a haircut. A late model Cadillac pulled up and unleashed exactly 69 rounds out of the magazine of an AK-47. The statement was made. Black was devastated at the loss of the guy he considered to be his OG and mentor.

In the midst of all the drama the rapper Seagram from the Village released his freshman album on Rap-A-Lot Records titled *The Dark Roads*. The album was an instant success and sold over eighty thousand copies. It was an ode to all the fallen soldiers in the recent drug war.

Seagram made reference to several factors that would now be in the Mob's crosshairs. His ill threats were duly noted by these millionaire gangstas and they put a bounty out on his head. One day while Seagram was sitting in his candy green Mercury Cougar waiting on a hooker in the Murder Dubs, he was lit up by gunfire. He never made it to the hospital, he died instantly.

The bodies were stacking up in the county morgue and the Feds decided to step in. They got warrants for numerous wiretaps on Black and A.F. Manuel was too elusive and strayed away from cell phones completely.

The Feds recorded hundreds of hours of cell phone conversations on the two kingpins. Black was overheard barking orders to his henchmen. He made several threats that were recorded, one of which the Feds found very ominous. His exact words were, "I want A.F.'s whole family, including his momma, dead."

On the west side of Oakland there was a young hustla named Meechie that would find himself in the middle of the whole situation. Although he was a freelance baller doing his thang in Campbell Village, he was playing both sides of the fence. Sometimes he would cop keys from A.F. and sometimes he would purchase his work from Black.

During their wiretap surveillance, the Feds overheard several conversations where Meechie was the topic of discussion. It became evident that he was doomed to be the target of an assassination attempt. When they notified the local authorities, the lieutenant decided it would be appropriate to at least notify the young man that his safety was at risk. During a routine traffic stop Meechie was detained and brought into the homicide division, at which time they informed him of the intel they received and how he needed to take it seriously. They let him listen to the tapes. Meechie let it go in one ear and out the other. Once he left the cop shop, he continued with his regular program, stating, "I ain't hard to find; I'll be on the turf."

The Fed's prophecy proved to be true in the early morning hours at a West Oakland stoplight. Meechie was ridin' in his fire engine red Chevy Corvette ZR1 bumpin' his music. All of a sudden a car slid up next to him and three armed men exited the vehicle with guns blazing. Meechie didn't have a chance, his life was over before he knew what happened. When police arrived, he was a block away slumped over the steering wheel with the horn blowing. His car had jumped the curb and crashed into a BART station fence. The shooters hopped back in their vehicle and sped away on the wrong side of the street.

Black was still making money at a rapid rate, but it was evident that all the drama was having an adverse effect on his business interests. A lot of other major ballers in the Town became reluctant to do business with him or his constituents for fear of getting caught up in the crossfire.

The Village squad was on the warpath on behalf of Black. They had suffered several casualties as well. The streets had hell to pay. Black relocated his headquarters to a neighborhood in the 50s and assigned another one his close patnas by the name of Rab to be his lead enforcer. Rab stepped up to the plate and started knockin' shit down immediately.

Kilos of cocaine were at an all time low of 14.5 per. The Columbians and the Paisanos were flooding the Town. Several freelance ballas started inserting theirselves into the dope game and filling the gaps that the A-Team and the Mob left wide open. Black expanded his operation into Berkeley's waterfront. He let a cat by the name of Lovell run the area. This proved lucrative for a short period of time until Lovell got knocked down. Apparently, the A-Team already had roots down there and wasn't feeling the competition.

By early 1991 the Feds had enough. They moved in and captured Black and charged him with continuing a criminal enterprise and major drug distribution conspiracy. He could only be linked to two kilos of heroin and one kilo of high grade cocaine. He was also suspected of being the orchestrator of at least thirty killings in 1990, an extremely bloody year in which the homicide rate reached 161 murders.

In the following two years after Black's arrest, Oakland would see its highest murder rates on record, 165 in 1991 and 175 in 1992. This was due to remaining factions volleying for power, the Lacy/Flowers Gang and the leftover Village crew.

Meanwhile, Gangsta Black was being held at Santa Rita County jail in Dublin with a federal hold. While in trial he was being escorted to court one morning down a long hallway. He was shackled by his hands and feet in full waist chains. Another inmate worker came toward him under escort, he broke the k-line and attacked Black. Apparently, the other inmate was a family member of the A-Team. As the deputies got the situation under control, Black struggled to get loose but couldn't. He started yelling at the other inmate and swore to have his family killed.

As the months went by, Black fought his case tooth and nail. He even followed in Big Fee's footsteps and rewarded one of his lawyers with one of his vehicles, his blacked-out Buick Grand National GNX. None of the murders could be linked directly to him, however, he would still be convicted on the charge of possession and conspiracy to distribute narcotics and sentenced to twenty-five years in a federal penitentiary. He was twenty-seven years old. Black's reign of terror was over.

While he was in custody, his older brother Norb would be murdered in another drug dispute on 84th Avenue. This would hurt him to the core.

Black served twenty-three years and was released in 2016 to a federal halfway house in Fresno, California. He remained there for six months before he was released completely. He went on to marry the mother of his children in a Palm Springs wedding ceremony.

Black was the most vicious drug lord in Oakland history next to Big Fee.

CHAPTER 8 -- ANT

When crack cocaine hit Oakland in early 1982, hardly anybody knew how to convert cocaine powder into crack rocks. Dorothy had been trained as a professional chef, and she figured out the best method for cooking the coke using ginger ale or 7-Up that would bring back extra on every batch. Her revolutionary method would become referred to as bouncing. She was one of the first cookers in Oakland that knew how to manufacture the substance and prepare it for street use.

For a fee, she would cook up major weight for all the local D-boys that didn't know how. If she really had love for them, she showed them how to whip it up theyself. When she cooked for individuals that was green and game goofy, she would charge them to whip it up and then keep the extras in the pot. This was what she called the gypsy twist.

She was basically a queenpin in her own right. Her stompin' grounds was an area of East Oakland on a strip of Macarthur Boulevard where she plied her trade in all of the rundown hotels that were lined up from 90th Avenue to 105th.

Dorothy's favorite nephew was a young teenager, Anthony, but everyone just called him Ant. She spoiled him rotten and liked to keep him with her every chance she could. He was a spry young man that was always bright eyed and bushy tailed. He had a special affection for his big auntie and stuck to her like glue. He watched closely how she conducted business with all the players and hustlas she came in contact with.

Ant was raised on a strip of Plymouth Street in between 98th and 99th in a three bedroom, single family home, right down the block from the Dirt Road, Oakland's first and most prominent rock spot.

By the time Ant decided to come off the porch in 1984 and get his feet wet in the D game, he was already laced up, thanks to Dorothy. Not only did he have a direct line on some of the best blow that money could buy, but he already knew how to cook the coke, cut the coke, package it up and sell it. When it was time to make his debut on the block, all he had to do was come out of his front door and walk to the corner and post up. Nobody would even attempt to dispute his presence out there on the Dirt Road because he was the nephew of the top chick in the Town.

Ant didn't waste no time stacking his paper up. To keep him company out there while he was grindin' he decided to have his best friend watch his back. His name just so happened to be Anthony too, so he was called by his initials A.B.

Initially both of them only had aspirations to flip a clean car on Stars and Vogues. The car game in Oakland was at an all time high, and the block that started it all was right around the corner from where they was hustling.

The Falcon Boyz car club was on Sunnyside and 96th Avenue. They used to line their two-tone Falcons up and down the block. All the Falcons had rims and music and when they hit the strip they were a sight to see. Ant was infatuated with the spectacle and couldn't wait to get his scratch together so he could put him something together to hit the strip.

Ant started killin' the block with his special blend of pink coke. He was top secret about his special blend during the cooking process. Nobody else had his quality of product. All the dope fiends started looking for the little teenager with the pink dope. Even when he was at school they would be waiting outside of Elmhurst Junior High to get their slugs. Since the OGs on the spot couldn't compete with his work, they just started buying him out as soon as he hit the block. This was a win/win for them because he had the fattest slugs in a five mile radius. All they had to do was chop his dubs down to double their money.

This gave Ant the leeway to start venturing out and networking on other turfs nearby. He was killing the game with that Pepto Bismol colored Mother of Pearl. Once he put the bounce twist on it with that ginger ale or 7-Up, no other grade of coke could light a match to his.

He started spending most of his time hanging with some of his schoolmates that lived in the Oakland Hills. One of his buddies, Jerrin, had an older brother who was already gettin' real money in the dope game named Jed. Ant and A.B. used to go ride mini bikes and YZ80's with Jerrin on the weekends up behind Knowland Park. Jed took a liking to the hustling youngstas and started picking them up and taking them to the skating rink at Foothill Square, all the while lacing them on how to stack their money in the dope game. Little did Ant and A.B. know that they were in the presence of a millionaire; he just wasn't a so-called turf nigga.

The whole town would soon find out about Jed's status when he got apprehended at the Tijuana border with a briefcase filled with a million dollars cash. He was taking it down to Mexico to cop nearly a hundred kilos from his cartel buddies. Jed could account for the money because he was also a music producer. He would later produce hits by the legendary Oakland rapper Richie Rich, who just so happened to be his neighbor in the Oakland Hills.

Teenage Ant was rubbing shoulders with the upper echelon of the Town's drug trade. He would slide thru his Auntie Dorothy's house on 100th and C Street and just watch the ballers come and go to do business with her. Ant was soaking it all up.

Aunt Dorothy's house was where all the moneymaking took place. All day long her clientele would be picking up and dropping off money and merchandise. Her house was a combination stash house, cook spot, and where they counted dough.

Ant would be there with A.B. and his younger brothers Joe Joe, Sammy, and Hennessey by his side. One of their young playmates took a liking to Ant and stuck to him like glue. His name was Dario and he would eventually become Ant's right hand and protégé. Between his family circle and his tight knit cadre of friends, they all became pretty popular around the area of the 90's, 100's and the alphabets. People started referring to them as the A-Team.

Before anybody knew it, Ant became the kilo man. With his ability to bounce one kilo into two, his profit margins were outrageous. He started flooding all his clientele with the best A-1 cola on the market. He was also able to provide the cheapest prices per kilo around. Even cheaper than his only competition from 69 Village, the one and only Lil D.

Ant had amassed more than enough money to start putting together some of the prettiest Mustangs and Cougars the Town ever would see. One of his drop Ford Mustangs would be custom equipped with right-hand steering. He gave a black hardtop '67 Stang to Dario for his birthday. Ant's next trophy would be a '67 Mercury Cougar XR7. He took it to Yarboroughs and had them chop the top. They fitted it with a peanut butter convertible buckskin top. Then he took it to Mico's and had it sprayed candy brandy wine burgundy on gold Daytons and Vogues. His love for Mustangs was evident when he flipped another '67 drop Stang and painted it candy apple green on Zeniths and Vogues with lambskin interior. He rode it till he got tired of it, then he sold it to a gangsta nigga out of West Oakland named D-Folks.

For the most part, Ant and his crew were just hustlas and playas. All they liked to do was get money, ride their cars, and fuck with bitches. He learned a long time ago that funk and money didn't mix when he witnessed the Funktown Boyz take over the Dirt Road temporarily in the earlier 80s.

He decided to relocate the majority of his family that wasn't in the game to a neighborhood in Sacramento. This would keep them out the way while he was getting money in the Town and provide them with a better way of life. He invested in a small store and had it remodeled into a restaurant. The restaurant was named Flowers Fish Market and it was located in a predominantly black neighborhood called Oak Park.

Around late 1987 Ant took what everybody thought would be a major hit. The Oakland Police Department had been watching his Aunt Dorothy's house and decided to obtain a warrant to hit the spot. For the most part they came up empty handed until one overzealous task force officer decided to search the backyard and stumbled onto approximately one million dollars in cash and a money counter buried under the doghouse. The money was Ant's. He couldn't be tied to it personally, however, because the place was clearly not his residence. News of the find hit the morning papers and the whole town knew whose dough it was.

Ant took the loss and kept on pushing. Not too long after that, his closest competitor Lil D would be apprehended by the Feds and sent away. Lil D and Ant had a fairly decent rapport and didn't step on each other's toes. Lil D respected all the Dirt Road niggas because they were the ones he was buying dope from when he got started. He would eventually blow up to levels far surpassing them, but he still tipped his hat to them cats.

However, his mentality did not get passed on to his lieutenant. Black from the Mob would take the reins from Lil D when he fell. His mind state was that whoever wasn't with him was against him.

Black's crew and the A-Team would co-exist peacefully until 1989, the day of one of Oakland's annual picnics. The picnic was held at Fruitvale's Diamond Park. It was given by another major factor named Fat Hub. Ant and one of Black's young headbustas got into a squabble. Ant wasn't happy about the results and attempted to go to his trunk and grab a pistol. The nigga that put hands on him, Lil Squeeze, told him to put the gun down and they could chunk them again. Ant decided to let it go right then because it was too many witnesses around. This incident would soon spark the second most vicious war in Oakland history that would spill over into several different neighborhoods.

Although Lil Squeeze was a Mob affiliate, his original stomping grounds was on 77th and Rudsdale. Later that night (after the picnic), Ant dispatched one of his hired hittas named Dirty Red to slide down the 700 block and hunt Squeeze down. Dirty Red pulled up on a Kawasaki Ninja and let off with two 9 millimeters on a crowd of people standing on 77th. He missed Squeeze by inches but hit an old lady standing next to him. This was the beginning of all out mayhem.

Dario had been known to put a little work in for the A-team when necessary. Since the funk jumped off between his squad and the 700 Club, he decided this was the perfect time for him to put a move down. He had been selling bricks of coke to one of the main ballers on 77th, Black Leon. Leon was an independent baller that didn't really declare his alliance to the 6-9 Boyz like everybody else on his turf.

This would prove to be a nearly critical mistake on his behalf. During the midst of the breakout war between the two rival factions, Black Leon decided to call Dario to grab a few bricks. Dario kept it cool with him over the phone and told Leon to meet him on Golf Links Road past Grass Valley Elementary. Leon agreed and said he could be there in thirty minutes. When Leon pulled up, Dario was already there leaning up against his car. Leon handed him a bag with over forty-three thousand dollars in it. Dario reached down on his car seat as if he was going to grab the bricks of coke. When his hand appeared again it was holding a 45 caliber pistol. He shot Leon straight in the face, then jumped in his car and drove off, leaving Leon for dead.

Black Leon managed to maintain consciousness. He struggled to put his still running car in neutral and roll down the hill to the nearest gas station at the bottom of Golf Links Road. When he pulled up to the gas pump, one of the customers noticed immediately that he was bleeding profusely out his mouth and jaw and ran to the attendant to call for help. Black Leon's face had a gash in it the size of a recently fucked vagina. The ambulance and fire department arrived within minutes and rushed Black Leon to the nearest hospital. Surprisingly, he would live.

The war was starting to heat up, requiring Ant to drop his player persona and pick up the guns and put in his own work. He started purchasing guns by the dozens to arm himself and his crew with. For his own protection he started riding around with assault rifles on his seat wherever he went.

The 69 Mob boss was Ant's arch enemy. Him and Black could not stand each other and declared to hit each other on site. In late 1990,

Black was attending a funeral for two of his close friends from West Oakland's Campbell Village. Fila and Tracy were best friends that were murdered attempting to purchase two kilos of coke in a KFC parking lot in Carson, California. Black had been tight with Fila and Tracy since their childhood when Fila's Aunt Sheila went with 6-9's Big Fee.

Ant and the A-Team got wind of the funeral and decided that this would be his opportunity to assassinate Black. As the funeral was letting out, Ant pulled up to the front of the funeral parlor in an Oldsmobile wagon. He spotted Black coming down the front stairs and bounced out with an Israeli Uzi. When he pulled the trigger nothing happened. Just as he was about to pull the trigger again, a police cruiser rounded the corner. Meanwhile, everybody was taking cover and grabbing their weapons. The pallbearers froze and struggled to hold the caskets up. Ant jumped in the wagon and the police gave chase.

The Oakland Police cordoned off the area. Ant turned a few corners then bounced out on foot. He was eventually sniffed out by a police K-9 hiding in somebody's backyard garbage can. He was cuffed and stuffed in the back of the police car and taken down to the station to face charges. He quickly made bail.

Everybody in the Town knew that Ant had pulled this failed attempt on Black's life. This upped the ante in the back and forth shootouts between the Mob Boyz and the A-Team. Both crews were on the warpath.

The A-Team would soon prove themselves to be a rich and deadly organized crime family. They put so many people's heads to bed that they started being known as the Flower Boyz. So many families had sent flowers to their loved ones graves and it was because of that the name stuck. The actual murderers responsible for these misfortunes were three of Oakland's worst killas on record; Dirty Red, P-Dub, and Lock-Lock, straight motherfuckin' killas.

The A-Team-Flower Boyz had recently developed a partnership with another million dollar organization, the Lacy Family. This organization was a behemoth in its own right with ties to the Murder Dub neighborhood and the Black Muslims. Their leader was a criminal genius by the name of Manuel, M.L. for short. When these two squads hooked up, it was understood that whatever funk each team had would be a part of the deal.

The notorious Pondo (aka P-Dub) was initially a hitter for the Lacy Clan. He was an ex-military marksman and a real live serial killa. He would act on the orders of M.L. and make anybody in the 23rd Avenue area that was selling dope either hook up or book up. If they refused, the only thing that would beat them to the morgue was the headlights on the hearse. P-Dub was a major acquisition in the Flower Boyz ranks.

Dirty Red was a juvenile delinquent from 85th Vlllage known for bustin' heads. He had close ties to the alphabets, the 90's and the 100's. His resume included robber, dope dealer, killa for hire. His MO was to get paid by a rich dope dealer for knocking an enemy down, but first robbing the victim for multiple kilos of dope, thousands of dollars in cash, making the hit, then riding off into the sunset. He would then funnel his newfound proceeds through the streets of Oakland and San Francisco's Tenderloin District. Ant knew he would be an asset to the A-Team and didn't waste no time putting him on the payroll. Out of all of Ant's hired hittas, he paid Dirty Red the best.

Lock-Lock was a whole other monster all his own. He was originally from a fairly unknown spot in the Fruitvale District, School Street and Plietner. Plietner gained a little momentum as a crack spot but Lock-Lock decided to venture out and seek his reputation elsewhere. The earth was his turf and he would bust his gun for the highest bidder. Ant and Manuel liked his work and put him on the payroll as a freelance enforcer

Ant started to maintain a low profile. What began as a little bitty fist fight blew up into a full fledged drug war over drug prices and territory.

North Oakland's Bushrod neighborhood had long been associated with the 69 Mob ever since Lil D had been in high school and was copping keys from Big Rudy. Black had been using the Bushrod area as a sanctuary during the funk season. When word of this got back to Ant, he sent the hounds through there. Dirty Red pulled up on 59th and Cannon street and let his cannon speak. The only person hit was Bushrod's number one stunner, Hillbilly. His finger was shot off in the gunfire but he managed to survive without the bullets doing any major damage.

The Feds had started to pay attention to the upswing of violence in the Town and decided to obtain a wiretap warrant for Ant's cell phone. Ant was then recorded discussing the distribution of several automatic weapons while he was shopping at San Leandro's Bayfair Mall. They traced the location of the call and decided that this would be the prime time to move in on the drug king.

Agents located Ant inside the mall then took him into custody. Inside his pocket were the keys to a rented minivan loaded to the gills with an assortment of Mac 10s, AK47s and Uzi machine guns. The vehicle was secured and Ant was taken into custody for illegal gun possession.

As soon as Ant was allowed his phone privileges, he contacted one of the Bay Area's most successful criminal attorneys, the infamous Tony Serra. Ant had kept him on a very hefty retainer specifically for occasions like this. Serra was an expert in dealing with the Feds and was instrumental in getting Ant's case dismissed earlier on the attempted assassination of Black. Now he was back on the job to get his client out on bail for these weapons charges. Ant was granted bail within days and was back on the scene.

The ATF and FBI were frustrated by this time and were pooling their resources to put together a multi-count indictment aimed at the upper echelon of the Lacy/Flowers organization, which took several months of investigative work to put together.

Manuel was the first one to get snatched up on the indictment. He quickly made bail and fled. He was eventually captured nearly a year later in Denver, Colorado while scalping tickets to a Broncos game at Mile High Stadium. Once Manuel was extradited back to the Bay Area, he would fight his charges by appearing in court in pro per without an attorney representing him. He single handedly beat the rap and would be released back to the streets.

Ant would once again defeat the Feds with the help of his hi-powered attorney. Only one member of the A-Team would actually have to sit down for a period of ten years. His name was Deandre and he basically took the fall for both the Lacy and the Flowers organization.

Black from the Village would find himself in custody not too long after this. His crew would not be able to carry on without his presence and they would become defunct after several back-and-forth shootouts with the Flower Boyz in 1992.

Due to these occurrences, Ant and the Flower Boyz were the undisputed kings of the drug trade in Oakland California. Ant's number one priority was to filter the blow back into the Town and to keep a peaceful flow of things. He put a new twist on all the kilos he sold hard. It was a spinoff of the earlier pink dope he used to serve in his Dirt Road days. Now he hit the streets with his new and improved form of pineapple dope, named for its bright yellow hue.

Ant had also gotten himself a new connect with a Mexican out of San Jose named Jerry the Mec. Jerry was a young man like Ant but he had kilos coming out of his ears. He was also an avid bodybuilder and a high level steroid dealer with ties to Mexico. Jerry was handing Ant like sixty keys a month. The Flower Boyz was back in business. They were basically the only game in town with the exception of a few independent ballers, some of whom had just recently bubbled during the drought.

Down in the dubs Manuel was undergoing several major setbacks. One of his closest buddies, Snoop, had just came out from under several hot-ones. Not too long after he touched down, he died behind the wheel of his Stingray Vet when he passed out from an overdose. He had been one of the Lacy Clan's most efficient enforcers.

To add insult to injury, P-Dub was gunned down while attending his baby daughter's birthday party in the Fruitvale district. When he arrived to attend the affair, his killers were lying in wait. As soon as he exited the vehicle, they started letting off with semi automatic handguns. He attempted to run down the street and knock on a neighbor's door. When they opened the door and realized what was going on, they slammed it in his face. The gunmen finally caught up with him on foot and unloaded. P-Dub was still breathing when the police and EMTs got to the scene. One of the officers took one look at him and was quoted as saying: *Oh that's P Dub, He's better off dead anyway.* He died on the scene.

Rumors started circulating as to the source of the hit. P-Dub had been robbing, killing, and extorting everybody in the 23rd Avenue area for some time now. An informant in a separate trial for another drug dealer made an astonishing accusation under oath concerning the P-Dub murder. He was quoted as saying that the Lacy Clan killed P Dub. This was never proven, however. These recent turn of events took a major toll on Manuel's crew.

In 1994, Ant and Manuel's entire organizations ran into another bump in the road. During several recent wiretaps they were all overheard discussing in code a late delivery of approximately seventy kilos from some Hispanics out of L.A. Ant had already sent the Hispanics seven hundred thousand dollars for the shipment, yet it hadn't arrived. Jerry from San Jose was instructing Ant on how to deal with the situation.

During several months to come, several hours of recorded conversations would be documented as the A Team, the Flower Boyz, the Lacy Clan and the Jerry the Mec felt comfortable talking openly on what they thought to be untraceable cloned cell phones. Drugs would be referred to as Gucci bags and zippers. The Feds cracked their code and convinced a grand jury to hand down a number of indictments in August of 1994. When it came down, a number of residences throughout the Bay Area would have their doors kicked off the hinges in early morning raids. Taken into custody were Ant, Dario, Joe Joe, Lil Rob, Jerry and his counterpart Blondie. They were all charged with conspiracy to distribute multiple kilos of cocaine, fraudulent use of a counterfeit access device, possession of cocaine base for sale, with a weight clause enhancement. Jerry was charged separately with possession of large amounts of steroids.

The only actual evidence recovered were six kilos from a residence linked to Lil Robert as well as eight hundred sixty grams located at a spot belonging to his partner in crime, Big Sheldon. Ant did not personally get caught with a crumb of anything. Phone conversations alone linked him to the conspiracy. He would be charged as the founder and the leader of the entire conspiracy, however.

During the trial, several issues would be brought up that would somewhat affect the trial. There was a conflict of interest in reference to Ant's attorney of record, Tony Serra. He had been going thru his own legal troubles in a separate tax evasion trial. He also had represented more than one of the defendants on entirely separate occasions.

They would finally begin the trial phase in 1996. It would go on for a period of four months until a mistrial was declared. The US Government would refile immediately and start the entire process all over again. This time it took three years but they would be successful and come down with a conviction against all of the defendants on all counts. In 1999 Ant was given the mandatory sentence of twenty-seven years in federal prison. Oakland's Mayor Jerry Brown attended the sentencing and held a press conference afterward. He swore on a stack of bibles that kingpins like Ant would not be tolerated in Oakland, California. His brash statement would fall on deaf ears. Whenever one drug lord fell to the wayside, two more stepped up to take his place.

Ant had the best prices (per kilogram) and some of the cleanest classic cars of any other drug lord in Oakland's lineage of D-Boyz.

PHOTOS

Big Fee (right rear)

Big Fee & Sheila with Tootie & his wife

Big Fee 1978 Mugshot

Big Fee's Hollywood Mansion
formerly owned by Clark Gable

Big Fee's ornate bronze casket on horse-drawn carriage

Big Fee's funeral procession

Mick Mo (kneeling center)
Numonics Album Cover

Funktown Harv

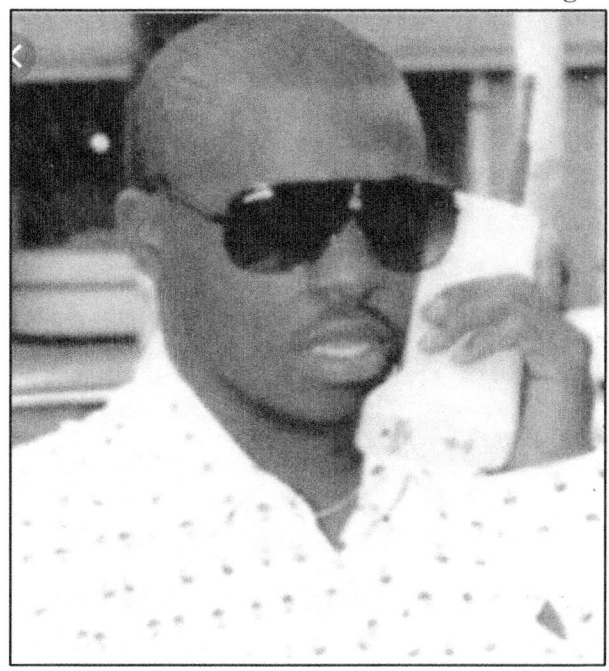

Lil D, Big Fee's Nephew

Lil D in the Feds
(Three River Texas 2002)

Lil D (kneeling) & Big Will

Lil D's 20th Birthday Party, 1988

Fila & Ricky Cheater, far right

Red Walker (right) and the Author

Tracy & Fila from Campbell Village
(murdered in Carson, California)

Black from the Village (3rd from left) in the Feds 2006

Ant

Wheelchair Will (before shooting)

Wheelchair Will (after shooting)

Fat Twin, Lil Twin (on right & left)

Brookfield Charles & Griselda Blanco

Cuzzo Kev (right)

(L-R) Mack Major, Magic & Fed
from Tray-Seven

Big Rudy's Rolls Royce

Ant's custom '68 Cougar

D-Folk's '67 Mustang

K.K.'s infamous Cadillac Brougham

The Acorn Housing Projects

The Acorn Hi-Rises

The Mohr Houses (near Acorns)

Twin Towers Federal Building
downtown Oakland

Oakland

32nd & West Street
Ghost Town U.S.A.

West Oakland Housing Projects

West Oakland Housing Projects

Oakland Taskforce Vehicle

Huey P. Newton (left)
Black Panther Leader

OAKLAND HOMICIDES

- 2009: 110*
- 2008: 125
- 2007: 127
- 2006: 148
- 2005: 94
- 2004: 88
- 2003: 114
- 2002: 113
- 2001: 87
- 2000: 85
- 1999: 68
- 1998: 81
- 1997: 111
- 1996: 103
- 1995: 153
- 1994: 151
- 1993: 157
- 1992: 175
- 1991: 165
- 1990: 161
- 1989: 148

* Includes two investigated by BART police

Oakland Annual Homicide Chart
1989 to 2009

CHAPTER 9 -- HOLLYROCK

Little James was born to a beautiful pint-sized lady named Johnnie Mae. She was every bit of five feet tall and ninety pounds soaking wet. She was a brown skinned, street smart, outspoken little firecracker. Since the moment that Little James was born, Johnnie Mae struggled with heroin addiction.

Big James basically left Johnnie Mae with the task of raising James by herself. Due to her addiction, she struggled immensely to make sure that her baby's basic necessities were met. Keeping a roof over the both of their heads was nearly impossible for the first few years of James's life. They ventured from pillow to post and ultimately found themselves homeless. As prideful as Johnnie Mae was, she would be forced to pitch a tent in downtown Oakland at Old Man's Park for her and her baby, right across the street from the North County Jail and the Police Department.

Old Man's Park was dope fiend central. It was in a prime location only two blocks away from Swans, an indoor shopping center that sold clothes and other items for bargain basement prices. Only three blocks in another direction was the Salvation Army. Every day at noon the Salvation Army would open up the soup kitchen and feed the homeless for free. James and Johnnie Mae would be there faithfully.

The public bathroom area of Old Man's Park was literally a shooting gallery. Numerous overdoses occurred there on a daily basis. Used needles would be found strewn all throughout the children's play area and near the swing sets, some even in the sandbox.

Regardless of their station in life, James stuck to Johnnie Mae like glue and loved her more than anything in the world. Johnnie Mae didn't hide none of the sad realities of the world from her baby boy and always told him the truth about the way things were, whether good or bad.

She was well known and loved by all the drug addicts, dealers and hustlers who looked out for her and little James alike. Some of them would even help wash his clothes by hand, then hang them up on a nearby fence, making sure that nobody would steal them. If they had food, they would feed him. If they had spare change, they would walk him to the nearest candy store and purchase him some penny candies.

Eventually Johnnie Mae would catch the eye of a hardcore ex-convict recently released from Folsom State Prison by the name of

Big Eric. He was six-four with twenty-two inch arms on the hang. He was head over heels for Johnnie Mae and took to little James right away. Johnnie Mae liked Big Eric equally and not soon after he expressed his love for her they all three became a team.

Eric moved Johnnie Mae and James into his mother's house on 34th Street and before they knew it, Johnnie Mae was pregnant with her second child. Little James was about four years old when his little sister arrived. They named the brown eyed baby girl Ericka. and she was beautiful.

Life was going smoothly for the family of four. James was enrolled into pre-school at nearby Hoover Elementary. The school was just a block away and was just recently built. It took up an entire city block and the playground was massive, providing the children with plenty of space to play sports, horse around and fight.

James was a short little runt of a kid that had to fight all the time because of his lighter complexion. The children at Hoover were a rough bunch and could be cruel at times. They would talk about each other's mommas and call Johnnie Mae a dope fiend and a hooker. This would get an instant reaction out of James and he didn't mind picking up a stick or something to get his point across.

For the most part, he was smart in school and all the teachers loved him. He learned how to use his lighter skin to his advantage and started sweet talking the teachers to get his way. The little girls in his class started paying attention to him at an early age. By the time he was in the first grade he had two or three girlfriends already.

James and his little schoolhouse buddies started getting into mischief. It started before school when they would all crowd inside the corner stores and stuff their pockets with all the zu-zus and wam-wams they could. After school they would go to Alameda and steal bikes and snatch purses. Sometimes they would run errands for the hookers on San Pablo. James used to love to see the hookers sashay to a car window and couldn't wait to sneak a peek at their ass cheeks when they leaned in to make the deal. He had dreams of being a pimp one day himself.

By the time he was ten years old, James had witnessed so much that nothing seemed to surprise him. He carried himself with the maturity of a teenager much wiser and older than his years. Around his neighborhood he started being known as Icy because of his ice cold stare in the face of danger. Little did anyone know that he was mentally recording all their moves for future reference.

At the age of twelve, Icy would start having his first run-ins with the law. All the vice cops knew him by name and had driven him home to his momma on several occasions. Big Red and Suzie Q were the neighborhood vice cops and told him to get off the ho stroll every time they seen him out there.

Icy would find himself in 4th and Broadway, Juvenile Hall and Los Cerros Boy's Camp all by the time he was fifteen. The straw that broke the camel's back was when he shot one of his schoolmates at Marcus Foster Middle school and then threw the gun on the roof of the school. His schoolmate would live, but this episode would get Little Icy James sent to California's Youth Authority. While he was away he would hone his skills as a master manipulator, a gangster and a hustler.

In 1984 James would be paroled. His momma, Eric and Ericka were all living in a rat infested, piss smelling hotel on the ho stroll called the Silver Dollar. It was a four story sugar shack of a building with communal bathrooms on every floor and a communal kitchen on the third floor. Johnnie Mae managed the place and their family lived there free of charge.

The drug of choice had changed entirely while James was locked up. The entire country had jumped from heroin to crack cocaine. One of his running buddies from back in the day, Charlie C, had rose up and pioneered the first crack houses ever in Ghost Town USA, the neighborhood that James called home.

The neighborhood was called Ghost Town due to all the abandoned houses in the area. This became prime real estate for Charlie C and his brothers, Dino and Marquise. They would open up shop in the abandos and serve rocks out of the clothing dryer slots so the buyers couldn't see their faces. Once one abando got too hot, they would relocate to another one nearby.

As soon as word hit that Lil Icy James was back on the scene, Charlie C slid thru the Silver Dollar to give him a jug. He laced Icy up on the new and improved money stream. Selling crack was the new business. Icy was all for it based on he didn't have two wooden nickels to rub together at the time.

Charlie C went outside to his Cougar and returned with a chunky white nugget of cocaina. He threw Icy his first ever quarter ounce worth about four hundred fifty bucks wholesale, nine hundred retail. He gave the work to Icy free of charge and showed him how to chop it up and serve it. The Silver Dollar, Icy's parole address, turned out to be his first rock spot.

Icy gave his mother and Eric a sample of the substance to promote to the other tenants in the hotel. Crack wasn't really they thing but they were known to take a mack-blast every now and then.

He cut up all dub rocks, put them on a all white dinner plate and waited for the first knock on the door. It didn't take long for the word to get around. When the knocks started coming, Icy would let the dope fiends choose which one they wanted after they handed him the money. Unknowingly, Icy had accidently cut his first batch of rocks so fat that the knocks started calling them Hubbas after the Bubblicious chewing gum, the largest pieces of gum on the market at the time.

James shared his area of the hotel with the love of his life, Antoinette. She was a high-yellow, long-legged beauty with freckles and a bubble butt. She was a couple years Icy's senior with a voracious pussy. When Icy came home from CYA she was pregnant by another dude, but Icy decided to adopt the baby once it was born and do the real nigga thang. The baby boy's name was Jermel. Icy and Antoinette went down to city hall and killed two birds with one stone. They got married and had baby Jermel's last name changed to his.

The first two soldiers to jump on Icy's team was both little hard heads from Ghost Town, Grady-Bo and Young Julian. They both had just got out of juvie and wanted to get in on the ground floor with the new money making movement. Young Julian was the oldest at fourteen and Grady-bo was thirteen. In the beginning, they would sit in the spot twenty-four hours a day trying to bubble.

All they had was a .22 caliber rifle with three bullets in it that they took turns holding while the other one answered the door and served the knocks. This thwarted all potential robber smokers that might even consider running up in the spot and bustin' a dope fiend move. Some of the fiends still found ingenious ways to fandangle the youngstas. Sometimes they would ask to taste the dope then spit out a lemonhead candy in its place. Or sometimes they would cuff the real rock between their fingers then drop a piece of sheetrock on the carpet, then decline to buy it. Sometimes they would try to shortchange the youngstas or pass counterfeit bills. All of these sneaky tricks would get them beat the fuck up once Grady-Bo and Young Julian discovered their sheisty actions.

As traffic started boomin' Icy realized it was time to expand. One of Julian and Grady-Bo's classmates named Shalon lived on 30th between MLK and West. It just so happened that her mom was one of their best customers. Once she found out that the two of them knew her daughter, she invited them to stop by the house. Shalon's momma knew that this was an opportunity for her to smoke for free so she enticed them with the prospect of posting up at her house and serving the clientele of smokers that she had stopping by already. Young Julian ran it by Icy and he signed off on it, giving Julian free reign to run the spot. He armed him with a .22 caliber pee shooter and gave him a bundle every day after school to take over there.

The next spot that they opened up was at a Broadway hustla's apartment named Hollywood. He lived a couple blocks up from Shalon's house on 30th near Telegraph Avenue. Hollywood was a real cool player type dude that used to come by and shoot the shit with Icy and them then buy a few rocks. They all liked him because he still kept his wits about himself and used to talk real slick. Icy assigned. Grady-Bo to commandeer Hollywood's spot.

By this time a few other Ghost Town Boyz came on board to get some money with Icy, Grady and Julian. Antoinette's brother L.A was the next man on the team that stepped up to run the Silver Dollar. Then came Black Chris and Big Waco. Big Waco stood about six-two and all muscle. He would prove to be a good addition to the up and coming group of youngstas. Paps was a new recruit to Holly's organization. He knew how to move lots a coke all over the Town, so Holly brought him on as a field marshal

People in West Oakland started going crazy over crack. Once their money ran out, they would pawn everything for another piece of the rock. Dope fiends in The Lower Bottom region started burglarizing the trains that were stopped at the naval base shipping yards delivering goods. They would be coming up with all kinds of military issued clothing and guns still in shipping crates. Then they would come to the Silver Dollar and trade it all for a fist full of hubbas.

Most of the cars that Icy and the crew drove in the beginning were dope fiend rentals. The knocks would tweak-off their cars for a dub-pop at the drop of a hat. Cadillacs, Iroc Z's, Monte Carlos, you name it. Julian, Grady and L.A. would bring the cars back with the brakes squeaking, the tranny slippin, and the tires smoking.

There was so many crackhead women running in and out of the Silver Dollar that the hos got put out of business. Some of them were even working class women that worked at the nearby city hall and the Clorox building. They would power walk to the Silver Dollar and suck a dick on they lunch break for a kibble of crack. Some of them, like Two Minute Tanya, were infamous for their dick sucking skills. If she couldn't make one of the dealers bust a nut in two minutes, she would give them the crack back. That never happened. Her head was hotter than fish grease and the hustlas would let her keep it anyway.

The crew started calling Icy by an abbreviated version of his last name, because calling him Icy attracted too much attention in public, so he became known as Holly.

Holly's crew was raking in a few thousand a day. He paid all his workers weekly and told them to just stick to the script because it'll be greater later. They had a total of five rock spots throughout West Oakland and the North, one in Golden ViIlage and the other on 45th and MLK at a knock named Curtis house.

Holly's grandmother passed away in early 1985. Holly, Johnnie Mae, Eric and Ericka put on their Sunday best for the funeral of the family matriarch in East Oakland, where they ran into some of their long lost relatives from the east, another major factor in the dope game, the infamous Lacy Family, led by Manuel, a distant cousin. Holly told Manuel that he had a lil something of his own going on and they exchanged numbers. A few days after the funeral, Manuel called Holly and summoned him to a hotel off High Street and Macarthur next to a 7-Eleven.

Holly had Julian and Grady slide with him strapped up for protection. Family or not, niggas was shady. When they got to the hotel, Holly went in by his self while Julian and Grady stayed in the car with the engine running. When Holly returned, he had an entire kilogram wrapped in a funky hotel towel. Manuel had instructed him that this was just a test run and if he could move that in a timely fashion, there was more where that came from.

Holly and them returned to the Silver Dollar with Olympic speed. He had Charlie C and Dino slide thru to help him put the cook down. Holly had never cooked up that much dope and he wanted to make sure he didn't fuck it up. After they put the whammy on it, they cut the whole kick down into rocks, lumps and chunks. The slugs was so fat that Holly told all his workers to cut them in half and give all the knocks two for one. Traffic started coming from all over the Bay Area to purchase these big fat double-ups.

Now that his clientele was up, Holly thought it was the perfect time for him to treat himself to a luxury vehicle. He took Curtis the dope fiend with him to Pat Patterson Cadillac by Lake Merritt. Curtis had a good job, so Holly thought it would be wise to put whatever he bought in his name. Holly fell in love with a '78 starburst blue Cadillac Seville with a peanut butter top and interior, already sitting on Tru Classics and Vogues. When he came thru the neighborhood in his Sea Monster all you could hear was the whistle that the car made when it passed by.

Holly was a flashy character. He kept his shoulder length hair whipped in a perm, usually wearing wet waves, oceans or pull curls. His hair dresser was an old school player that owned Jenkins Hair Shop on the corner of 29th and Pablo at the bottom of a four story hotel. Jenkins started smokin' and used to make house calls at the Silver Dollar and do Holly's hair in exchange for a dub.

Holly had to stop going to Jenkins to get his hair done because Jenkins got too far gone off the base rocks to do quality work. He almost burned one of his client's hair off when he was smoking a cigarette while working. The cherry from the Newport Long fell into the perm butter on their head and the customer screamed to the high heavens and took off running out the shop looking like Michael Jackson with his hair on fire.

Glamours Hair Salon was where all the boss players and celebrities went. It was located on 43rd and Telegraph. The shop was owned by Elsie and Jennifer. Going to Glamours was like being at a red carpet affair. When Holly and Julian were in there they would be treated like kings.

Rock star Sheila E. was also a client and used to get her hair done before she went on tour with Prince and the Revolution. She was a local girl and liked to have fun. She seen Holly there getting his hair done and was amazed at how much he resembled the legendary Prince. She decided to take a trip on the wild side and bend a few corners with Holly. They spent a few days holed up in her luxury suite at the Hyatt Regency getting buck wild. When the ride was over, she dropped Holly off in her limousine at the Silver Dollar. As he was exiting the limo she said, *Hey, what is it that you do?* He responded back and said, *I sell rocks bitch, I thought you knew.* She smiled and said, *Hollyrock, I like that. I'm gonna name my next song after you.* A couple of months later Holly and his crew were riding in his Sea Monsta and the song by Sheila E. came on the radio. *Rock, Rock, Hollyrock. Everybody say*

Hollyrock. He couldn't believe it. That became his new moniker and anthem from that day on, courtesy of Sheila E.

Hollyrock was on a mission to take over the Town and get rich in the process. He had rock spots all over West Oakland and had recruited an all girl click to deal for him on Mead street. Their names were Kimmie, Carol, Lavette and Carla. All stone cold gangsta bitches.

Hos was flocking to Hollyrock by the dozens. He had always flirted with the pimp game as a youth. When he was in YA back in the day he had sent Antoinette a Ho Contract. She signed it and sent it back but it was all a joke to her. Now that Hollyrock was back on the streets, it was only right that he start capitalizing on every ho he came in contact with. His momma even said that she knew he was gonna be a pimp one day. Every drug free bitch on San Pablo, West Macarthur and Telegraph belonged to Hollyrock. They would work out of the Silver Dollar, the Isabella, the San Pablo and the California Hotels.

Big Waco talked Hollyrock into going to see a dentist that specialized in putting gold teeth in. The doc had started poofing and would hook the whole crew up for the right amount of hard white. Waco was from New Orleans where everybody wore gold teeth. He sold Hollyrock on the idea and they went to get fitted for their gold ones. Hollyrock gave the doc a couple ounces of his best product to put all diamonds and rubies in his six top teeth. When you looked at Hollyrock's mouth closely, the diamonds spelled out ROCK and the rubies were added as highlights.

One of Hollyrock's biggest competitors was a gorilla looking cat by the name of Benny Hop. He had a rickety little dope house in some housing authority apartments behind Marcus Foster Middle School on 27[th.] His crew consisted of his one and only best friend and lieutenant named Mercel. Nobody in the area particularly dug Benny Hop because he was a bully and used to harass all the little middle school kids when they got out of class.

Multiple members of the Hollyrock crew went to Marcus Foster when they were kids. Benny Hop knew this and used to go out of his way to fuck with them specifically. It wasn't until Benny Hop made the mistake of dissing Hollyrock's sister Ericka that the shit would hit the fan. He called her a bitch one day as she was walking by. She told him that he was a bitch made motherfucker and that if he didn't leave her alone she would tell her brother. Benny Hop lost it and said *Fuck your brother bitch.* Then hauled off and slapped her. Ericka took off running and when she got to the Silver Dollar she was crying her eyes out. Her face was red and Hollyrock wanted to know what happened and who did it. When she calmed down enough to explain to him what went down, he knew what he had to do.

He told his crew to gather up the choppers and pull the mob cars around. Then he sent a dope fiend to the gas station to fill up a couple three-gallon gas cans. For the rest of the daylight hours they sat around drinking forty-ouncers and filling the empty bottles with gasoline and torn sheets.

When it got dark thirty, they loaded up the choppers and the cocktails in the mob vessels and pulled up to Benny Hop's spot with the lights out. They could tell that shop was open because there was dope fiends running in and out. They waited till the dope fiend traffic slowed down then got out and lit the cocktails and started throwing them through the windows one by one. Then the shooters started letting off until the clips on the Israeli Uzis was empty. Benny Hop and Mercel jumped out the back window with smoke comin' off their shoes. Benny Hop got grazed in his left ass cheek and Mercel got a lock shot out of his dusty ass matted-up perm. The fire department and ambulances rushed to the scene, followed closely by a Channel 2 News van. Dennis Richmond labeled the incident an act of street terrorism by feuding rival drug gangs. The spot was burnt to a crisp.

Benny Hop's career in Ghost Town was over. Everybody knew that the Hollyrock Crew had put the mob move down. Hollyrock let everybody on the turf know that if he even seen Benny Hop trying to visit his momma, he would make him run past her house at gunpoint.

Hollyrock was getting so much money that it was only appropriate to put the icing on the cake. He went and flipped a brand new '86 Mercedes Benz 450 SEL off the showroom floor from Import Motors on 40th and Broadway. He took it to Blanca's House of Candy and had it sprayed with ten coats of candy apple red. When it hit the streets it was the cleanest Benzola in the entire Bay. Fully equipped with gold Daytons and Vogues, plush white leather interior and limo tints. Hollyrock became famous for paintin' the town, bumpin' Prince's Pop Life and Sheila E's ode to him *Rock, Rock, Hollyrock* with four twelves in the trunk sounding like a concert.

Hollyrock was worth a cool million easy. He had rock spots all over West Oakland, North Oakland, East Oakland, Berkeley, Richmond, Pittsburg, and Stockton. Not to mention his infamous stable of ho bitches that he sent across the water to Frisco nightly. The Rock Man was twenty deep with no sleep. All Asians, Caucasians, Hispanics and ducks (black bitches).

In a short matter of two years out of California's Youth Authority, Little James aka Icy aka Hollyrock became a cult figure, purchasing nearly a hundred kilos at a time. Even though he didn't mind getting his hands dirty, when it came to the gangsta shit, he knew he would have to outsource for some more muscle. His popularity had reached far beyond the levels he had ever imagined.

He reached out to a couple of the most heinous killas in the Town at the time, Fat Dave and Spicy Mike. Fat Dave was originally from 2-4 Village but had migrated to Funktown to fuck with Big Harv. Spicy Mike was a freelance hitter from the North. He was known for carrying two Tech 9s in a violin case everywhere he went. He had just beat two murders that he put down in MB Mall in broad daylight.

Hollyrock put both of these killas on his payroll to keep the streets clean. Their job was to keep all the side busters, jackas and shortstops away from any of Hollyrock's territories. If anybody got caught sneak dealing in Rock's areas, their orders were to rob 'em, smoke 'em, and make them come up missing. Whatever they got, they could keep on top of the grand a day he was already paying them.

Fat Dave would ride by each spot every day at a certain time and give all the suckas one warning: *If you don't get Hollyrock dope, don't be out here when I come back.* Sometimes he would just snatch them up and do something bad to them like take their butt cheeks in a back alley at gunpoint, then drop them back off buck naked. All the Shortstops had a curfew.

Niggas from other crews started hatin' the Ghost Town Hollyrock Crew. Rock and them started bumpin' heads with hella other turfs all over the Bay Area. People was starting to get offended when they found out they baby mamas was hoing and selling dope for Hollyrock or one of his peoples.

The Hollyrock Gang was over a hundred deep, all gangsta niggas and bitches included. His immediate circle was shinin'. He kept Boss Man, Grady-Bo, Gunny, Young Julian and Paps close to him at all times.

K.K. from Acorn pushed up on Rock at a gas station one day. A light scuffle took place and Hollyrock felt like he had been disrespected. The next day he had Curtis rent a big ass U-Haul. He slid thru the Ghost and gathered up as many shooters as he could and loaded them up in the back. He rode shotgun up front with an A-K with a bayonet on it. When they turned down 10th street, the Acorns was lit up, niggas was everywhere. Hollyrock jumped on top of the roof of the U-Haul and started bangin' on it with the butt of the AK. Niggas started filing out the back of the U-Haul by the dozens with yoppers and the Acorn niggas started scattering. A police car passed by at the intersection and Rock put his fingers in his mouth and whistled hella loud then waved his hand in a circle and all the shooters jumped back in and they drove off without firing a shot. K.K. got word of this and sent one of his baby mammas that knew Hollyrock to ask him to squash the shit. Rock told the bitch he wasn't trippin' and let the shit go.

Wendy Tokuda from Channel 2 News seen Hollyrock at Nations Burgers downtown Oakland one day. He was waiting for Boss Man to be released from the juvenile detention center across the street. She was amazed at him and the black youths with him all draped in gold and diamonds with long perms and Fila sweatsuits. She approached Hollyrock and fell for his charm immediately. Her pussy juices was flowing down her leg. She gave him her card. She was a newscaster. Rock called her and picked her up after work and took her out to dinner. She insisted on paying the bill when the check came. Hollyrock spent weeks lacing her up with his ism. She wanted to hand him the world in a hand basket by the time he had finished running his game past her. She asked him if she could do a segment on him for the ten o'clock news. He agreed and they set a date.

On a clear Bay Area day in 1988, Hollyrock came riding through Ghost Town with Wendy Tokuda in the passenger seat and a camera man in the backseat. He stopped on 34th and MLK where Boss Man and the rest of the crew had two drop cougars parked nose to nose with the tops down, bumpin' the Hollyrock anthem and dancin' throwin' up R's to represent the Rock man.

During the interview, Wendy asked Hollyrock what he did for a living, and he told her he hustled doing whatever he had to do. He told her he wanted to be Oakland's next Big Fee. She asked him whose pretty red Benz were they ridin' in, and he told her it was his sister Ericka's car and she was a student in high school. Hollyrock explained to her how he had came from the gutter to making hundreds of thousands of dollars a week. He showed her several stacks of money he had in the car under the floorboards. He took her to an auto shop that he had invested in and let her meet his workers. The interview aired a few weeks later on KTVU News and Hollyrock became a household name.

Not soon after the interview, Hollyrock and Charlie Rock started catching cases. The police started sweating everybody they thought was associated with the Hollyrock crew. Rock was out on three bails at the same time. Finally his run would be at an end. His lawyer would get all the cases compounded and he would be sentenced to five years state prison. Hollyrock served out his sentence at Duell Vocational Institution in Tracy California. After a total of thirty months the infamous Rock was back.

When he touched down he opened up a small t-shirt shop on 37th Street and MLK and used his newfound Swahili name Way-Way as the store's name. Way Ways House of Goodies would become his headquarters and base of operations.

In an effort to reinvent himself, Hollyrock had his biggest trophy, the Benz, repainted candy apple green. Then he purchased a fire engine red corvette and a Vandenplaus four door Jaguar. This was his way of letting the Town know that he was still made of money.

His first order of business was to reclaim his old flame from another nigga that had popped up on the scene and knocked his wife from him. Antoinette had chosen up on a Hollyrock wannabe named A-Zone while Holly was gone. A-Zone was an L.A. transplant that had moved to the Town and got turned out on real live organized crime and decided to leave all that petty gang bangin' shit behind. Him and his brothers and sisters worked out of the motels on West Macarthur on the outskirts of what Hollyrock considered his territory.

Hollyrock launched a war effort against A-Zone and his family and ran them completely out of the area. He wasn't able to get Antoinette back, but that was just something he would have to live with. He already knew that hos went from man to man like money changed from hand to hand.

A bad lil bitch named Dae Dae seen Hollyrock one day and jumped on his nutsack. She was Mick Mo's illegitimate daughter. She was tall and skinny with beautiful long wavy hair down her back. Dae Dae and Hollyrock were a match made in heaven. Rock was an admirer of her daddy back when he was a kid. His favorite song to this day was *Time Brings About Change* by Mick Mo's group the Numonics.

Dae Dae was the shit. Although she was raised in Ghost Town, she spent all her time in the Murder Dubs with her daddy's family the

Mo-Mos. Gangsta shit was all she knew. Hollyrock started sending her up in clubs to lure major dope dealers to an undisclosed area so he could kidnap them and take them home to open their safes. Dae Dae even faked her own kidnappin' so her and Rock could extract a hundred thousand dollars out of her uncle's pockets. She was like Bonnie to Hollyrock's Clyde. She even played her own position when it came to his stable of hookers.

He had started turning it back up with the pimp game and had a few stomp down mudkickers from Richmond and Berkeley that he used to set down over in San Francisco on O'Farrell by the Mitchell Brothers Theater. Hollyrock started knocking reputable pimps off left and right. He knocked Pimpin' Doe Doe from 37th off for his bottom bitch Terri out of Berkeley. Then he knocked Mack Rio out of Richmond for a two piece salt and pepper team, one white bitch and one black bitch.

Hollyrock and his squadron went to the Candlelight Club in Richmond one night campaignin' and some South Richmond hittas stepped to him on behalf of Mack Rio. Grady-Bo went outside and popped the trunk. Once Hollyrock and the rest of the crew was in the car safely, Grady-Bo shot everybody coming out of the club like ducks in a pond.

It was evident that Hollyrock and company still were moving the crowd. One of Hollyrock's favorite sayings was *Once you start being a gangsta, you gotta stay a gangsta, cause if you don't, they gone kill you.* This was the code that Hollyrock lived by.

When shit got funky, Hollyrock had a crew of body doubles that looked almost exactly like him, perms, gold teeth and the whole nine. Before he showed his face in the Town, he would have them go gas his cars up and take them to the detail shop to get washed. This would let him know if the Town was hot or not. One day one of his body doubles was warming up his hardtop red Vet in front of Way Ways House of Goodies when a car slid up and Swiss cheesed the Vet thinking it was Rock. Mike Mike looked exactly like his boss. Unfortunately, he would make the ultimate sacrifice. He died instantly.

After this incident, Hollyrock started taking his show on the road. He hooked back up with Charlie Rock in Stockton's south area. A dike bitch named Japor bought his Benz from him and started rockin' for him. Rock's specialty was slidin' into a town and sellin' the locals bunk kilos or just robbing them blind at gunpoint with the ski mask down.

He was a tactician and a con artist extraordinaire. To this day Hollyrock has never been stabbed with a knife or shot with a bullet.

Once again he would get apprehended, this time while fleeing the scene of a jewelry store heist. The robbers entered the store during the midnight hours thru a ventilation duct on top of the roof. They made off with hundreds of thousands in merchandise. Rock was the getaway driver and was surrounded several blocks away. None of the merchandise was found on his person or in his vehicle, however, a British .30 caliber bullet casing found in the glove compartment that was linked to an unsolved crime would get him sent to the Feds for five years. Hollyrock held his mud and laid it down again.

When he returned back to the Town, he was no longer Hollyrock, he was just James. He married his bottom bitch Terri. She was the best thing that ever happened to him and had cleaned up her act in his absence. She was a whiz with the paper game and her business acumen was through the roof. Together they purchased several properties in the Ghost Town zone as well as a detail shop formerly owned by Rock's cousin Manuel. The detail shop was called Classy & Classics on the corner of Market and West Macarthur. They reside in a three story luxury home hanging off a hillside in Contra Costa County.

Hollyrock was one of the most all around gangstas in the lineage of drug lords that ever touched the streets of Oakland.

CHAPTER 10 -- SLOW MOTION

Eighty-fourth Avenue was a tree lined street located directly behind Castlemont High School. Most of the homes on the block were owned by older retirees that could be seen outside sweeping up the maple leaves in the fall or barbecuing in the summer. Bancroft Avenue was the nearest thoroughfare and Dowling Street borderlines the small block on its upper end. This was where a wiry young man with bifocal glasses that was never in a rush to do anything was raised. For that reason alone, his mother nicknamed him Slow Motion. His momma was a hustla. She did what she had to do to keep the lights on and food in his stomach. Occasionally she would sell a few rocks here and there. Her brothers would be a major influence in Slow's life. They were always around and taught him all the things that being a man was about.

Eighty-fourth was about as close as you could get to the suburbs in East Oakland. There wasn't a lot of crime on their portion of the block. Sometimes drama would spill onto Dowling in the form of a high speed chase that ended in a car wreck, or the high school kids would cut school and smoke weed and drink under the tree at the corner of Dowling and 84th. Besides that, a person could still hear the birds chirping on a bright Sunday morning.

Slow and all his childhood buddies had it good. The 7-Eleven was within walking distance and they could ride their bikes down Bancroft to the Eastmont Mall only eleven blocks away to see a movie or just hang out. The rec center on 82nd and East 14th provided several activities and even sent them to Camp Mendocino for two weeks every summer. Arroyo Park was only two blocks away with a creek running through it for the kids to play in.

This was the place where Slow would first get a glimpse of the game. The park was bustling with a bunch of pretty young girls in pigtails gliding around on roller skates and chewing bubble gum. The older niggas would be pulling up in their whipped up cars and bouncing out with big fat joints of choker weed in they mouths, wearing perms and Shirley Temples. The snack bar sold all kinds of goodies like nachos, French fries, icees and hot links. People would be pulling up buying sherm sticks and weed right in plain view of the kids. Arroyo Park was crackin'. You could hear the music from the parked car speakers and the boom boxes all the way up on Bancroft Avenue.

Slow's best friends were Beamon and Timilo. They did what all the other little kids their age did, play sports, ride bikes, play video games, and climb the neighborhood fruit trees. They would crash at each other's houses regularly and have wrestling matches before they raided the refrigerator. Slow had the coolest of mommas on the block. She used to drive them around in her bright yellow Camaro and drop them off at their destinations. She wouldn't get mad when she caught them in her house bumping her records that she had just got from the House of Music on 77th and Bancroft, or when she caught them trying to sneak a couple young girls into Slow's bedroom so they could hump on them.

Slow had a beautiful childhood. His block was a breath of fresh air compared to the crime ridden areas nearby like 82nd, East 14th, and Macarthur. The old folks on Slow's block did their best to maintain the curb appeal of their homes and keep their eyes on each other's children and property. There was one apartment building on the block, however, that would start to become a haven for mid level dope dealers. The D-boys started parking all their flamboyant cars up and down the driveway of the bright yellow two story building. Just like all little kids, Slow, Beam, and Timilo used to stand by whichever car they liked and say it was theirs. It didn't take long for the old school D-boys to get to know the youngsters and take a liking to them.

By the time Slow made it to junior high, crack cocaine was rearing its ugly head. Heroin had always been the dominant drug being sold in the 82nd Avenue area and weed was a close second, being pushed on 83rd by the Hooker Family. This gave Slow several options to choose from when he finally figured out he wanted to get in the D-game. Ironically, it would be his own momma that seen the dollar signs in her baby boy's eyes and welcomed him into the family business. She threw him his first bundle to get him some change with.

Slow and Beam started making a few dollars selling weed on their block. Next thing you know, 84th started being known as East Oakland's safest weed spot. After work all the traffic coming off 82nd and Bancroft would make pit stops on Slow's block to grab a fat twenty sack of some dank. This went on undetected for years because all the major drug traffic on the other spots overshadowed theirs; 77th and Greenside, 82nd including Macarthur, Olive, East 14th, Arroyo Park, 85th mini park, and Fat Gene's spot on 88th. All these spots were super boomin' and kept the heat off 8-4. These were the coke, weed and hop spots that allowed 8-4 to fly under the radar for several years.

Slow, Beam, and Timilo stacked their change up tremendously during this time. They all had came together and invested in the crack game. Pretty soon they were selling weight. Beam and Timilo were the most flamboyant of the crew. Timilo put together a turquoise '68 hardtop Cougar on Zs and Vs, and Beam flipped a candy brandy wine burgundy '68. Slow's momma gave him her bright yellow Camaro and he rode around in that.

He wasn't a materialistic individual at all. When all the rest of the fellas were wearing all the latest fly gear from Mr. Z's, Slow would be on the turf in his gym clothes from school. He started to take an interest in buying, restoring and souping up hi-performance vehicles. A lot of D-boys was showing everybody what their turf was worth by flipping hi-po shit. Then they would race for pink slips down on San Leandro Boulevard.

Slow started hanging around at an auto shop on 90th and Mac that was owned by Fat Johnny and Indian Tone. Both of these cats was major figures in the east and avid classic car enthusiasts. Rubbing shoulders with niggas of their caliber allowed Slow the opportunity to do some networking of his own. People started to hear his name and see him around. Once word got out that he had decent prices and was consistent with his work, they started seeking him out and spending money with him.

By the time Slow got out of high school, he had his change up. His uncles had always told him that the game wasn't gonna last forever, so he decided to start up a rap label. A young rapper named Axkari X from 72nd and Lacey had just got out of CYA. He would hang out at the Uhuru House on Mac by the red fence. He was a phenomenal rapper and most of his lyrics were based on his allegiance to the Muslim splinter group Ansar el Muhammeds. Slow heard some of his demo tapes and seen the potential in him. He took the young righteous black guerilla under his wing and released his first album *Ward of the State* on his upstart record label, Slow Motion Records. Askari X's debut album was a runaway success with hit singles like *All the Peckerwoods Better Hide Tonite* and the title track, *Ward of the State*. Askari was way ahead of his time and well educated in race, religion and politics.

Oakland's burgeoning rap scene was on an upward trajectory. Most of the well known artists started collaborating and would congregate at a number of studios in the town, like Too Short's, and turn them into a party scene. There would be dice games, boxing matches, wrestling matches, smokeouts, cookouts, capp sessions, orgies, barbecues and car races on any given day. Some of the Town's best music was produced as a result of this golden era.

Too Short would often be around and developed a good rapport with Slow, Timilo and Beam. Sometimes Short would slide thru 8-4 and hang out with the crew while they would be out there hustling. Eight-Four became known as a celebrity hangout spot: J.R. Ryder, Gary Payton, and several other NBA players would pull up in their Bentleys and bounce out and chill. Ice Cube from NWA had family in the area and brought his female rapper Yo-Yo thru there one year. While she was on the block, she chose up on one of Slow's young player patnas named Bill.

Slow Motion had risen to the top of the food chain in the dope game. He had his youngstas out with garbage bags full of twenty sacks of potent dank. Meanwhile, he would have a bucket parked on the block with a trunk full of kilos that he would run thru on a daily basis. Due to the fact that he was damn near the only game in town, for a short period of time he became the kilo man. The Feds had rolled up numerous other kingpins, but Slow was so low key that he was able to keep eating without attracting attention to himself.

His record label was doing good numbers. Askari X released his sophomore LP titled: *Message to the Black Man*, with features by 3X Krazy, The Luniz, Cydal and Seagram, on the hit song *Three Strikes*. Slow Motion Records put up a billboard on 73rd and Bancroft above Church's Chicken with a picture of Askari X looking up at a Muslim star and a crescent with the title of the album in black set against a red background.

Oakland, California was on fire and several new booty turfs started poppin' up nearby. A small click from Funktown set up a heroin machine around the corner on 82nd and Olive. They called themselves the Burnout Boyz and the ring leader was a money hungry motherfucker named Deddy-Bo. He ran his machine like the old school, with spitters, lookouts and shooters. When the spot got hot, they would relocate the traffic to nearby Webster Elementary School ground or Arroyo Park.

Down on 81st several members of Too Short's entourage mobbed up and took over the block. They put down a heroin machine that opened the door for the rest of the Sobrante Park crew to come post up and get money in the shady 80s. Fat Virg was the man with the plan and was pushing a line on that spot along with his patnas Curt and Roy.

A stone cold headbusta by the name of Skully-G from Sobrante Park had just touched down from doing a jolt in New Folsom. While he was down, he read the book by John Grisham titled *The Firm*, and decided to start a movement bearing the name when he got out. He came home like King Arthur and sat all the major factors in the deep east down at the Round Table. The word of the day was *You couldn't grind if you wasn't on The Firm's time.* Niggas from hella different spots all over East Oakland jumped on board and fell up under The Firm's umbrella. Criddy-Bo from Funktown, Polly from 85th, and Slow-Mo from 8-4 would all be touted as knights and sit strategically at the table.

Slow had knocked up a young Mexican bitch whose family owned a street corner fruit stand on 74th and Bancroft. Her uncles had all the Mexican mud and coca-cola that The Firm needed to compete on a nationwide scale. Sobrante Park was sewed up immediately, then Arroyo Park, then the Shady 80s. A few hard heads tried to buck the system but found out real fast that they didn't have no win against The Firm's movement.

J.R. Ryder came on board and started funneling NBA money into the organization. He enjoyed being around all these gangsta ass street niggas and had a lightweight temper of his own that had him labeled as a thug in the league. Him, Beam and Timilo would pull up to functions dippin' and yokin' in his purple Bentley Azure with the top down. High-sidin'!

Too Short and Polly were best friends. Every year they would invite everybody who was anybody down to the ATL to attend the Freaknik. All the bossy ass Town niggas had their cars shipped down there to Atlanta to show them country bumpkins how the Town did it. Mustangs, Cougars, Benzes, Vets, Lexo's, Beamers and Bentleys with candy paint, bump and rims on everything. The only niggas that could even keep up with the Town at the Freaknik was the BMF. The Freaknik opened up several other doors for The Firm to put their people into play down south.

Slow Motion was making millions as a D-Boy and entertainment mogul. He was the CEO of his own label and started investing in property. He purchased a fairly modest home on a cul-de-sac in an upscale community of Walnut Creek, California. He married his high school sweetheart and they were the proud parents of two small children. At home Slow and his wife presented themselves as the quintessential middle class black American family.

The Mexican bitch Christine started flying to Detroit to handle some of The Firm's business interests. She had basically reached queenpin status in her own right and with the approval of The Firm she had Arroyo Park on lock with their special blend of burgundy heroin, never before seen in the Town. Their newest form of tar hop would have a dope fiend pissin, shittin, throwin' up and sucking his own dick when he nodded.

During one of Christine's distribution trips to Detroit, she was set up and robbed for a kilo by one of her clients out there. He stripped her for the kick and a few measly thousand that she had on her. Christine escaped with her life and caught a red-eye flight back to the Town immediately. She got one of her main gunners named T-Roy from 84th and flew back to Detroit. When they arrived at their hotel, a package was waiting for them at the front desk with two Glock 9 millis. Christine knew her client's routine and rocked up on him in true Town fashion while he was coming out of a soul food spot. They lit him up like the Fourth of July and skirted off in the rental back to the airport.

The Detroit homicide investigators would soon put two and two together and put a nationwide warrant out for the arrest of Christine and T-Roy. OPD caught up with her at her parent's fruit stand and extradited her back to Detroit immediately to face charges. T-Roy would be apprehended weeks later at a picnic and extradited as well. The Firm's dominance in Oakland's drug trade started to become recognizable by the fuzz. Several heavy hitters that recently paroled from high security level four institutions started using their connections inside and out of prison to advance the lines of The Firm. If a person inside the joint needed to be touched, that was not a problem. They also flooded the prisons with hi-grade heroin at a hundred percent markup.

Arroyo Park became the location for several boxing matches set up by Hot Lips from Sunnyside. He was an amateur boxer and a knockout artist. He used to have all the knockout artists from all the major turfs in the Town come up there and put the gloves on. All the major ballers like Slow and them used to be up there on the sidelines betting big money on who they thought was going to win. Slow liked to gamble and he had more than enough money to jack off on street bets.

Slow Motion and his Firm buddies started taking expensive trips to places like Cancun Mexico. They would invite their rappers out and have a blast. Too Short would fly out and bring along groups like Lil Jon and the Eastside Boyz. The town would follow suit and jump on Southwest Airlines and come support The Firm and party with them. Local D-boys baby mammas would spend they rent checks to come get loose with the bosses. Oakland's rapper Richie Rich talked about it in one of his songs stating *What happens in Cancun stays in Cancun.*

When Slow was in the Town he still drove around in his hand-me-down Camaro. Occasionally he would pull out one of his hi-performance Novas or Grand National to go blow the doors off somebody who wanted to race him on San Leandro Boulevard. He would also ship his cars to the Barrett-Jackson and Mecum Auctions to get top dollar for them from the rich white folks.

For the most part, Slow's life surrounded around his wife and kids. He would slide to the Town and conduct his business, then get right on the freeway during rush hour traffic to make it home in time to help his kids with their homework. On the weekends he could be spotted by his neighbors mowing his lawn or throwing a football back and forth with his son.

His low profile would soon come to the attention of the DEA at downtown Oakland's Twin Towers Building. They would launch an investigation into his record label and into his operations in association with being a drug lord and the main driving force behind The Firm's organization and hit squad. Slow Motion was a tough cookie to pin a tail on, however. First of all, he was a legitimate businessman and a shrewd hustler that didn't flaunt his riches.

The multi-count indictment against Slow Motion, Christine, Criddy-Bo and several others finally got rubber stamped by the federal magistrate in the late 1990's. Slow-Mo was taken into custody peacefully during an early morning raid at his Walnut Creek home. Several of his neighbors (all professional white people) were interviewed by KTVU News. They all had nothing but good things to say about the young father and husband. None of them even had the slightest idea that they were living next door to a real live drug lord.

No drugs were seized at the property, just tens of thousands of dollars in cereal boxes in the kitchen cabinets and some handguns The Feds towed his black Buick Grand National GNX out of the garage and impounded it. His wife was arrested, questioned, then released.

Christine was flown back to the Bay Area by Air Marshals to answer to her charges in the indictment. She was already serving a life sentence in Michigan for her murder conviction, so she quickly struck a plea bargain and took her time for her role in the conspiracy. Her family built a shrine for her next to Jesus Malverde, the patron saint to drug dealers, in their fruit stand on Bancroft Avenue.

The Firm's number one lead enforcer, Criddy Bo from Funktown, got a ten piece Feds for his role in The Firm. He took his time on the chin and did it moving. The Feds didn't have nothing on him anyway.

The Feds wanted Slow. After a couple of years of being held in custody with no bail, Slow-Mo would be convicted for being the ringleader of a major cocaine, heroin and marijuana distribution ring that reached several U.S. cities. He was sentenced to life in federal prison. His lawyer filed an appeal immediately.

The Firm would continue to be a powerhouse operation in the Town until the early 2000's, at which time the remaining Firm members would go radio silent. During Slow Motion's career he proved to be a phantom in the dope game and the most elusive in Oakland, California's line of drug lords.

CHAPTER 11 -- BROOKFIELD CHARLES

Brookfield Village was the second to last stop on East Oakland's border. It was a two-sided neighborhood that was split down the middle by 98th Avenue. On the southern side of 98th was Douglas Street and the Columbia Gardens. On the northern side was Edes Street and the Dag Village area. Together, they made up the Brookfield Flatlands.

The entire area was made up of single story homes that sat on streets that wound around like a combination of mazes. Brookfield Elementary sat stately on Edes Street next to the Brookfield Recreation Center. This was the reason the entire neighborhood took on the title of Brookfield Village.

The young children in the area ran amok in a world basically all their own. Their parents didn't have to watch them constantly because everybody basically knew each other. While most of the parents were at work, the youngstas would terrorize the back streets like wild hyenas. The older cats started calling them the Jungle Boyz. They grasped onto this title with pride and went to the Eastmont Mall and had the name Jungle Boyz ironed on their derby jackets, their t-shirts and their beanie hats. When they travelled out of their comfort zone they always travelled in groups. They would meet up on 98th after school and get in scuffles with other school kids from other turfs.

Their closest rival was Sobrante Park. Some of the Jungle Boyz suffered the misfortune of having to go to elementary school in Sobrante. If they stayed on the Douglas side of 9-8, going to Sobrante Park Elementary or Madison Junior High was a nightmare because the Sobrante Park children were a little bit deeper and a little bit rougher than they were.

The Brookfield Jungle was home to a young man by the name of Lil Charles. He was just one of many little hard headed boys growing up in the area that was running rampant in the Jungle. Everybody knew him and he seemed to be well liked. He did pretty good in school and lived in a house owned by his grandmother. He hung out but enjoyed riding bikes and talking to girls more than fighting and bumping heads with other kids his age. Early on, it was evident that he was a thinker.

By the time Lil Charles hit junior high school age, Brookfield, Dag and Columbia Gardens were infested with drug activity. It started with weed being sold at the corner store on Edes. Then it snowballed into sherm, mescaline, red devils, bennies, heroin, cocaine, then crack. Lots of teens his age used to hang out at the store and work for the older members of the biggest family in Brookfield, the Wilsons.

When crack hit, a lot of his peers started dabblin' and smokin' base rock. Lil Charles wasn't above cutting class and smoking the occasional joint of good gold weed but basing really wasn't his thang.

Overnight Lil Charles seen his middle class neighborhood turn from sugar to shit. People would leave the butts of Newports filled with powder coke strewn all over the playground area of the rec center. The little hip kids would collect them and roll them back up for an after school blaster.

The Brookfield flatlands started to look like the night of the living dead. Even the most popular youngsters started smoking crack crushed up in weed. They called these joints gremies because after you blew one you would damn near turn into a gremlin.

Choka Mike and Lil Scooby was the first young Jungle Boyz that really started makin' a name for themselves. Charles was a late bloomer but eventually started selling a little weed at the Brookfield store after school. When cars rode by he would put two fingers to his lips to symbolize that he had weed for sale.

The older niggas used to pull up in they duece-n-a-quarters and buy a bag from the young whippersnapper just to put a few chips in his pocket. They would shoot the shit with him and give him a few pointers on where and how to stash his bundle and what escape routes to use when the taskforce hit.

Charles got tired of wearing French braids and went and got his hair fried, dyed, and laid to the side. He had the hairdresser put a gold streak down the side of his finger waves like all the other Jungle Boyz with perms had, representing a tiger stripe.

The skating rinks was crackin' and on the weekend some of the Jungle Boyz would hop on the bus with they personalized skates and go get loose on the roller rink floor. Niggas from Brookfield and Sobrante used to have skate-offs to see who could do the most on the floor. Toddy-Bo from Brookfield and Big Cee-Cee from Sobrante were the best skaters in all of Oakland. An hour before the skating rink shut down they would turn on the strobe lights and turn the rink into a dance floor. Chuck Johnson from Soulbeat would be filming while all the youngsters did dances like the Polio and the Dogcatcher to songs like *Jeckyll & Hyde* and *the Smurph Beat*.

After the Foothill Square let out, all the turfs would gather in the parking lot and pick fights with each other. Charles would be right in the thick of all the shit with his schoolboy glasses, his 501's with sewed-in creases, and his surfers on. His grandmama started to notice the change in her grandbaby's behavior and warned him that if he didn't knock it off she would send him down to the Central Valley to live with some of his family members. He just shrugged it off and continued doing what he was doing.

The weed game got outranked by the crack cocaine that was being sold on nearly every corner in Oakland. Charles fell right in and started pushin' a few stones here and there around the neighborhood. He was nickel and dimin', sellin' a hubba here and a hubba there. He managed to get up to a few zippas and was doing alright for himself.

One of his runnin' buddies talked him into pulling a robbery on a D-boy down the block. After they went and tore the D-boy's pockets off, they thought it was over with. Two days later Charles' partner in the robbery got found shot to death behind the rec center. Charles' granny got wind of this and his involvement in the robbery and put him on the first thang smokin' to Fresno.

Fresno was a far cry from the fast moving streets of Oakland. Charles felt like he had been shipped off to the country. He put his nose in the books, got himself a little after school job, and stayed out of trouble. A couple years went by and Charles drove himself back to Oakland in a little bucket that he had saved up and bought while working at his after school gig.

When he got back to the Town the dope game was moving a hundred miles a minute. Several individuals his age from all over Oakland had already gotten nigga rich selling the hard white candy cola. On the flipside, some of the older cats in Brookfield had fell victim to the hooter and was walking on the back of they shoes pushing grocery baskets and begging for change.

Charles had sprouted up to a cool six feet. He still had his old school perm and his playeristic mentality. He wasn't in a rush to get back into the streets so he spent his time at his granny's house in the Brookfield/Dag area. One night while he was kickin' back watching the news and nursing a budda Thai doobie, a special report came on. It was a thirty minute segment about Griselda Blanco, the Godmother of Cocaine aka the Black Widow. Pronounced La Madrina de la Cocaina aka La Vuida Negra in Espanol.

She was the most powerful female cocaine queenpin in the world.

Originally from Medellin Columbia where she began her career as a drug dealer and sparked the career of Pablo Escobar as well. She migrated to Miami, Florida in the mid-70s where she controlled the cocaine market for nearly fifteen years, ordering several contract killings and distributing thousands of tons of coke in the process. She was nicknamed La Vuida Negra (the Black Widow) due to the fact that she had singlehandedly assassinated two of her previous husbands for their disloyalty.

Griselda was forced to flee the Miami area after she got word that several warrants for capital murder and cocaine conspiracy were coming down the pike aimed at her. She was also the target of several six figure contracts with a price on her head by rival dealers.

California seemed like the perfect place for her to seek refuge and continue on with her nefarious activities. She landed in Hawthorne, California and didn't waste any time getting her network back in motion. Her bloodthirsty ways would finally get the best of her when she decided to have the niece of her Columbian connection robbed and murdered for a thousand kilos. The young lady was delivering the package on behalf of her uncles, the infamous Ochoa Family. Her decomposed body was found on the side of the 105 Freeway.

The DEA finally caught up with Griselda and she was being housed at the federal facility in Dublin California.

Charles was sitting there entranced by the magnitude of this woman's story. He couldn't believe that this elderly lady of Columbian descent could be the mastermind and driving force behind a cartel of vicious cold killers and drug lords. As he was sitting there feeling the effects of the Thai weed, it dawned on him that this lady was being housed right here in Northern California directly across the street from Alameda County's Santa Rita Jail. A place he knew very well because his momma had took him to visit family members there in the past. A bright light went off in his head and he grabbed a pen and some paper and started writing this lady a letter. He had to call information to get the number to the prison so he could get the correct address, but he thought that maybe he could boost her spirits by dropping her a line. The next day as he was passing a mailbox he dropped the letter in sealed with his best regards.

A couple of weeks later when Charles came in the house after he had been on the block hustling, his grandmother told him there was a letter on the kitchen table for him. The letter was stamped from the federal prison at Dublin and in a scribbly chicken scratch he could see the name Griselda Blanco in the upper left hand corner. He couldn't believe that she had wrote him back.

When he read the letter, he was amazed at how humble and sweet this notorious queenpin was. She was actually very grateful that he had reached out to her. She went on to express how lonely prison was no matter how much money you had or who you were. Inside the letter she had enclosed for him a visiting form for him to fill out and send back with a open invitation for him to visit her.

In Charles' next letter he expressed to her that he didn't believe any of the terrible things the media said about her. He enclosed the completed visiting form and gave her a number to call in case she needed someone to talk to.

Within a week La Madrina called him and they would talk deep into the wee hours of the night. They would have wonderful conversations about her travels and her pride and joys, her two sons. He even had a separate phone line installed in his room specifically for her to call him on.

Charles and Griselda's visiting form got approved. She called him in an extremely chipper mood and informed him of the good news. He was just as happy as she was and let her know that he would be up there on the nearest visiting day available.

On his first visit to see Griselda, Charles was a little bit nervous. He didn't know what to expect from a woman of her caliber and influence. When she entered the visiting room she was glowing. He could tell that her upkeep was far greater than the other female prisoners there. She looked very different from her mug shots on TV.

Although there was a considerable age difference between them, they found it easy to talk to each other. They were able to see eye to eye on several topics, including the drug game. Charles let her know that he wasn't no stranger to the game and that he had peddled a few pebbles of coca on occasions. Nothing near what she was used to.

La Madrina was a woman of authority, even in her prison garb. Being that she was almost a billionaire, there wasn't too much of anything that she couldn't pay the CO's to bring her or let her get away with.

When Charles arrived on their second visit, Griselda made it very clear to him that she needed some dick. She had already pre-arranged with the correctional officers to allow the two of them to access a mop closet. It cost her fifteen hundred bucks, but that was just a drop in the bucket to her.

Charles could tell that La Madrina was not someone a person said no to, so he decided to oblige her and entered the closet with her. Before he could get his shirt off she attacked his zipper, pulled his dick out and started sucking it sideways like she was playing a harmonica. Her hunger for his pole was evident by the sounds she made as she ran her lips and tongue up and down his swipe. Once his dick was at full extension, she pulled one leg out of her pants and straddled him with her legs around his waist and her arms around his shoulders. She rode him ferociously for fifteen minutes until she was about to nut. Charles spun her around and pushed her against the wall while he was lightly choking her with one hand. That made her squirt pussy juice everywhere. Then he bent her over and spit on her asshole before he plunged his dick into it until he was balls deep. As he pounded her asshole full throttle and pulled her hair, he spanked her bottom like she was a disobedient child. When he finally nutted, she pulled out his halfway limp dick and deep throated it until she sucked all the remaining cum droppings and shit particles off of it. This would be their routine during every visit.

After Charles returned home from his third visit, he noticed a mysterious box on his grandmother's porch with his name on the top of it. He opened it up slowly and all he seen was kilos on top of kilos inside the box. When he looked around to see if anybody was looking, he noticed two Columbian looking guys sitting in a car across the street. One of them gave him a thumbs up as he put the car in gear and drove off. Charles picked up the box and took it straight to his room in the house. Griselda called him a half hour later and asked him if he had gotten his present from her. He confirmed that he did and she hung up.

Charles counted out the bricks on his bed and there were fifty keys total. He couldn't believe his luck. This was more dope than he had ever seen in his life. He knew he wouldn't have any problems moving it because the city of Oakland was in a frenzy over cocaine crack.

The next day he went to a neighbor's house that was a known smoker and gave him a few dollars to let him use the spot as a cookhouse. He sat there for nearly a week cooking the product and bagging it up into half thangs, nine-packs, Q-Pees, and zippas. He slow cooked all the work and turned the fifty keys into sixty-five by the time he was finished without compromising the quality of the coke that had came straight from South America.

The Brookfield Jungle was already boomin' with rocks being sold on every corner. Charles had a plan, though. He would approach all the hustlas and inquire about what they were copping. Then he would make a proposition that they couldn't refuse. He would sell them whatever they needed cheaper than what they were paying, and then he would front them that amount as well. This blew his clientele through the roof. Once everybody in the Brookfield, Dag and Columbia Gardens found out that he was The Man, everybody jumped on board.

The Jungle was flooded. The knocks came from San Leandro and Hayward to purchase the doom-dooms that the Brookfield Boyz had. These were working class people that would pull up and spend two and three hundred dollars at a time instead of a measly twenty. In less than a month's time, Charles had sewed up the entire area.

He had always admired an old school player by the name of Charlie Clacks, who was one of the only people in his neighborhood that drove Rolls Royces and Excaliburs and wore tailored suits and gator cowboy boots. So Charles started dressing like his namesake with the cowboy boots to match, and some folks started calling him Cowboy.

On his next visit to see Griselda, she told him that she needed him to take on more responsibility within her organization. From that day on, he would be her representative and act as her voice during all the meetings with her nationwide network of contacts as well as in South America. Charles would be dispatched to cities like Chicago, Detroit, Minneapolis, Dallas, D.C., Atlanta and Miami. He would answer only to Griselda and be the only black man in history to ever be in charge of a Columbian drug cartel.

La Madrina had two living sons. Her oldest son had previously been murdered in Medellin in a shootout at a club. Her second youngest was embarking on a career as a drug smuggler in his own right and was thought to be in Bogotá. Her youngest and her pride and joy, Michael Corleone, was in Belize with friends of Griselda's.

She was desperately wanting to see her baby boy, so she asked Charles if he could arrange for Michael to come stay with him so he could bring him to visit her. Charles thought it was the least he could do after all she had done for him.

Michael Corleone was still a growing teenager and spoke English very well. He had spent most of his formative years in Miami when his mother was the queen of cocaine out there. Him and Charles had talked on the phone on several occasions and he couldn't wait to get on the plane back to the states. Charles picked the young man up in true Oakland style from the Oakland International Airport riding in a drop top '68 Mustang on gold Zeniths and Vogues with the beat bumpin'. Michael Corleone was in heaven. He immediately fell in love with the Town and was surprised at how much it reminded him of the black neighborhoods in Miami. The Friday night before their visit with Griselda, Charles had some of his young folks from Brookfield take Michael Corleone to the sideshow. They converged around the young Columbian like he was a prince and made sure he enjoyed himself and nothing happened to him the whole night.

The next day when they arrived at the prison, La Madrina broke down in tears at the sight of her youngest baby boy. She loved him more than anything on the earth's surface and wanted him to be nearer to her from that day forward. Before the visit was over, she asked Charles if he would do her the honor of acting as Michael's godfather and legal guardian and let him remain in Oakland with him. He agreed. She gave both of them her blessings and left the visit with a new lease on life.

A so-called drought hit the Town when Manuel and A.F. got caught up in an indictment. The only turf in the city that still had a steady stream of dope was Brookfield courtesy of Cowboy Charles. He would fly in and drop like twenty or thirty bricks on his crew and then board a plane and fly back out to tend to La Madrina's business interests in other states.

Charles started purchasing property in several different places. He bought a house in Fresno, a condo in Chicago, and a mansion in Belize. Michael Corleone visited the South American country with him and they decided on a Spanish style stucco villa on waterfront property. This would be their vacation home during the winter months because it was still sunny in Belize during that time of year.

Back in Oakland, Charles' car collection started to rival a celebrity's. Every other month he would buy a new car. He had a Corvette that was formerly used as a national pace car, a drop Benz, an Excalibur, two Lincoln Town Cars, a Cadillac Biarritz, a Cadillac Seville, and a XJ6 V12 Jaguar. He gave his grandmother one of his Town Cars and Michael Corleone his drop top Mustang.

Corleone's older brother began to resent Charles' role in his mother's life. He knew that they were officially a couple and that Charles had custody of his little brother. He just couldn't accept those facts, mainly because Charles was black. He also had a lot of animosity in his heart because his own dad was no longer alive courtesy of his mother.

In an act of rebellion he struck out on his own and started a separate faction outside of his mother's organization and against her will. She warned him that he was making a big mistake in her phone conversations with him.

During one of his trips down to Columbia, he was assassinated in what was said to be a message from the Ochoa Family in retaliation for their niece being murdered by the Black Widow. Griselda was devastated and furious at the same time. She swore on a stack of Santa Biblias to seek retribution on anybody she thought had anything to do with her son's murder. In her angry and deranged state, she started having delusions about the United States government having something to do with her son's murder. She made a personal vow to seek deadly vengeance against the entire system for keeping her away from her children in their most vulnerable period. Based on the location of the murder, she was not allowed to attend her son's funeral.

Charles was living the dream of a cocaine cowboy, flying first class and staying in penthouse suites at the Ritz Carlton. He developed an affinity for alligator cowboy boots from JB Hill in Texas. All his meals were cooked by his personal chef. He lounged poolside in his own cabana while he made million dollar moves for La Madrina's Cartel.

During one of his visits to Dublin to see Griselda, he caught the eye of another visitor. She was a blonde haired, blue eyed siren that was there visiting her husband at the coed Institution. As they were both leaving the visiting area, she slid Charles her number on a piece of paper and licked her tongue at him. This white bitch was stacked like a shit brickhouse. His dick stood up like an angry python thru his jeans.

Later on that night he called the young lady and they had a rendezvous at one of his hideouts. This chance encounter developed into a relationship that he tried to keep a secret. When word got back to La Madrina, she was infuriated. The black widow inside her started to reveal itself. After all that she had done for this man, he had proved to be just like the rest of them. Therefore, she would deal with him as such.

One night while Charles was driving home down 98th Avenue, the train crossing started to light up. As traffic came to a halt, he noticed what appeared to be the same two Columbians he had seen when the box with fifty bricks was left on his porch riding in the car right next to him. When he went to wave, that's when a man in the back seat rose up and aimed a machine gun right at him. Pop, pop, pop was all he heard before he started ducking and slamming his Corvette in reverse. He aimed the rear of the Vet toward the island in the middle of the street and jumped the curb, then swung the car around and slammed it into first gear all in one swift motion. He took off down 98th doing a hundred miles an hour. When he got to his granny's house, he was shaking like a bomb specialist.

He went in his room and grabbed his Mac 90 out of the closet and stood by the window like Malcolm X. The phone started to ring and he knew right away who it was. When he picked it up, La Madrina was on the other end spewing profanities in her broken Columbian form of Spanish. All he could understand was Tu'Pinche Miaté, *You fiuckin' nigger.* He begged her to calm down and she finally told him that the COs at the prison had told her about his new love interest. Charles had been spotted riding in the same car with the voluptuous vixen to and from the institution on visiting days.

Griselda explained to Charles that it wasn't the fact that he had a lil side piece, because he was a young man and she understood his desires. She was upset that he didn't have enough decency not to rub it in her face. She felt like her reputation had been tarnished by his blatant disrespect. He promised her that he would break it off immediately. This seemed to pacify her for the time being.

The next time Cowboy Charles seen Griselda, she looked like a broken shell of her former self. She was a nervous wreck and was speaking erratically, mumbling something about her life was in danger and she needed to escape. She instructed him to pass a coded message to her top enforcers with orders to kidnap and hold the president of the United States hostage and demand her release immediately. After she was released and was safely on another continent, she would order the president killed. Charles was sitting there in his chair thinking to himself, *this bitch done lost her rabbit ass mind.* But he played along with her anyway. She didn't even ask for her usual dose of anaconda in the mop closet that day.

After the visit, as he was headed to his car, he was surrounded by

U.S. Marshals and escorted into a small holding room. The marshals read him his rights and notified him that they had been listening the whole time during all his visits. They even had the mop room bugged and joked with him about his prowess during his escapades with the queenpin. Charles was quietly arrested on the spot and shipped to an undisclosed location in Washington DC. For the next forty-eight hours he would be debriefed and interrogated during a recorded session.

He was the subject of a national conspiracy to kidnap and murder President Ronald Reagan as well as being the secondary defendant in an international indictment to distribute tons of cocaine in North and South America. The accusations against him would hold him in prison for the rest of his natural life if he was found guilty. The authorities decided to throw him a life raft and offered him a deal. Complete immunity for his cooperation against Griselda Blanco aka the Black Widow. Charles agreed to assist the government to foil La Madrina's plot to kidnap and assassinate the president. In doing so, he would be released from custody and flown back to California to visit the queenpin one last time.

On the day of his last visit, knowing he would never again see the queen of cocaine, he decided to give her his best performance inside and outside of the mop closet. He knew that the table they sat at would be equipped with high powered microphones, so he steered the conversation toward her recent plot to kidnap the president. She was none the wiser and spoke freely about the topic.

When they entered the mop closet, Charles didn't waste no time pulling her prison jumpsuit down around her ankles. He bent her over and commenced to sucking her pussy from the back with his nose in her ass crack. She moaned loudly as he twirled her titty nipples with his fingertips. La Madrina had one hand on the ground while her other hand was busy at work stroking his lightning rod of a dick in her backwards clenched fist. When she came, she subconsciously pushed his head against the wall as she maneuvered her hips in a circular motion, squirting hot cum all over his mustache, lips and chin. He stood up straight and dropped his pants down around his cowboy boots and inserted his penis into her soaking wet vagina from the back. Then he pounded her pussy hole for thirty minutes, making her cum four more times. When it was time for him to bust his load, he pulled out and shot white hot nut all over her big fat ass cheeks.

When he left the prison that day he felt a twinge of guilt about agreeing to testify against Griselda. He knew that once the trial phase started, she would become aware of his betrayal. His relationship with Michael Corleone would also be over, even though he was basically all the young man had left on this earth.

Charles went underground completely with the white bitch he had met at the prison. His grandmother took custody of Michael Corleone and made sure he did everything like all kids his age, such as go to school and do his chores.

Cocaine Cowboy Charles had amassed millions of dollars while he was in charge of Griselda's organization. He had coke lines all over South America and property worth several million dollars. He made sure his whole family and Brookfield loved ones were well taken care of.

La Madrina was given a plea deal in the most recent conspiracy, but was deported when she finished serving her federal prison sentence. The U.S. Attorney knew that her deportation would basically be a death sentence due to the fact that she had crossed Columbia's most powerful drug family and cartel.

Griselda Blanco was released in late 2010 and was flown back to Medellin Columbia by the U.S. Government. She was handed over to the Columbian Immigration Department who would be in charge of monitoring her whereabouts. A couple of years later, she was shot in the head by a motorcyclist while she was exiting a small town butcher shop. Her assassination made worldwide headlines and she would become the legend of many movies and documentaries to come.

Brookfield Charles, the Cocaine Cowboy, would resurface in a documentary about the Black Widow and tell his side of the story in detail on nationwide TV. He makes occasional appearances in Oakland, California to visit his friends and family. He was privileged enough to walk his daughter down the aisle when she married a local D-boy from his old stomping grounds in the Brookfield Jungle. He is said to be spending most of his time in Belize sippin' margaritas and enjoying the company of his white girlfriend.

Brookfield Charles had the closest ties to the Columbian Cartel than any other drug lord in Oakland history.

CHAPTER 12 -- D-FOLKS

The Ghost Town section of West Oakland was just a hop, skip and a jump away from downtown. This neighborhood was the closest street turf in proximity to the Town's nucleus. Ghost Town was a grand total of thirty city blocks that spanned all the way from West Grand Avenue and Martin Luther King Jr. Way all the way to West Macarthur Boulevard.

This area was one of the most centrally located areas in all of Oakland. From West Macarthur a person can be in San Francisco, Emeryville, Piedmont, or Berkeley in no more than ten minutes. Telegraph Avenue stretches from downtown thru the upper edge of Ghost Town all the way to UC Berkeley. San Pablo Avenue spans from downtown thru the bottom edge of Ghost Town and stretches thru ten cities until it peters out in Rodeo, California. The numbered streets begin on 24th and end on 37th. MLK and San Pablo sandwiches in West Street and Market Street.

31st thru 34th Streets were where all the magic began in this infamous territory that even the city officials refer to as Ghost Town. Martin Luther King Jr. Way was originally Grove street. The street was renamed in the mid-eighties after the well known civil rights leader. The entire neighborhood was built of Victorian style single family homes, duplexes and four-plexes with approximately ten or twelve Housing Authority buildings sprinkled throughout the whole area.

Initially, the area was a drive thru weed spot started by Miss Burrell, the matriarch and queen mother of five notorious hardheaded sons and the auntie of MC Hammer. From her corner house on 32nd and Grove, she sold nickel bags, half ounces and zips of good gold weed. If a person purchased marijuana to sell from her, he would be instructed to go a block down and sell it. If you were given a bundle by her or one of her sons, you would be given permission to sit in one of the abandoned vehicles across from her house in the empty lot and serve your sacks.

The neighborhood was bustling with activity because San Pablo Avenue, West Macarthur Boulevard and Telegraph Avenue were hosts to the glitzy nightlife and underworld of pimps, players and prostitutes. Eli's Mile High Club, the Doggie Diner, Flint's Bar-B-Que and Biff's Restaurant all acted as backdrops in the Ghost Town landscape and gave these street people a safe haven to frequent the area even if they didn't live there.

Everybody from around the area referred to their home turf as G Street, until one Halloween night at a party that Miss Burrell gave. The whole party was in the house dancing to the Parliament Funkadelics *Not Just Knee Deep*, when all of a sudden a power outage occurred. The music died and then it got deathly silent. Out of nowhere a young man named Titty-Bo yelled out *GHOST-TOWN...OOOHHH*. Everybody followed suit and said *GHOST-TOWN... OOOHHH*. Then the lights and the music came back on and they all started doing the Dog Dance, which became their signature dance. Miss Burrell's oldest son Aral gave Ghost Town its hand signal. It's the hand sign that Bootsy Collins made famous by holding your index, thumb and pinky fingers to the sky, with the two middle fingers down.

Geer's Liquors was where all the young street kids used to assemble. It was a bulletproofed Arab owned liquor store with two video games in the doorway area of the store, Pac-Man and Defender. This was where all the youths used to hang-out, sell their weed and test their boxing skills. They would fight each other all day until a side buster from somewhere else would come around there and start some shit. Then they would all team up and beat the brakes off whoever it was, then chase them off the block.

The older niggas in the Ghost Town area would back the youngster's play if it looked like they needed some help. The Burrells, the Palmers, the Tolins and the Allens were the biggest families in the area and they would all come on the corner of 31st and Grove just to fight.

Several major figures would rise up out of the Ghost and make a name for themselves in the game on a multitude of levels, selling dope, robbing, killing and rapping. Big Dex, Hollyrock, Charlie-C, Slick Roll, and MC Hammer. However, since a young man by the name of Derlin was in elementary school at Hoover, it was a known fact that Ghost Town would be his one day.

His older brother, Campy-Do aka Big Camp, was an original Ghost Town knockout artist. He ran with the best of them, Stictor Victor, Manny-Moe, Angie B., Aral, Jed, Titty Bo, Young Man, B.J., Black Cliff, Spadey, Puncho and Karate Melvin. These OG knockout artists would take turns teaching young Derlin how to throw them thangs every time they seen him just because he was Big Camp's lil brother.

When Derlin went to school and got in fights, he would put grown man hands on his classmates. This led him to be the undisputed king of the school in elementary throughout middle school. He stayed on 29th Street directly across from Marcus Foster Middle school. During lunch him and his buddies would escape thru the hole in the fence and go to the alleyway behind the park and smoke weed and drink brew. Sometimes they would go up on Pill Hill and snatch purses from the nurses that worked at Summit Hospital. The security guards would chase them as far as the tunnel that separated Telegraph Avenue from Martin Luther King. A few security guards had made the mistake of crossing the tunnel and got beat half to death by the older Ghost Town cats in the process.

Derlin stood out like a sore thumb in a crowd of his buddies. He was a wiry little red headed boy with freckles and big lips that stuttered. If any one of his classmates even attempted to poke fun at him for any of these reasons, he would beat them to within an inch of their life, then chase them home every day after school. He would also pit all the other students, male and female, against each other at lunch time for his own entertainment.

His leadership skills became evident when one of his best buddies, Kevin Fos, got transferred to another school nearby named Westlake. The kids up there didn't know Kevin was from Ghost Town and tried to jump him one day. Kev came back to Marcus Foster and Derlin orchestrated a military style assault on the entire Westlake Junior High. The whole Marcus Foster Middle school cut thru the hole in the fence and marched the nine blocks to Westlake wearing straw bowling green hats and golf gloves and jumped on the whole school. The teachers and the principal alike got hit upside their heads with croquet sticks, golf clubs, bats and bottles.

From that day on, at basketball games against Carter Junior High, Lowell Middle School, and Claremont, Derlin would be leading the pack. All the Ghost Town youngstas fought side by side and stuck together at all times.

It was around the eighth grade that Derlin decided to start sellin' a lil weed . He looked up to Miss Burrell's son Jed more than he did anybody else on the turf and asked him if he could grind for him. Jed put him on the payroll and gave him the corner of 31st to get his paper on. If Derlin had any problems, Jed would pull up on his MB5 motorcycle and bounce off with his burners on and put the smash down. Jed ran Ghost Town's weed trade until he was shot in the head with a shotgun. He lived but could no longer function the way he used to, so Derlin struck out on his own and put his stamp on 31st behind Geer's Liquors.

His original crew of grinders was Charlie Brown, Grady Bo, Boss Man, Lil Stoney, and a pretty little bitch named Denise that lived in the duplex behind the store where they used to stash their bundles. Her and her momma used to make airbrushed Ghost Town T-shirts on the side as a hustle, customized with the Pac Man Ghost and the person's nickname on it.

Everybody on the turf was loyal to Derlin and didn't even ask to get paid. They just liked being on the turf hustlin' with the boom box bumpin' on a sunny day, listenin' to songs like *Freakazoid* by Midnight Star and Pac Jam.

Charlie Brown, Derlin's favorite lil buddy, got murdered by some Jamaicans one night while he was on the turf alone. They chased him through the alley, robbed him and killed him. He was only fourteen years old and this made everybody in the Ghost start bringing guns on the turf. Grady Bo was one of the first people in West Oakland to sell a nickel bag of weed to a decoy and accept marked money. This left Derlin all by himself on the block. He would not long after start catching weed case after weed case until he found himself in juvenile hall's revolving door.

Once he was inside juvenile hall, he found himself surrounded by some of East, West and North Oakland's roughest teenagers. Based on the fact that he liked to fight and was good with them thangs, he started putting down demonstrations immediately. Once he had his recognition and respect, he assembled anybody and everybody who was from the Ghost Town Mob and challenged any other turfs in there from other parts of the city. He hooked up with another gang leader in the Hall named Art-E-Bo from 2-4 Village and they came together and called it the 2-4/Ghost Town mix-up, pitting East Oakland against West Oakland.

Derlin's hand game was notorious in juvie and he became a unit worker. He had all the counselors wrapped around his fingertips and he could do what he wanted. Whenever one of his associates got to the hall, all they had to do was tell one of the counselors that Derlin was they folks and they would get left alone. This applied to the other youth too. Nobody would fuck with Derlin's people. This was how he acquired the nickname, D-Folks from Ghost Town.

Every time D-Folks got out of the hall, he would go right back to 31st and MLK to reclaim his fame. His runs on the turf would be short-lived and he would find himself back in custody time and time again on some petty bullshit.

Unlike the other youths in the Ghost who had jumped on the Hollyrock Crew, D-Folks did his own thang. Hollyrock respected that and knew that D-Folks was the rightful heir to Ghost Town's throne. Whenever D-Folks was on the streets, Hollyrock would touch him with however much product he needed. And he instructed all of his workers to stay off of 31st cause that was D-Folk's spot. This made D-Folks feel like when the Mob gave Chicago to Al Capone.

It wasn't long before D-folks would find himself back in custody on a gun case. This time he would ultimately find himself on his way to CYA. One morning while he was going to court, him and Young Julian, another Ghost Town nigga, spotted Lil D. D-Folks had bumped heads previously with Lil D at a party Larry-P gave in the Acorns. Lil D had been trying to holla at D-Folks' girl Lavette. The whole Ghost Town crew at the party stepped to Lil D and told him to let that go because Lavette was Ghost Town property. Lil D was from 69 Mob and wasn't used to being talked to like that. The Ghost Town niggas didn't give a fuck where he was from and mugged him the whole night long. After the party, when the Ghost Town crew got ready to make the trek back to the Ghost on foot, a car pulled up with Larry P driving. Lil D hopped out with a rusty ass .38 and yelled: *Hey Patna, remember me? I'm Lil D.* Then he started taking potshots at the crowd with his pee shooter. Everybody took off running and D-Folks dropped to the ground like he was hit. When Lil D ran out of bullets, D-Folks jumped back up and yelled: *Ghost Town..OOOHHH*, threw up the Ghost Town sign and took off running.

Seeing Lil D in lockup was right up D-Folks and Julian's alley, because they knew Lil D wasn't gonna have no win in there. After breakfast, D-Folks told Young Julian to go to Lil D's cell and tell him to have the counselors pop his door so he could meet him in the bathroom. Lil D wasn't no peanut about it and met D-Folks in the bathroom so they could holla. When they got in there, they talked it out and Lil D told D-folks that he wanted to squash the shit. He gave D-Folks his number and told him to holla at him when he got out and he would put him on with some major work. They shook hands and it was over. This was a major feather in D-Folks cap having the richer and more well established gang leader personally ask him to squash some funk. When word of this reached back to 150th juvenile hall, all the other big boys in D Unit tipped they hat to the Ghost Town general.

D-Folks' gun case would lead him to California's Youth Authority at Preston. He would be housed there with the Town's most high ranking gang leaders. Niggas like Big Criddy-Bo from Funk, Greg-G from 50th, Mack Glass from 3-7, Big Calshawn from the Acorns, Black Day Day from Greenside, Melle Mel from 8-5, and Lil Wayne, Big Fee's son. Together they would represent the Town and go to war with the L.A. Crips, the White boys and the Southern Mexicans. By the time D-Folks got out, he was a certified beast off the leash. His return to the streets would be well received and he had his mind set on one mission, to organize his team and sew up Ghost Town.

Once again he inserted himself on 31st and MLK. He summoned all the neighborhood headbustas and grinders and told them about his plans to put the smash down. Then he gave anybody that didn't agree the option to step in the middle of the street and chunk 'em with him. For the rest of the day D-Folks put on a clinic of knocking motherfuckers out, only stopping to use his asthma inhaler in between brawls. This was a feat of epic proportions because Ghost Town only bred two things, pit bulls and knockout artists.

After D-Folks made his statement, he started opening up shops in local dope fiends' apartments. Hollyrock and Charlie-C had gotten wrapped up in his absence so the majority of their workers thought it would be a bright idea to jump on D-Folks' band wagon. With his immediate soldiers and some of his family members, Dino and Ira, he started moving like a quarter pound a day in rocks. He stacked all his money in the beginning and didn't even buy a car. He paid a local cab driver who was on cream to chauffer him around to tend to his business and make all his moves.

His girl Lavette had moved on to other niggas while he was gone but still had his back as a friend. He used to slide over to her momma's house on Mead Street and holla at her. By this time Lavette was selling dope for a neighborhood D-girl named Dee-Dee. Dee-Dee was a bad little yellow bitch from the biggest family in West Oakland. She was raised right down the street from Lavette in 2-4 Village. She ran an all girl crew of her cousins and drove a white '77 Seville with a pink fade on the bottom sitting on Daytons and Vogues. Occasionally D-Folks would bump into Dee-Dee while he was over there chopping it up with

Lavette. He always kept it cordial and went out his way to speak to the beautiful young lady. He never tried to overstep his boundaries and really holla at her because he didn't think he had a snowball's chance in hell at knocking something that bad.

Dee-Dee had been hearing about D-Folks ever since she was in grade school. She knew he was a straight laced gangsta but was intrigued at how nice and polite he was every time she seen him. She herself had gotten into the male dominated crack trade as a natural progression. Her father was an ex-pimp turned smoker, and her momma was an ex-ho turned smoker. She grew up drinking sugar water and wearing hand-me-downs, so she thought that it was only right that she use the game that ruined her family to get ahead.

Her and her cousins were famous in West Oakland for letting the male dope fiends suck their pussies and eat their booty holes for crack. They started being known as the Saran Wrap Gurls because that's what they made the male toss-ups use as protection when they was giving them that head clinic. Dee-Dee's present boyfriend at the time named Weaver was from Bushrod in the north. He was doing a county bullet for wearing a bulletproof vest when he went to see his PO. He had been gone now for a few months and Dee-Dee's little hot pink pussy was screamin' for some attention.

One day when she was making a drop over Lavette's house she seen D-Folks. He had on one of his signature velour Lotto sweatsuits with the shoes to match. She couldn't help but to notice his gigantic dick print. Her snap dragon got hotter and wetter than molten lava, and on her way out she went on and slid D-Folks her number. She had gotten tired of letting the late nite hypes suck on her body parts and was ready for some real dick.

D-Folks couldn't believe it and asked his little patna Boss Man what he should do. Boss Man was a straight player and told him to call the bitch and blow her back out. Boss Man told him that all the bitch wanted was some dick anyway.

Later on that night, D-Folks called her and they hooked up. Just like Boss Man said, she was fiendin' for some dick. D-Folks blew her pussy hole out the socket and left her on the bed with her knees tremblin'. She had never had no gangsta dick of that magnitude before. D-Folks thought that it was just a one night stand, but Dee Dee kept coming back for more. Before he knew it, he was in love with the bitch and she was in love with him. Dee Dee was only the second female that

D-Folks had ever been with except for the neighborhood toss-ups. Everybody on the turf knew this and used to ride him about it. D-Folks and Dee Dee became connected at the hips from that point on. This turned out to be a major merger as far as the West Oakland drug trade was concerned. She would be the brains and he and his crew would be the brawn. Her ex-boyfriend Weaver would be the last to know.

Together they started opening fifty rock spots all over West Oakland. The dope would be signature wrapped in aluminum foil complete with two Roman capital letter D's stamped on the outside of it. She convinced D-Folks to go buy himself a sky blue Caddie Seville like hers. He put chrome Zeniths and Elite white walls on it just to make it stand out. Most of the time he just left it parked on 34th and MLK in front of his headquarters.

D-Folks rarely left Ghost Town because he was too busy assembling his team. When he was on the turf he would usually be surrounded by fifty to sixty soldiers on any given day, all ready to attack on his command. He purchased all his top lieutenants Mercury Cougars with all the bells and whistles. Boss Man had a starburst blue '67 on gold Daytons and Vogues. Grady-Bo had a drop-top '71 Cougar, black on black with Zeniths and Vogues.

The money was coming in from every direction. Dee-Dee had 2-4 Village on lock and D-Folks had the whole Ghost Town on smash mode. Now it was time for them to make the ultimate statement. They got married in a lavish ceremony on a bright sunny day at St. Andrews Baptist Church on West Street. All of the Who's Who in West Oakland was in attendance. When they came outside to the limousine, the pastor released two white doves into the sky. Their honeymoon lasted two weeks on the Hawaiian island of Oahu. They spent their nights on the beach lounging and fucking each other's brains out.

When they returned, they leased a four bedroom penthouse in Lake Merritt's Park Bellevue Towers for five grand a month, complete with a doorman and valet parking. The view from their penthouse was magnificent. When there wasn't any fog, it looked like you could reach out and touch the Bay Bridge.

In just a matter of months after their marriage they had accumulated several more vehicles. D-Folks purchased a candy green drop '67 Mustang from Ant of the Flower Boyz. Then he bought Dee Dee a candy emerald green drop 5.0 with matching BBS rims and Pirellis. To put icing on the cake, they both agreed on a '88 drop top

Vet ZR1.

D-Folks usually wore his short perm in two French braids down the side with a part in the middle. He had recently started going to Glamours and having Elsie put wet waves in his hair. He stepped his crew's dress code up and started taking the whole crew to Oxford Street to cop all the latest in sportswear and fly shit. They bought Bally shoes, quarter length leather jackets, Cross cords and Guess Jeans. This would be known as the Ghost Town ensemble.

Jun's jewelers made all the top Ghost Town soldiers custom medallions with the Pac Man Ghost flooded with diamonds. D-Folks paid for everything and made sure that they were all made to fit the big fat donkey ropes that everybody had in his crew. His four finger ring sat on top of his hand like some brass knuckles and spelled out Folks in blue diamonds.

He had reached the epitome of the game. Not only that, he had the richest and the baddest bitch in the entire Bay Area. Dee Dee was considered an ugly duckling growing up, but now she had blossomed into a showstopper. Along with the money that she had acquired, she could afford herself the luxuries of all the pampering that money could buy; mud baths at Napa Valley's Calistoga Ranch, mani-pedis at the best spas in Frisco, and shopping sprees at Nordstrom and I. Magnum. She came to be respectfully known throughout the Bay Area as the Dee Dee Bitch. She would zip around the Town in her drop Corvette with her mink hat and mink shawl on over nothing but a bikini and heels. Her diamonds would be turning the colors of the rainbow and her sandy brown hair would be whipping back and forth in the wind.

Nobody in their right mind would even think about robbing her. Not only was she Oakland's number one queenpin, she was also the first lady in charge of not one but two of West Oakland's most powerful drug gangs, Ghost Town and 2-4 Village. With the assistance of a bunch of her male family members, she had infiltrated and began setting up fifty rock spots all throughout the Lower Bottom region of the west.

D-Folks' only concern was Ghost Town. Him and his crew was smashing on anybody who didn't have Ghost Town dope. Some OG cats down on 32nd and Market came up with an ingenious way to compete with D-Folks fifty rock spots. They started weighing up fifty rocks, then cutting them in half and selling them for twenty-five dollars. This generated a lot of traffic toward their spot and they became known as the Solid Boyz because everybody called the twenty five dollar rocks solids.

When D-Folks heard about this, he told Boss Man to go down there and find a dope fiend's house that they could open up on the block so they could shut they OG asses down. Boss Man found the spot they could use and started making preparations to put some workers in there. When Lil Mike, Twon, Petey, and Yogi, the OGs on 32nd, found out about this, they knew they had to do something quick. They knew they couldn't go to war with the Ghost so they just went on and torched the dope fiend's spot so nobody could get money out of there.

The next day when Boss Man slid thru the block to set up shop, all he seen was the fire department. The spot was burnt down completely. When he reported back to D-Folks, he already had heard what happened.

The boys on 32nd thought all their problems were solved. The very next day they were all congregating in front of their dope spot when they spotted D-Folks' drop 5.0 coming down the block. They all hustled their way up the stairs into the spot. Yogi was already inside the top floor apartment bagging up some solids for the next rush hour. When he seen everybody come running in the spot, he went to the window to look out. D-Folks and two of his hitters was sitting outside in the 5.0 with the top down. D-Folks told Yogi to come downstairs so he could holla at him for a minute. Yogi bit. He went outside thinking he was just gonna talk to his longtime schoolmate. That's when the two other niggas with D-Folks bounced out and drew down on him with fat ass AP-9's. They told Yogi to get inside the back of the 5.0 and they drove off. When they got to an unincorporated section of the Lower Bottoms by the abandoned Amtrak station, they pulled him out the car and shot him at point blank range, then left him for dead. By the grace of God, Yogi survived. D-Folks message was clear: Anybody can get it.

A couple of days later, one of Yogi's patnas went to holla at D-Folks at his headquarters on 34th and MLK. His name was Barbarian and he was one of D-Folks old schoolmates just like Yogi. Based on that fact alone, he thought he could talk it out peacefully and get the entire issue resolved. They didn't call him Barbarian for no reason. He was six feet, two-fifty, with twenty inch arms on the hang. D-Folks was not trying to hear nothing he had to say and told one of his shooters to pop that nigga and get him off the block. When the young gunner pulled out the hammer, Barbarian took off running, but it was too late. He caught two slugs in his thigh and his ass cheek.

Dee Dee's ex-boyfriend Weaver finally got released from Santa Rita County Jail. The whole time he was down, all he heard about was how his old bitch Dee Dee had hooked up with D-Folks and took over West Oakland. Together they were officially the West's royal couple. Weaver was broker than the Ten Commandments and felt like Dee Dee Bitch had violated the rules by not properly serving him the news. Instead, he had to hear about her disloyalty in jailhouse bullpens.

He was still connected to several of her family members due to the fact that he had been with her for so long before she chose up on the Ghost Town general. Her younger brother Ducky was still a part of Weave's North Oakland Bushrod Crew. Even though Ducky was from 2-4 Village like his sister, he still held his allegiance to Weave because he had laced him up on the gangsta game as a youngster, teaching him how to use guns, break them down and dispose of them after puttin' in work.

A major drought occurred in the Town in 1989. Nobody could find any dope anywhere, especially multiple kilos. Dee Dee and D-Folks were looking all over the place for some work to supply their spots with. Dee Dee went against her husband's advice and called Weaver to see if he had some coke. Weave thought this would be his perfect opportunity to get some payback. He played the role with her and told her he could get his hands on one kilo. She said that would work and they made arrangements to hook up at Bos'n Locker, a bar and restaurant on 59th and Shattuck. She got the money together, seventeen and a half grand, and put it in her handbag, then went to the location. When she got there, they made the exchange and she returned back to the penthouse to surprise her hubby with the package. When she got inside, she went to bust the kick open on the kitchen table. Lo and behold, it was fake. When D-Folks came into the kitchen, she knew she had to tell him the news. He was upset but was more transfixed with the fact that he was looking at a See's candy box filled with dirt wrapped in masking tape. Who would of ever thought of that? When he told Dee Dee to call Weaver back, he had changed his number.

D-Folks held a meeting on 31st the next morning and notified all his soldiers that it was on site with any and everybody from Bushrod Park. They jumped in a couple of stolos and slid through everywhere they thought Weaver might be. He was nowhere to be found so they shot up Bushrod every day for a week straight hoping they could smoke him out.

On November 20th, 1989, Charlie-C's little brother Marquis from Ghost Town got out of the pen. D-Folks went and picked him up from the Greyhound station on San Pablo in the drop Vet. When they got on MLK, all the Ghost Town Boyz was waiting for him with bottles of drank and big joints of weed to welcome him back to the Ghost. D-Folks threw him the keys to the sky blue Seville and put a few thousand dollars in his pocket so he could get back on his feet. Marquis jumped in the Ville and went and snatched up his baby mama and her best friend. As they were riding in the sea monsta on their way to get something to eat, they entered the 29th Street underpass on MLK. A dark gray old school Pontiac came speeding up behind them and rear ended the Cadillac, making them crash into the side of the tunnel. The next thing they knew, gunshots flashed in the tunnel and the young lady sitting in the backseat's head exploded. Then a Toyota Camry slid onto the sidewalk next to them and more shots rang out. Blop, pop, pop, pop, pop, pop, pop, Boom, pop, pop, pop, bloom. Marquis and his baby mama Aloma were both hit while trying to duck down in the front seat. Both vehicles sped off and got found abandoned a few blocks away. The Highway Patrol and the Oakland Police department cordoned off the area and apprehended three of the shooters while they were hiding in backyards nearby.

Upon capturing the three shooters, the police did a thorough sweep of the neighborhood surrounding the incident and located a Beretta .380 semi automatic pistol, a 12 gauge shotgun, an AK-47, and a .38 Special. Another .357 was located inside a potted plant by one of the detectives later on that evening.

Marquis and his baby mama both survived but were hit with several gunshots. Sharea, who was sitting in the backseat, died instantly. Forensic investigators at the scene discovered that, along with the shell casings from the handguns, over forty bullet casings from the AK-47 had been discharged during the course of the attack.

The gunmen in the assault were blasted across every news station in the Bay Area. They were listed as Weaver, Tallmadge, and a young man by the nickname of Patty Cake, all Bushrod Boyz. Another assailant eluded police but was said to be none other than Dee Dee's younger brother, Little Ducky. A warrant had been issued for his arrest but he remained at large. Weaver and his hitters were all booked and charged with one count of murder in the second degree, two counts of attempted murder, and several firearms charges.

When news of this hit the Ghost, the whole area went into a state of shock. Weaver and his crew had literally mistaken Marquis, Aloma and Sharea for D-Folks, Dee Dee, and one of her girl cousins. The car had belonged to D-Folks and Marquis had a long perm just like his. The irony of the whole situation was the fact that Lil Ducky had been involved in an attempted assassination of his own sister and her husband.

When Lil Ducky was apprehended, he contacted his sister and adamantly denied this outrageous act of betrayal. Out of the love and compassion that Dee Dee had for her baby brother, she desperately wanted to believe him. In fact, her and D-Folks even assisted him with bail money as well as his lawyer fees. Once he bailed out, he would maintain a low profile for months while putting together a killa crew of his own.

D-Folks and Dee Dee continued to get money like the Mob. The drought was over and the kilos were readily available again. As the two of them were making a drop in Emeryville's Food Co parking lot one afternoon, they were lit up by the Emeryville PD as they were pulling out of the lot in their drop 5.0. They had just collected a hundred thousand dollars in a transaction and pulling over was just not an option. With D-Folks behind the wheel, they took off on what would become a high speed chase. As they entered Oakland, the Oakland Police Department and the Highway Patrol joined in the pursuit. They drove up West Macarthur doing a hundred and made a sharp right onto MLK. The sun was out and there were people on every corner. Dee Dee reached into the duffle bag full of money and started throwing it out the drop top as they passed each group of people standing on the corners. Twenties, fifties and hundred dollar bills started wisping into the air as the pedestrians started scrambling into the middle of the street to retrieve them. This caused a virtual roadblock and the pursuing law enforcement agencies couldn't continue their chase. The infamous power couple got away.

Ghost Town was on fire. Everybody within D-Folks faction was shining. Word of the car chase had circulated and other D-boys started trying to infiltrate the Ghost Town area. A major factor from the Murder Dubs started trying to filter some of his work into the Ghost Town network through some of his family members who stayed on

Martin Luther King and 31st. Based on his family was raised in the area, the drug boss thought that this would go undetected. When one of D-Folks play cousins named Kenya discovered the sneak dealing that was going on, him and about twenty other Ghost Town members started posting up in front of the family's house every day selling rocks. When the niggas that was shortstopping saw this, they called their family member from the Murder Dubs to slide thru and try to check these people outside. When he pulled up in his drop Saab Turbo, he bounced out and told everybody in the crowd that they couldn't stand in front of his granny's house.

D-Folks pulled up and quietly got out of his drop Stang and walked up to him. The nigga didn't know that he was in the presence of the Ghost Town general himself. He started to get louder and more animated, stating *Ya'll motherfuckas gotta lift up from out front my folk's house.* D-Folks seen that he was just woofing and told him that he didn't give a fuck who lived there, *This Ghost Town, nigga, we run this.* Then he told Kenya Cuzzo*, whup this nigga.*

The nigga looked at Kenya and thought because he was younger and slimmer than him that he was gonna have an easy fight, so he came up out his shirt and started squarin' off. Kenya started bobbin' and weavin', then hit him with a flurry of well placed uppercuts, jabs, and hooks that lifted him out his shoes. His whole family started pouring out the house to witness the debacle. A Ghost Town chick named Shalon took off on one of the females in the family and, next thing you know, the whole block was dragging the family in the street. A gunshot went off and Shalon dropped. Everybody started ducking and pulling their straps out. By this time the police came and everybody took off in their cars and on foot.

As a result of this incident, the Oakland Police started parking the mobile police tactical bus on 31st and MLK for weeks at a time. Shalon lived but would walk with a pronounced limp for the rest of her life. The rest of the family members got the message and never again sold a crumb out of the house for fear of retribution.

D-Folks had a fender bender down at Esther's liquor store in the Lower Bottoms. By coincidence, the driver of the other vehicle was none other than his old YA crony, Big Crid. Both had mutual respect for each other and knew they couldn't involve the police in the incident, so they decided to chunk them thangs just to resolve it. This would also end the age old question about who had the best hands when they was in the Youth Authority, D-Folks or Big Crid? The two of them went at it for about ten minutes and drew a crowd in the process. The squabble ended in a tie. Just to send a message, D-Folks sent a few of his Ghost Nuts through the funk to pop off a few shots later on that day.

On a bright summer day in 1991 Boss Man was riding around bumpin' his music in his starburst blue hardtop Cougar. As he was sliding up 24th passing by the Village, somebody sprayed his car with a super soaker water gun. When he hit his brakes and backed up, he noticed the water gun being held by a nigga named Lil Rodgee. He put his car in park, bounced out and started fighting with him. Rodgee was little but had too much energy for Boss Man to handle. He beat the brakes off Boss Man and told him to get up out the ViII. Boss Man stumbled to his Cougar and burnt rubber straight to the turf to get D-Folks and the rest of the crew.

D-Folks jumped in the car with him and told another car with Kenya and Garland and a few more niggas to follow them. When they got there, a crowd had already gathered in anticipation of their return. D-Folks told Boss Man to fight Rodgee again. Once again Lil Rodgee put the mix tape down on Boss Man. D-Folks got tired of watching his patna get scraped and started to unbutton his shirt so he could squabble with Rodgee.

Right then D-Folks so-called brother-in-law Ducky pulled up in a rental car and popped the trunk. He pulled an AK-47 out the trunk and started yelling; *Y'all Ghost Town niggas is way too deep in this Village.* D-Folks told Ducky to put the gun up, *We ain't down here for that.* Ducky looked at D-Folks and said *Alright.* Then he handed the gun to Lil Rodgee. Lil Rodgee started chasing Boss Man and the rest of the Ghost Town Boyz busting at them with the kayta. D-Folks stood there and looked at him and said, *Lil nigga, you ain't gonna shoot me.* Rodgee responded by shooting him eight times with the AK and killing him.

The D-Folks era was over. Two weeks later when Dee Dee, who had been ostracized by all of her husband's family and friends, entered the funeral parlor, CP Bannon, everybody got quiet while she kissed her deceased husband on his ice cold forehead and then placed a poster sized wedding picture inside the casket. Boss Man jumped up and pushed her out the way, then grabbed the photo out of the casket, tore it in two, threw it on the ground, spit on it and stomped on it. He told Dee Dee, *Bitch, get up out of here. You the reason why D-Folks dead in the*

165

first place. Dee Dee was hurt and humiliated and broke down in tears, then took off running to her vehicle. When she returned, she was clutching a 9 millimeter pistol and shooting in the direction of Boss Man. Several other Ghost Town members in the funeral home pulled out their pistols and shot Dee Dee in her arms and stomach. The whole funeral parlor broke out in mayhem and the police had to seal off the area in riot gear. Dee Dee was taken to the hospital and arrested. D-Folks casket was searched by the funeral director and several ounces of crack cocaine and thousands of dollars were found on his corpse as well as one of the pistols used during the melee.

When the newscasters did the evening news about the drug lord's death and the actions surrounding his funeral, they mispronounced his name and eerily referred to him as the Ghost Town leader named Devilin, one of West Oakland's worst and most notorious gang leaders in the city's history.

D-Folks would move on to his final resting place at Rolling Hills Memorial Lawn in Richmond, California. His headstone would be a lasting testament from his loving wife, the Dee Dee Bitch. The inscription says it all: *To D-Folks My Loving Husband.* Paid for by the queenpin herself.

Dee Dee would continue on as a major drug distributor for a few more years. She would be associated with large scale drug kingpins in Oakland and East Palo Alto. Finally she would catch the eye of the Golden State Warriors star center C. Webb. They would become an item for a short time until she would be apprehended at his townhouse in San Leandro, California in possession of over a hundred ounces of individually wrapped zippas in a Louis Vuiton suitcase. C-Webb's custom Harley Davidson would get impounded in the process. When news of this hit the airwaves, C-Webb did his best to separate himself from Northern California's largest female cocaine distributor.

Dee Dee bailed out on a seven figure bond and fought the case with the help of a high powered attorney. Ironically, she beat all the charges on a technicality due to the fact that the townhouse could not be linked to her in the first place. Therefore, whatever was found inside could not be directly attributed to her. Once she put that case behind her, she enrolled in Cal Berkeley and put the dope game in her rearview mirror entirely. While attending the college she began a relationship with another up and coming basketball player that was destined for the NBA. They would eventually become husband and wife after carrying on a relationship for several years after he was drafted by the Toronto Raptors. They are now married with children and he has since became a general manager for a California NBA franchise. They reside in the lap of luxury in a minimalist mansion in a Northern California gated community.

Dee Dee went on to complete her studies and obtained a bachelors and a law degree from Cal Berkeley. She is now a practicing lawyer and a female activist in charge of a non-profit organization for women. Her brother Ducky was released after serving time for his part in the two murders that took place. Upon his release, he took over the Lower Bottoms heroin trade until he was savagely gunned down on his birthday on 10th and Center street in West Oakland. Lil Rodgee was given twenty-five to life for the murder of D-Folks and is being held at New Folsom State Prison in Represa, California.

D-Folks was definitely one of the most fearless drug lords to ever grace the streets of Oakland.

CHAPTER 13 -- MAESTRO

Maestro's given name was Phillip. He was born and raised in the Shady 80's section of the Alphabets on 88th Avenue and A Street. He lived with his momma and his older sister Kym in a corner apartment a block away from the East Bay Dragons clubhouse. His mother spoiled him rotten and Kym doted on him from the moment he was born. His other family members resided in Richmond, California, and he and his sister Kym used to spend a lot of weekends and summers out there with their cousins.

He was a little charmer and had all the women dancing to his tune since he was knee high to a fly guy. He had a smooth way with the ladies and even the little girls at his school couldn't deny him anything. They all started calling him the Little Music Man. When he got a little older he became known as Maestro.

The Alphabets was a blue collar neighborhood. Mostly working class people that had capitalized on the opportunity to buy a home after what some historians like to refer to as White Flight took place. The East Bay Dragons opened their clubhouse in 1959 and their presence as the first black biker club in the USA held a lot of weight in the Town. They made sure that they kept any drama off the block.

Maestro went to Highland Elementary on 85th and A Street with all the hardheads from 85th Village. Since he didn't have any brothers to protect him, he had to fend for himself in battles. He was forced to stand and fight when he was challenged by not just one but sometimes groups of kids that wanted to jump on him. He learned how to defend himself real quick and earned a certain amount of respect from the 8-5 Boyz.

After school, him and his patna Phats used to go to the Tassaforanga Recreation Center right in front of the Village to play ping-pong, foosball, and wrestle. This kept him out of trouble and developed the friendships and bonds with the other kids in the neighborhood that would help him later in life.

By the time Maestro became a teenager, East Oakland was at a turning point. What used to be a beautiful middle class neighborhood turned into a scene right out of Rod Serling's Twilight Zone. Crack cocaine came on the scene and took over. Rap music was coming out of the speakers of every passing car. The 8-5 Boyz had taken over the mini park, and Cadillac Frog was the man about town. He had a '70 drop top and a '73 Brougham that he rode around in with the rest of his crew crowded up inside. Frog was Maestro's idol.

East 14th Street was the ho stroll. When Maestro and his playground buddies used to ride their bikes up to East 14th it seemed like the whole world opened up into a complete circus. There would be dope fiends, alcoholics, con artists, hookers, tricks and pimps all moving and grooving up and down the street.

Maestro's sister Kym was the first one to actually get into the game. Her boyfriend at the time was a mid level dope dealer and gave Kym her initial package to sell. She had a lot of female companions that used to hang with her and help her get rid of her product. Meanwhile, Maestro was still keeping his games on the playground and at the Tassaforanga rec center. Him and his buddies favorite pastime was chasing the little pissy tailed girls around and playing hide and go get it.

His favorite cousin Marvin lived in the Hilltop section of Richmond. Maestro liked hanging out there because all the neighborhood girls would be outside on hot summer days roller skating up and down the hills in short skirts and pigtails. This was a far cry from the area around the 85th Village where he and his family lived.

When it came time for school to start back in the fall of his ninth grade year, he talked his momma into letting him go to El Cerrito High in a plush white neighborhood in the Richmond School District. He used his cousin's address and him and Marvin both were enrolled there. El Cerrito High was like Beverly Hills compared to the Oakland public school system. The student population was a diverse combination of rich white kids, Asians and blacks from the other side of the tracks. The school had two football fields, a baseball field, tennis courts, and a radio station provided by a former student turned rock star in the Creed band.

At lunch time all the cool kids used to hang out in the front of the school and sell weed to the students that smoked. Many of the students came from the south side of Richmond and represented projects like Easter Hill and Crescent Park. Their style was a lot different to what Maestro was used to in East Oakland, but he blended in just as well. His cousin Marvin was one of the more popular Richmond students and introduced him to everybody he needed to know.

The high school was an open campus, so on a good day the kids used to walk to the nearby 7-Eleven and fraternize in front of the store with a bottle of Andre Champagne and some Indica joints. The campus security guard, Mr. Smalls, used to pull up and attempt to shake them down but they would all end up capping on his ancient ass Jheri curl and run him off.

Maestro and Marvin went in on a quarter ounce of Indica bud and rolled up a bunch of joints to sell at school. The little white kids from the nearby suburbs of Kensington, Albany, and El Sobrante used to buy them out on a daily basis. This was Maestro's first taste of what the hustle game had to offer.

During the summer he would be left to his own devices in East Oakland. His sister Kym was still doing her thang selling a few rocks to the fiends. Maestro used to sit in his momma's kitchen and watch his big sis weigh and chop her dope up. He learned the metric system well and how it applied to the dope game. He knew that there were ten tenths in a gram, twenty-eight grams in an ounce, sixteen ounces in a pound, and 2.2 pounds in a kilo, which weighs a thousand grams total. Now all he needed was a razor blade.

With the couple hundred dollars that he had saved during his ninth grade year selling two dollar joints, he invested into the crack game. His sister sold him some bubble to break down and double his money with. He was a new booty to the game so he would go through all kinds of trials and tribulations before he actually started making some money. The Shady 80's where he lived and started hustling crack had some notorious jackas that would not spare anybody regardless of their age if they caught them out of pocket slippin', so he knew that he was gonna need some security on his side. He purchased a .25 semi-auto pistol with the firing pin missing just to keep the cheat off of him while he was out there on 88th.

Things were going cool for a month or two and Maestro put up a nice lil stack that he was gonna use to buy him some of the latest gear for the upcoming school year. One unlucky day while he was on the block, a customer walked up that Maestro didn't know. Maestro had been posted up for about an hour and this was the first person that even came on the block looking for anything. The customer was a healthy looking brother that could of played for the Oakland A's or something. He politely asked Maestro if he was doing something. Maestro said yeah, then asked him what he needed. The customer asked if he had a twenty. Maestro told him he did and the customer handed him a twenty dollar bill that looked brand new like it just came from the United

171

States Mint. Maestro reached behind his back and dug his bundle out of his ass crack where he kept it and gave the knock the fattest dub rock out of the bag.

As soon as the customer got the rock he turned around and took his baseball hat off and put it right back on his head backwards while he was walking away. That was the signal. Before Maestro knew what happened, all he heard was the four barrel carburetors from the black Crown Victorias coming down the street directly toward him from both directions. More than fifteen big burly redneck white men with blue windbreakers that had OAKLAND POLICE in bold yellow writing on the back of them bounced out and hemmed him up against a fence. Sergeant Midyett got out of his cruiser with a clipboard and told the officers to frisk him. When they did, they located the crispy twenty and the pistol. Sergeant Midyett held the twenty up to the clipboard. The serial numbers matched a bill that was already copied down on the clipboard. Maestro was cuffed and stuffed into the back of a black-and-white and taken in for sales to a decoy and possession of a firearm. He had accepted marked money.

Maestro did several months in juvenile hall before he was sent up the hill to Los Cerros Boys Camp. The Judge wanted to teach him a lesson and give him a break all at the same time. The camp was considered a privilege because it didn't have any bars or gates .After a few months of good behavior, the youngsters could obtain weekend home visits until they were released back into the community.

The year was 1986 and there were several other juvenile delinquents from different turfs in the Town that were being housed at Los Cerros along with Maestro. They would stand around and take turns lacing each other on how to become better dope dealers, killas, and hustlas each and every day. The youngstas from East Oakland were deep. There was Indian Tone from 77th, Lil Wayne from 6-9, Ice T from 96th, Dario from the Flower Boyz, Dirty Red from 85th, Scooby from Brookfield, Black Day Day from Greenside, and a whole bunch of other knuckleheads from East Oakland. West and North Oakland representatives were Jon Jon and Meechie from Campbell Village, Stack-A-Dolla and Jamie Wallace from the Acorns, Young Julian from Ghost Town, Buji from Dogtown, Kenny Mac from 63rd, Dionne Grandison from Keller Plaza, and many, many more. The majority of these youths would become the future of the dope game in Oakland, California's ghettos once they were released, Maestro being one of the most notable.

He spent most of his time in the weight room with Indian Tone and Dario. Maestro's arms got so big that he couldn't hold them straight down at his sides. He played basketball, watched movies and went to school. At night he would lie on his bunk and read nothing but Donald Goines books. He was fascinated by all the paperback mackin' that the famed author portrayed in his novels. Maestro couldn't wait until he got out so he could get right back to his game plan when he touched down.

Every Friday all the young would be hustlers would compete against each other about whose family would pick them up in the cleanest cars. They would also make bets about who would come back in the freshest fits.

Maestro's sister Kym would pull up on Friday nights in her Ford Granada on color Keys and Vogues with the beat bumpin' to pick her little brother up for the weekend. When she dropped him off, he would be kitted from top to bottom in his favorite brand, Reebok, with the velour sweatsuit and Reebok Classic shoes to match. Maestro and all the other young men that had home visits on weekends would stash their weed in the trees that lined the road near the camp where they would sneak and go retrieve it while they were on their way to see the nurse during the week at the hall. Sometimes they would sneak down to the girl's jinny barn and get the little chicken heads high so they would get freaky enough to let them suck their titties and play with their pussies before the counselors realized they were gone. Maestro developed a relationship with one of the girls at the camp named Rhonda Downs. He would write her love letters and send them to her thru the jail mail at the camps.

When Maestro finally graduated from Los Cerros, his sister picked him up as usual and took him straight to Bayfair Mall so he could go on a shopping spree. When they got back to the Shady 80's were they lived, she threw him the keys to a '77 old school four door, dark green LTD. After he went inside the house and kissed his momma and ate one of her famous home cooked meals, he went outside and jumped in the LTD and bent some corners. He was enjoying himself bumping to the sound of the two twelves when he seen his patnas Phats and Fat June hanging out on 87th. He pulled over and bounced out and they was juiced to see they young playa patna. He told them that he had just touched down and was ready to get money and they was with it. They jumped in the LTD and rode around for the rest of the day chopping it up about how they was gonna put it down.

Rhonda Downs had already got out a couple of months before he did. She stayed in contact with him and told him to hit her up as soon as he touched down. She wanted to be the first bitch to get a dose of that jailhouse dick before the other hos in the Town did. She was originally from the Acorns of Larry P lore. After she got out of girls camp, she relocated with her four brothers to 7th Avenue in Funktown. Her cousin Fat Dave gave her a ghetto pass in the area and let her know it was cool for her and her brothers to put some dope down around there.

Everybody knew her as Rhonda Red now, and by the time Maestro got out she was already up to about a half a key of coke (18 ounces). Maestro called her and they hooked up at the Lakeside Hotel on 1st Avenue. The two of them laid up freakin' in the hot tub room for two whole days before they came up for air. After that, Rhonda went to her car and came back with a quarter pound of hard white crack. She threw it on the nightstand and told Maestro that it was for him to get on his feet with. She told him that she knew a spot in Funktown that he could open up shop on 6th Avenue and East 18th in a smoker named Rob's apartment.

When she took him by Big Rob's spot to introduce him to the hustler/smoker, Maestro and Rob hit it off instantly. Big Rob told him that all Maestro had to do was provide the dope and he would do all the selling. He already had a steady flow of clientele that came by the joint to spend money and smoke. On top of that, Big Rob's brother Gill was a functioning smoker that had a good job and liked to jack his whole check off on cream. Maestro jumped on the new business opportunity and told Big Rob that he would be back the next day to open up shop.

The very next day, Maestro pulled up in the apartment building parking lot and popped the trunk. He pulled a long barreled 12 gauge shotgun out of the trunk and walked to Big Rob's door and knocked on the door with the butt of the gun. His roll dogs Phats and Big June jumped out the car and joined him at the door with a pistol in each of their hands. When Big Rob opened the door his eyes got big. Maestro told him to be cool, the guns was only for security, and entered the spot. He leaned the shottie against the wall next to a chair and pulled a sack full of rocks out of his sock the size of a softball. Shop was open.

Before nightfall, Maestro had to make two trips back to the 80's to get some more coke. Big Rob's house was smackin. He left Phats and

Big June in the spot twenty-four hours a day, seven days a week, and gave Big Rob a booyah here and there for allowing them to use the spot. Rob's brother Gill would tweak his whole check off and then get credit all month from Maestro to keep his habit up. Two local smokers named Baldy B and Ski started running for the crew and bringing more customers to the spot. Maestro recruited one of his younger patnas Jenal to do all the store runs for baking soda and food to feed the rest of the crew and to be a lookout. Jenal was crosseyed, so he could look both ways down the street at the same time to see if the police was coming.

Maestro and Rhonda Red were still a team. They lived together in a cozy little apartment in the hills of Broadway Terrace. Between her brothers and cousins and Maestro's crew, they ran a squad about fifteen deep. Aside from the original Funktown Gang, their only competition was three miscellaneous crews.

Their steepest competition was a million dollar nigga from 69 Mob named Utsi. He was in charge of several 50-rock spots sprinkled throughout the upper and lower Funktown areas. How Utsi infiltrated the area, nobody knew; however, he used to ride around in a stepside truck with members of his crew in the back ready to bounce out and deal with anybody shortstopping on his spots. Sometimes he would pull out his burgundy slant nose Porsche and his matching brandy wine burgundy McLaren and campaign around the Funk to let everybody know he was eatin' real tough. Maestro and Rhonda weren't exactly on his level yet so they didn't bump heads in the beginning.

The next crew in close proximity to Maestro and Rhonda was a group of major ballers from Alameda's Buena Vista housing projects. They had migrated to the Funktown area after hooking up with a major Mexican kilo dealer named Easy. They called themselves the Fila Funk Crew. The two individuals that ran the crew was an ex-military policeman named Keith and his son-in-law, Green Eyed Mike. They crew was about ten deep and functioned out of an apartment building on 8th Avenue.

The third click that was getting a little money in the area right up the street on 6th Avenue was an old school Funktown family ran by the oldest brother Red. He had been paralyzed in a shooting that took place during a robbery and had temporarily moved away to Fresno. When he returned, him and his brother Lamont sold dope out of a motor home with a couple more of their family members.

The neighborhood was a treacherous place. The old school funksters didn't approve of anybody freelancing anywhere in the area and would rob and kill at the drop of a dime. Most of them were now crackheads so they preyed on the up and coming slew of hustlas who encroached on their territory.

One early morning when Maestro, Phats, Jenal and Big Rob was in the spot sacking up some cream for the next flurry of customers, the metal door came off the hinges. Two gigantic dope fiends came in with pistols in both hands and told everybody to strip out. After everybody did as they was told, they grabbed all the dope and money they could find in plain view, slapped Big Rob on his left ass cheek and took off out the door. As soon as they left, Maestro took off into the bedroom and came back out in his boxers holding a Mac 90 with the clip in his other hand. He ran outside with Phats right behind him holding a .45 semi-auto. When he got to the sidewalk, he took a knee and slapped the magazine into the chopper. The knocks that had just robbed them were only a half a block away. Maestro jacked the Mac 90 off and started yanking on the trigger as him and Phats chased the dope fiends up the street.

When word of this spread around, everybody including the OG funksters knew that Maestro meant business. He realized that he had to incorporate more soldiers onto his team and went back to his home turf of the 80's and put about ten more foot soldiers on patrol outside his spot. Before anybody knew what happened, he had sewn up everything from 5th Ave to 8th Ave. With the help of Rhonda Red he took over the Lakeside Hotel, which was infested with drug traffic as well.

Bouncing dope had become extremely popular in the Town. If a dealer could stretch his product during the cook-up, this would increase his profit margins incredibly and give him a natural advantage over the ones who couldn't. One of the Fila Funk boys was a master at cooking dope. Green-Eyed Mike would charge other D-boys to bounce they shit, but he was somewhat spooked of Maestro so he taught him the game for free. They were connected through their dope line Mexican Easy.

When Maestro learned the bounce game, he would spend days and nights inside of a kitchenette in the Lakeside whippin' up keys. He had a bad habit of scratching his head with the powdery residue still on his fingertips. This gave him bald spots on the back of his head.

He was rakin' in hundreds of thousands by this time and went and flipped a '69 drop Cougar. It was royal blue on gold Zeniths and Vogues. His right hand man Phats bought himself a gold '73 Chevy Impala four door. Maestro spent thousands of dollars at Harputs on the latest outfits for him and his crew.

The Foothill Strip was lit one afternoon and Maestro was out paintin' the town in his drop Coug. He pulled into a gas station mini mart on Havenscourt to grab some zu-zu's and some gas. As he was pulling out the station, a passing car with a gunman hanging out the passenger window started bustin' at him. Maestro ducked but got hit once in his forearm and one more time in his shoulder. He was wounded but was able to drive himself to the hospital, bleeding the entire way. He survived the shooting but had a few ideas about who was responsible.

A couple of weeks later, him and Jenal was ridin' by Lake Merritt and spotted the individual whom they thought was responsible for the attempted hit in a truck in front of them. As they rounded the light by the Grand Lake Theater, Maestro started poppin' at the truck in afternoon traffic. The hot slugs started bouncing off the metal, making ping-ping sounds. The driver swerved onto the sidewalk and knocked over a parking meter, then ran the stoplight and hopped on the freeway headed toward the Bay Bridge. Maestro and Jenal made an illegal U-turn and drove the other way laughing at the coward.

About a month later, the spot on East 18th got raided by the OPD. The OPD brought the bat out for the occasion and rammed thru the fence and the dual sliding doors in the front of the unit. Maestro tried to escape out of the back window in the alley behind the apartment, but was apprehended by awaiting officers. Maestro and the rest of the crew that were inside the spot were all carted off to jail. Large sums of cocaine and money were found inside the apartment as well as guns. Maestro, Big Rob, and two more of his crew members all received prison sentences as a result.

Maestro spent over two years in prison. Two of his closest confidants would no longer be amongst the living when he returned. Rhonda Red was brutally murdered in an East Oakland shooting. Maestro's right hand man Phats would soon after meet his end in a shootout as well. Maestro came home and had to restructure his entire crew from scratch.

The 6th Avenue spot was burnt up and too hot to try to fire back up, so he focused his attention on another part of the Town, North Oakland.

He knew a few people on a spot called the Wild Web. The turf was right off the beaten path of West Macarthur. The individual who previously ran the spot named B.J. had been gunned down by a jealous lover so the spot was wide open for a takeover. Maestro was the man with the plan. He went through Funktown and snatched up a few youngsters that was having problems with a kingpin named Davey-Dee over there. He put them under his wing along with Jenal and the local cats who were raised on the Webster street block. This worked like a charm.

During the day they would post up at Mosswood Park and on the Web in the apartments. Then at night they would grind out of the rinky dink hotels on West Mac and on Broadway; the Imperial Inn, Westwind, Regency, and Sleepy Hollow.

A neighborhood chick named Sugar chose up on Maestro and started gettin' down for him out of her grandmother's house on 37th Street. This would cause a rift between Maestro and the original Tray Seven crew. One of Sugar's baby daddies had a brother named Dust that was moving major weight in the area. His right hand man, Mack Major, wasn't feeling the Webster Street niggas hanging out at Sugar's house. Both of these blocks had a history of bad blood that stemmed back decades.

Tray-Seven and the Wild Web used to bump heads at the Mosswood Park Carnivals. They used to have full fledge riots before guns got introduced into the picture. The hardest niggas from each of their spots used to knuckle up and chunk them thangs from the shoulders. Now that years had passed and the Webster Street Boyz had hooked up with Maestro, they was feeling their Cheerios and thought they could start steppin' on the Tray Seven Boyz' toes by selling dope at Sugar's house.

Mack Major and Dust was riding around strapped trying to catch any of the Webster Street Boyz slipping if they could. During a three-on-three tournament at Mosswood Park, hella Webster Street Boyz was up there watching Hook Mitchell (the legend) jump over cars and do all kinds of tricks in the slam dunk contest. Mack Major just happened to be passing by in his sky blue Brougham. He had on a bulletproof vest with his Tech 9 on the seat. As soon as he spotted a nigga named Leaf in the park, he pulled over and parked the car. Then he tiptoed along the side of the public bathroom until he reached the basketball courts. He aimed the yopper at Leaf and the crew he was with and pulled the trigger. The whole park went haywire and people was trampling over each other trying to get out the way. Major jumped back in his Brougham and skirted off.

It was on. Maestro had Fat June acting as his sergeant at arms in charge of all his weapons. Jenal got promoted to lieutenant and La-La and Dae-Dae, formerly from Funktown, were his field marshals. Leaf and his brother were in charge of the apartments on the Web since they grew up there. Big Little, Philly Bo and Baby E had Mosswood and would take turns supplying the hotels On West Mac. Sugar, Malika, and Black Vera, along with a couple other chicks, all got down out of her house with her.

A freelance hustla named Magic Mike started fucking around with the paper game real tough. He was writing bad checks all over Oakland and the entire Bay Area. He was originally from Tray Seven but pledged allegiance to the almighty dollar. Magic Mike had been buying guns out of a nearby gun store on West Macarthur named Siegels. He would go in there every day with a disguise on and a fake ID and purchase any kind of gun you could think of. When Maestro found out about this, he had Sugar call Mike to her spot so he could spend some money with him on some heat. Magic Mike sold Maestro so many guns out of Siegels that the landmark gun store had to file bankruptcy and went out of business. With Maestro and company's newfound arsenal, they armed everybody in their crew with a gun of some sort.

Dust and Mack Major realized that they were outmatched and outgunned and had a sit down with the Maestro. Maestro was a businessman and had to respect the fact that they had been raised around there. He agreed to squash the funk and keep his workers off the bend of Tray Seven below Telegraph. This part of the block was sacred to them because that was where they had lost a lot of loved ones and got a lot of money too.

One of their older folks had just got out of the pen, Big C-Note. He was legendary on Tray Seven because he had the white apartments locked down like the Carter on New Jack City back in the day, serving fifteen rocks for a hundred. C-Note got together with Maestro and smoothed out the drama even more to the point that Mack Major and Dust used to even cop from Maestro on occasions.

Maestro and the legendary Hollyrock would start bumping heads over control of the many hotels on West Macarthur. The Hollyrock crew and Maestro's crew from the Web would both be grinding out of the same motels at the same time. The dope fiends would go to whatever door had the fattest rocks that day. A few of Maestro's soldiers popped off a few shots at Hollyrock's grinders and vice versa. This went on for months until they finally reached a stalemate. Maestro agreed to keep his grinders in the motels above Telegraph and Hollyrock agreed to keep his workers in the motels below Telegraph.

Maestro and the Wild Web started balling out of control. They started pulling their whips out and going to all the events twenty deep with all their clean ass diamond jewelry on. They wore earrings that looked like miniature plasma TV screens hanging off the side of their faces from a distance.

A local chick that lived on 38th right off the Web gave a house party every year on her birthday. Her name was Pya and she had fucked damn near every nigga in West Oakland, North Oakland and Berkeley. Her parties would be off the hook because everybody knew her. On this night in particular her party was going off without a hitch. The Webster Street Boyz was in there and had all they bitches in the party smoking weed, drinking and having a good time.

Fat June was playing the doorman with his pistol in his belt behind his back. Fat Clarence from 34th pulled up in his candy green stingray Corvette with his crew trailing behind him in a purple Chevy Blazer on rims with the bump. When they pulled up they sideswiped Fat June's old school Goose. He had just got his '72 Monte Carlo (Goose) out of the paint shop and went out to the Blazer and told the nigga driving that he had to pay for his shit. The niggas in the Blazer jumped out and started jumping Fat June, not knowing he was strapped.

The rest of the people inside of Pya's house flooded out into the street to see what the bullshit was all about. As soon as the Webster Street niggas realized it was Fat June getting jumped, they all started whipping their pistols out and busting at Fat Clarence and the niggas in the Blazer. One of the niggas tried to run into Pya's house and Fat June lit him up on the staircase with the blower he had in his belt. The nigga dropped and rolled back down the stairs DOA. The party was over. Fat June went on the run after somebody revealed his identity as the shooter in the homicide. He was apprehended a couple of months later and charged with a 187 PC, Murder.

Now that Maestro's sergeant at arms was in custody, he started spending a lot more time at Sugar's house and it became his headquarters. Some L.A. niggas had just recently moved on the block and noticed all the traffic coming in and out of Sugar's house and started trying to holla at Maestro, Jenal and La-La's bitches who they had working for them.

As Maestro pulled up one day to check his trap, one of the L.A. Crips was posted up in front of Sugar's house having an argument with her. When Maestro bounced out the car he whipped his .45 out and cocked it back, then slapped the Crip nigga upside his temple with it. The nigga stumbled, then jumped back up holding his bleeding head saying *Cuzz why you do dat?* Maestro said *Nigga we ain't doing none of that ancient ass bangin' in Oakland, we gettin' money.* Then he walked the Crip nigga to the corner with his arm around his shoulder at gunpoint, kicked his blue rag up his ass and told him to get off the block.

One evening, Too Short, the Luniz and Dru Down was giving a party at Geoffrey's Inner Circle on 14th and Broadway. Maestro and the whole Webster Street Mob possied up and rode down there to have a good time. When they pulled up, the line was around the block. They got out they cars and all rushed to the front of the line. A loud mouth bitch in the line started complaining about them cutting in front of everybody. Maestro reached in his pocket and held up a wad of cash wrapped in a big red rubber band and said *When you start getting money like this, then you can go to the front of the line too, bitch.*

When they got inside of the club, it was packed to capacity with beautiful women scantily clad in mini dresses with their backs and cleavage out. Players from all over the Bay were there with their best pieces of jewelry on their necks, wrists and fingers. Dru Down and the Luniz performed their hit songs: *Pimp of the Year* and *Five On It.*

After their sets they mingled into the crowd and were surrounded by a group of bad ass bitches. The loud mouth bitch from outside started talking to Dru Down and pointing at the boys from the Web and Maestro. Maestro wasn't paying attention and continued to nurse his glass of Grand Marnier with cranberry juice and a twist of lime. Dru Down and C&H (his producer) started walking toward them with the bitch on his arm. When they got to where Maestro was at, Dru Down started yelling over the music at Maestro saying *Hey patna, you got something to say to my bitch, she said you was talking all that shit outside.* When Maestro finally realized that Dru was talking about the chick outside in the line, he dropped his drink and fired on Dru Down with a straight right hand that straightened his perm out. Then he got on his head with several more haymakers that looked like they came from way down south somewhere. Dru Down tried to duck. Maestro was socking him so hard you could see words coming off of his head like an old Batman episode; BOOM! POW! WHAP! The rest of the Webster Street Boyz mopped the floor with C&H, and the chick that started it took off running down the stairs of the club with everybody else.

Maestro and his squad left the club and jumped in their cars and drove by the club and pointed choppers out the window at the crowd of onlookers left over waiting for the police to come. A couple of months later, Too Short did a diss song aimed at Dru Down and the Luniz and rapped: *Dru Down I seen you get whupped at the club, ya talkin' hella shit and can't back it up.*

It was back to business as usual for Maestro. He started delving into the pimp game and venturing out to the City (Frisco) to set his stable of hos down every night. The ho money was fo sho money and he was feeling the extra paper. He had hookers dancing at the shaker clubs and turning tricks on the blade. During the day he would start off at Mosswood Park and line all his exotic cars down the block on West Mac. He had splurged on a 740IL BMW with Corinthian leather and suede interior. The Beamer was a ho catcher with three piece offset rims on it to accent the margarita burgundy paint job. His four door Peugeot was champagne gold and still had the European plates beneath the California ones.

Everybody else in the crew had Cadillacs, Lexos, and Benzes. The park would be lit up on a nice hot day and the chicks would be strolling up and down trying to catch the attention of a baller or an athlete.

While Maestro and his crew was in Frisco attending to his hookers one night, they noticed all the coke smokers headed toward the Tenderloin District. Being from Oakland, they weren't aware that the Tenderloin was a million dollar dope spot that was wide open for anybody to grind on. A spot like this was unheard of in Oakland. If a person wasn't from a spot or wasn't working for whoever ran the spot in Oakland, they would get smacked for just trying to grind. Maestro thought it might be a good idea to slide down there and see if he could make a few friends to see what was going on.

Amazingly, he ran into a couple of his loved ones who were part of the K-Mob in prison with him. They was from the city and stuck on stupid getting' their smoke on. When they seen Maestro pull up in his Beamer, they knew he was on like shit and gravitated to him instantly.

He chopped it up with them and threw a few numbers out there pertaining to his coke prices and they was sprung. A few D-girls was nearby and started inquiring about the kingpin when he drove off.

The San Francisco PD suffered a shortage of female officers in the 80's and 90's. This enabled droves of females to start selling drugs without getting harassed because it is illegal for a male officer to search a female suspect.

Maestro and La La started spending a lot of time out in the Tenderloin. Both of them ended up knocking two of the biggest D-girls out there, Dianne and Madame. Maestro put Madame in charge of his drug empire and his hooker bitches in the city. With her under his management, he took control of the drug trade in the Tenderloin District, selling over three to four kilos broke down a day. His organization was the biggest in Tenderloin history.

The Oakland Police raided Sugar's house one day. Inside was a cache of weapons along with a plethora of drugs and paraphernalia. Nearly half a kilo of dope and ten thousand dollars were stashed in the attic of the old Victorian. The house was owned by Sugar's grandmother. Under a brand new drug free ordinance that had just went into effect, the house was seized and put up for sale by the City of Oakland.

The DEA caught up with Maestro several days later in Mosswood Park. He was attending the Carijama Festival when six blacked out Suburbans jumped the curb and drove on the grass. Maestro seen the agents bounce out and come toward him in flak jackets and took off running. They chased him down and recovered a loaded .50 caliber Desert Eagle that he threw in the children's play area. After his arrest, they served warrants on his luxury apartment in Fruitvale's Diamond District. At this location they recovered three more kilos and a fully automatic German machine gun with a silencer attached. Maestro was tried and found guilty on all charges. With the help of his hi-powered lawyers, he got off easy with twelve years.

The Oakland Tribune and the San Francisco Chronicle both did big writeups on the drug lord's arrest. They described his multi-county drug distribution ring as the largest in San Francisco's Tenderloin District. Mayor Willie Brown was quoted as saying the Maestro definitely had everybody dancing to his tune.

After serving ten years, he was released in 2005 to a halfway house in Oakland. Before he was out of the halfway house completely,

Maestro purchased four homes in the greater Bay Area, two in Vallejo and two in Oakland, bought entirely with the millions left over from his run as a drug lord ten years prior.

Once he was released from the halfway house, he opened up a hip hop clothing store on Fruitvale and Macarthur Blvd. The store was located right nextdoor to the Southern Café and specialized in all the latest boys and girls fashions. He sold brands like Evisu, Bathing Ape, Red Monkey and LRG. He also opened up a lingerie store in Oklahoma City, Oklahoma with one of his bottom bitches that rode his jolt out with him, a blonde haired, blue eyed, six foot stallion. She danced at the shaker clubs and kept the kingpin laced up in all the newest trends. He treated himself to a brand new CLS Mercedes Benz fresh off the showroom floor. He also purchased a dually truck to pull his classic cars with. A first year flawless '64-1/2 Mustang was the first one he built after his release. Together with his ex-lieutenant Jenal he built and restored classic cars at Jenal's shop on 96th and International Boulevard called We Do Cars. The cars would be trailered to the Barrett-Jackson and Mecum Auctions to get top dollar throughout the year. Maestro's return was one of the most stellar of all the drug lords in the long list of gangstas, killas, and dope dealers in Oakland history.

CHAPTER 14 -- CUZZO KEV

Cuzzo Kev was raised in the Grand Lake section of Oakland by his paternal grandmother. His neighborhood was nestled beneath the foot of the Piedmont Hills. The street he lived on was lined with lush ivy plants and oak trees that spill out into the winding streets, shading the homes from the blazing sunrays that glisten off the water of Lake Merritt. His grandmother migrated to Oakland in 1942 from Greenwood, Mississippi along with her husband, James Sr. Their union spawned two children, a boy and a girl. In 1967 her husband passed. She was forced to carry on with nobody's help and eventually amassed a small fortune. During her career she worked as a schoolteacher, a seamstress, and an entrepreneur owning a Laundry mat, an apartment building and two homes.

Her son James Jr. grew up and fathered her one and only grandson, Kevin. The little box headed boy was like the reincarnation of his grandfather whom he'd never met, the spitting image. James Jr. together with his mom would raise Kevin with a silver spoon in his mouth. He would be taught the values of hard work and become his grandmother's little helper from the time he was old enough to walk. He enjoyed hanging around the kitchen and would be rewarded with meals served by his granny on her china out of the mahogany cabinets in the dining room of their five bedroom neo-classical home.

Kevin attended Crocker Highlands Elementary, McChesney Junior High, and Oakland High School. He collected soda bottles and maintained a paper route for the Oakland Tribune to save money for the extracurricular sports that he liked to participate in.

In high school Kevin would shine as a junior varsity and varsity running back for the O-High Wildcats. He got good grades and kept his nose clean for the most part by maintaining his circle of friends from elementary, junior high all the way thru high school, most of whom were squares like himself. They wore varsity jackets and hi-top fades and dreamt about what colleges they would go to once they graduated.

Kevin sprouted to a stocky six-two, weighing about one-ninety by the time he was in the eleventh grade. The other kids who went to the school who were from the other side of the tracks tended to take a liking to the gentle giant because he was smart and had a certain presence about himself that demanded respect. Nobody fucked with him and he became popular during his senior year. He loved cars and purchased a '75 Mustang from an old lady on his block whose yard he used to clean on the weekends. The car needed some work but he cleaned it up and installed eight eight-inch pyle drivers in the trunk himself. After school he would drive over the ramp in front of the school bumpin' his favorite songs by EPMD and Run DMC.

He started delivering pizzas after school for a local parlor owned by a Armenian guy named Raffi. Raffi was from Baghdad and left the war ravaged Middle East in the 70s with some money he inherited from his father and came to Oakland and opened Four Star Pizza on Lake Park Avenue right around the corner from Kevin's house. Kevin turned some of his childhood buddies on to the pizza parlor and they all got jobs there working for Raffi and his sister Dodi and their mother Arpi. The job paid cash and this was right up the teenagers alley.

Four Star Pizza was an after school hangout and a training ground all in one. Raffi was a karate expert and carried a 9 millimeter wherever he went. He let the boys basically run the place as long as the money was right and they didn't steal nothing out of the cash register.

Kevin's buddies were twins, Ronnel and Donnel. He'd known them since elementary school. Ronnel and Donnel were allegedly connected to Lil D's 69 Village crew through their cousin Derrick Fila and their Auntie Sheila. Big Twin and Lil Twin, as they were called, were always up to some kind of hustle scheme. They were already popular in school because of the fact that they had multiple vehicles to their credit, Mustangs, Cougars, box Chevys and a Honda Prelude that was lowered to the ground.

Big Twin was the first one to actually start selling dope. He got together along with his best friend Willie and pushed out to a spot in Pittsburg, California where the two of them started selling rocks. In three days flat, Big Twin had stacked enough money to flip himself a '77 Cadillac Seville on Elites and Starwires. When Kevin seen this, he knew he had to supplement his income by hustling.

He wasn't quite ready to start selling dope, so he started off by selling weed to his regular pizza delivery customers. This worked out great because most of the people who ordered pizza from Raffi's were working class white hippies that loved to partake of the herbal essence.

Kevin was on the cusp of graduating and had been accepted into UC Davis to play football. Upon walking the stage, his grandmother blessed him with a Nissan truck. With the money he had saved up from working and selling weed, he was able to get the truck painted, get the interior done, and put music and rims on it. He had it hooked up a lovely diamond white color with gold leafing on Centerlines and Yokohama tires with white leather and peanut butter suede interior with two twelves behind the seat running off of a Zapco board.

He continued to work and sell weed all summer until it was time for him to go off to college in September. Another one of his high school buddies started working at the pizza parlor that summer named Julian. Julian had just gotten out of Los Cerros Boy's Camp and was originally from Ghost Town's Hollyrock Crew. Between the Twins, Kevin and Julian, the pizza parlor turned into a virtual one stop drug spot.

In 1987, Kevin was off to college and was staying in the dorms at UC Davis. He would stop back through the pizza parlor on weekends and holidays to see what was going on, but was enjoying his college experience to the fullest. He spent most of his time attending his classes and going to football practice. UC Davis was a certified party school beneath its hick town exterior. Drugs of all kinds were being passed around like candy on the campus at parties in the dorms and at jamborees and games.

Once Kevin recognized this, his itch for the hustle game had to be scratched. This was the chance of a lifetime as far as he was concerned. He could sell all the rich white kids weed and coke and clean up while he was earning his degree. During one of his weekend trips back to the Town, he purchased some weed and powder coke from Fat Twin and went back to school that week and sold out in two days. Before he knew it, he was making runs back and forth like crazy, trying to keep up with the demand of these wacked out college kids.

His new business venture went undetected for months until one of his dorm mates ratted him out. The campus police reacted on the tip by searching his dorm room while he was out of town at a game with his team. They located a small amount of marijuana and powder cocaine and turned it in to the Davis California PD. When Kevin returned to the campus, he was promptly arrested and carted away to jail. When he was released after a few days, the dean of UC Davis summoned him to her office and told him to pack his shit because he was expelled from the school indefinitely.

When Kevin came back to the Town, he put college in his rearview mirror. Now it was time for him to face the real world head on. He went back to his old position at the pizza parlor and was welcomed with open arms. He picked right up where he left off selling weed and now coke to his customers that he delivered pizzas to.

After a few months back on the scene, Kevin and Lil Twin decided to become roommates at a new development in Emeryville called Emery Bay. The brand new apartments were luxury units that rented two bedrooms for a thousand a month. The both of them were working and hustling so that was affordable to them at the time. The condominium was as luxury as they come with a hot tub and sauna, a state of the art gym, and a mini mart on the premises. This would become the ultimate bachelor pad. All of their high school buddies and their immediate circle of friends would be given an open door policy at the spot to come by, party, kick it, smoke weed, cook dope, gamble, and toss bitches.

Big Twin, Willie, Julian, Turp-Dog, Crump and Q-Dog would be there on a regular basis playing Nintendo and networking out of the spot. Their cars would all be lined up outside of the complex sitting on Gold Thangs and Vogues. Mob Chevys, Cutlasses, Cougars, Stangs and Sevilles with candy paint would be highlighting the curb with their ambiance. The doormen to the complex knew all of them by name and would buzz them in without lifting an eyebrow. These former classmates had all started pushin' coke. Surprisingly, Kevin's father was an old school powder boy and would slide thru from time to time and drop a package of coke off with his son.

Four Star Pizza doubled as the group's unofficial headquarters and dope spot. They ran their operations out of there like a black upstart version of New York's Pizza Connection, buying and selling marijuana, cocaine, guns and merchandise of all sorts right there on the premises.

Willie became the first baller out of the group. Once he reached kilogram status, he became the supplier for all of them. Fat Twin had rock spots in East Oakland on Garfield Avenue, Walnut Street and at the Mel Ray Hotel. Lil Twin continued to work at the pizza parlor as the manager, but sold coke after work on 82nd and A Street out of his baby mama's house at night. Julian had clientele on 6th Avenue and East 18th, 50th and Melrose, and 37th Street. Kevin, however, followed in the footsteps of one his neighbors named Ron Ron, who had infiltrated a territory at the top of Funktown on 11th Avenue and East 24th.

Ron Ron was a preacher's son that was raised a block away from

Kevin in the Grand Lake suburbs. He sold nothing but weight to the youngsters on the 11th Avenue and 24th spot. Kevin would slide thru the area and sell to all the stragglers who couldn't catch up to Ron Ron.

One of the shining stars out of the area was a one legged bully named Fat Paris. He took a liking to Kevin and introduced him to a wider spectrum of the drug game. With Fat Paris he started spreading his hustle into the Twomps. Kevin's customers were enamored by the fact that he was a mobile one stop shop on wheels. They could call him for a pepperoni pizza, ounces of weed, and ounces of coke all at the same time.

Fat Paris and Kevin became so close that they started to call each other cuzzo. They would switch cars and Kevin would be sliding around the town in Paris' hardtop '67 Cougar and Paris would be dippin' around in Kevin's slam truck. Because of this, everybody started referring to him as Cuzzo Kev, the Big Dog.

Unfortunately, Fat Paris would meet an untimely death at the hands of a dope fiend in an alley on Junkie Hill in the Twomps. Cuzzo Kev was greatly impacted by the loss of his 'roll puppy. However, Fat Paris had opened up so many connections for him that it wasn't nothing for him to move on and expand his network.

The Emery Bay condo was still Cuzzo Kev and Lil Twin's party pad and headquarters. Some of the neighborhood women would stop by for a sack or two of weed and just to hang out. Kevin had even started serving the manager of the mini mart downstairs in the building. He was a white guy who looked like he liked to party and get high. He would hit Cuzzo Kev up when Kev came in there for his usual sandwich and a drink and cop his usual eighth of weed and sixteenth of powder.

Willie had gotten shot and was now confined to a wheelchair, earning him the nickname of Wheelchair Will. He was still able to maintain his status in the dope game selling multiple kilos and half thangs.

One night when Lil Twin, Cuzzo Kev, Crump, Big Twin and Wheelchair Will were all inside the condo cooking dope, counting money and smoking weed, a multi-jurisdictional task force walked in with a key provided to them by the management. Officers from Emeryville, Oakland, Berkeley, Albany and Richmond, all in flak jackets and riot gear, came thru the door with their guns held high. Wheelchair Will, thinking quick, spun around and threw a bag full of money in a nearby closet. The officers laid everybody down and zip tied their wrists, then escorted them down to an awaiting paddy wagon while they searched the premises.

The countywide task force found four pounds of bammer weed, two ounces of powder, along with three ounces of crack, an AR-15 rifle, a vintage musket, and a .357, plus the bag of money in the closet. The sergeant made a show of bringing the money downstairs to the paddy wagon, opening the door and asking all of the young men whose money it was. They all shrugged.

They were all taken to the Oakland City Jail and booked on drugs and gun charges. Almost every one of them would make bail the very next day. Big Twin violated his probation conditions as a result of getting caught up in the raid and had to stay in custody.

While Cuzzo Kev was on bail, he moved in with his high school sweetheart named Kenya in the Twomps. He continued his hustle thang and was in fact more accessible to his clientele in the area now that he lived so close by. This was a pivotal move on his part and he started expanding his tentacles even further into East Oakland's 30s neighborhood. Now he was serving the Funktown Boyz, the Twomps, and the 38th and Allendale Block.

Cuzzo Kev had risen up to copping a few keys. His cook game was fantastic. In fact, if the dope was of high quality, he could stretch it a little bit with his dry cooking method. When he purchased his kilos, he would take them home and use a box cutter to cut open a triangle like cut on the top side of the brick. He would then fold the opening back and scrape a total of three ounces out of the package. Then he would cook the three zips just to see if he lost or gained a few grams. If he lost, he would put the three cooked zips in a plastic sandwich baggie and tape it to the kilo, close the window on the brick and return it to the plug. If it was primo, he would cook the rest of them up and get to work.

Ron Ron the preacher's son had gotten shot up by a rival dealer named Utsi's crew as he was pulling up to the Arab market on 11th Avenue and East 24th in his drop '68 Camaro. A stepside truck pulled up with a bunch of gunmen hanging off the back who looked like angry Africans on a safari. They emptied their clips into the drop top and made a left at the corner whooping and hollering.

Ron Ron drove himself the four blocks to Highland Hospital and came within inches of his life as he pulled into the emergency trauma center. He had so many holes in him that if he drank water he'd look like a sprinkler system. He survived the attack but would stay far out of the way for a while.

Cuzzo Kev picked right up where he left off . He enveloped all the weight knocks and with the help of his young patna Julian he would flood East 18th Street as well. He got rid of his outdated slam truck and put together a '73 Chevy EI Camino muscle car from scratch. It was immaculate with a 454 racing engine fresh out of the crate. He painted it candy lime green and put Corvette Rallies on it. Cuzzo Kev rode around in his EIko day in and day out serving nothing but weight.

His relationship with his high school sweetheart Kenya came to an abrupt halt one day. She discovered a stash of neatly bagged up ounces in two Cap'n Crunch boxes in the kitchen cabinets. She flipped out and went thru the roof with rage. She had discussed his occupation with him on several occasions and had expressed her disdain with anything illicit. He just shrugged her off and figured he could keep it a secret from her as long as she didn't see it firsthand.

By the time Kevin returned home that night, she had packed up all his belongings and put them outside on the sidewalk unattended. When he pulled up he couldn't believe his eyes. When he went to the door, his key didn't work anymore; she changed the locks. She told him to put his shit in his truck and that he was no longer welcome there. Cuzzo Kev called her all kinds of bitches and hos, then went to the sidewalk and started placing all his stuff in the back of his Elko. Right as he placed his last box in the bed of the truck, Kenya came outside yelling, kicking and screaming. In his anger, Cuzzo Kev slapped the shit out of Kenya, then dog walked her all the way to the corner by her ponytail and her pants pocket until the neighbors started coming outside. Then he jumped into his Elko, put the slapstick in drive and drove off without ever looking back.

Cuzzo Kev stayed with some of his patnas who had a bachelor pad on a dead end right off of 38th and Allendale until he found a spot. He was already playing out of a kit of hundreds of thousands, so money wasn't the issue. He leased the hilltop home of the former kingpin Mick Mo on Sunkist Boulevard in the Oakland Hills. The home on Sunkist came equipped with closed circuit television security cameras, plus a hot tub on the balcony overlooking the Bay Area. Cuzzo Kev was living like the Godfather.

As his money started to pile up, he got heavy into building race cars. He put together a two door '70 Chevy Nova that had a 383 Stroker motor under the hood, balanced and blueprinted. He had it sprayed silver and black in an ode to the Oakland Raiders. During the week he would race this monster against some of the heavyweights like Indian Tone, Fat Johnny, and Ant Wash down on San Leandro Boulevard for G-stacks. On Friday nights he would trailer the Nova up to Sonoma at Sears Point Raceway and enter the amateur competitions.

Another one of his pastimes was breeding pit bulls. He had a hundred pound male brindle that he used to breed with females that were bloodlines. This beast's home was in the breezeway of his Sunkist house at night.

His father James would sadly lose his life in a choking incident that transpired when the Oakland Police were responding to a domestic disturbance at James' residence one evening. The loss of his father was a deafening blow to him and his entire family. He realized that he would have to step up to the plate and take the reins of his grandmother's business interests and multiple properties.

Cuzzo cancelled his lease on his hillside home and relocated to a three bedroom mixed use dwelling atop his granny's laundry mat on 55th Street and Genoa in North Oakland. He was also in charge of her six-plex apartment building right behind the laundry mat. His presence in the new location was welcomed by the neighborhood D-boys. It didn't take long for them to notice the two race cars and the pit bulls that roamed around in his driveway twenty-four hours a day.

He set up a weight set outside in his parking lot. Him and all his newfound friends and neighbors would be outside working out, shooting dice and talking drug prices into the wee hours of the nights. His prices were proven to be high but his quality was always A-1.

His new love interest was a light, bright and damn near white chick named Nicole that he knew from high school. She had one daughter already and they moved in with Cuzzo at his 55th Street residence. She was gainfully employed by the Oakland Police Department as a daytime dispatcher. Her presence in his life would open up many more doors because she came from a very large family in East Oakland. She was a down ass baller chick and had been with a few major players in her day, so she knew the game and played her position to a tee.

With the new additions to his life, Cuzzo added three more vehicles and a GSXR 1100 Motorcycle to his collection. He put together a lifted K5 Blazer with a removable snugtop and floodlights on top of the cab, a '75 Chevy Camaro with rollbars and a racing engine that became his first ten-second car, and a brand spanking new Infiniti Q45 for the lady in his life.

By 1995, Cuzzo Kev had expanded the scope of his operation to all four corners of the Town. His paper route started on 55th and Gaskill to Ghost Town, Center Street, the Acorns, Funktown, the Murder Dubs, the DIrty 30's, the 50's, 65th Village, and the Brookfield flatlands. He had large scale dealers on each one of these spots copping from him exclusively, moving kilos on top of kilos daily. This virtual square bear from no particular turf had inserted himself into the drug and violence ridden ghettos of one of the worst cities in the U.S. He did so successfully because he fed the wolves in the process.

Cuzzo Kev learned early on from Julian that a motherfucker had to stay strapped at all times when he was in the game. One day when Fat Twin, Cuzzo Kev, and Julian were sitting in Twin's bright red Pontiac GTO in front of one of their many dope spots in Ghost Town, Julian was sitting in the backseat with his pistol on his lap in plain view. Fat Twin instructed Julian to put the weapon up because it wasn't no need to have it out like that. Julian told Fat Twin and Cuzzo Kev *It's always a need for a strap on your lap, I'd rather be a suspect than a victim.* From that day forward, Cuzzo Kev kept a hammer on him at all times.

The three of them had commandeered an auto shop owned by an old fence named Mr. Red. The spot was a literal honey hole and acted as a refuge from the outdoor hustle. It had an apartment upstairs that they used as a cooking station for the multiple kilos they were juggling on a regular basis.

At first Cuzzo wrote everything down, but it didn't take long for him to realize that he had a photographic memory. If you owed him a penny or a pound, he would be able to recall the exact grain amount the next time he seen you. When he went to see his Mec, all of his work would be accounted for by the time he got back. Some of his customers would even drop their laundry off at the laundry mat to get washed and folded, then pick it up with their usual order of cocaine.

He married his fiance Nicole and celebrated his honeymoon in Lake Tahoe. His five karat wedding band weighed his hand down enormously. As a extra treat to himself, he bought a diamond studded Presidential blue faced Rolex with a five thousand dollar iced out band. Nicole's ring was a sparkling two karats that attracted plenty of attention in downtown Oakland at her jobsite.

An up and coming local boy turned hot shot cop started taking an awkward interest in Nicole. She let him know that she was happily married, but this officer just didn't seem to understand what that meant. He was a graduate from Oakland Tech and new the area well, including where Nicole and her husband lived. He had just recently gotten promoted to narcotics and was trying to make a name for himself.

Sometimes on her off day Nicole would be coming out her place getting into her Infiniti, and the officer would pull up in his unmarked vehicle and attempt to make small talk. He would comment on all the race cars that her husband had and inquire about what line of work he was in. Nicole thought this was odd but didn't want to upset Cuzzo Kev by telling him about these little interactions with Officer Joyner. In her mind, she just felt like the officer had a crush on her and she thought it was flattering.

One day as Cuzzo Kev was heading home down MLK passing Children's Hospital, he was lit up by a police cruiser's blueberries and cherries. He pulled over as he rounded the corner on his street, thinking this was just a random traffic stop. When he put the K5 in park, three more police cars blocked him in. They exited their vehicles with their guns drawn and instructed him to keep his hands in plain view and exit the truck slowly. He did as he was told and was placed in restraints, put into the back of a police car and driven down the street to his home and business. At this time, he was approached by Officer Joyner and informed that his residence was being searched as a result of a month's long investigation and presented the warrant to him. His wife and stepdaughter were safe upstairs being monitored by a female officer while the search of the unit was taking place. Apparently, the Oakland Police Department had acted on a tip from one of Cuzzo's associates and neighbors named Al that had ratted him out. According to Officer Joyner, the Department had to go to great lengths to keep the operation a complete secret due to the fact of his wifey being an employee there.

Over a hundred and eight ounces of hard and soft cocaine/crack were discovered and nearly forty thousand dollars in small denominations and a pistol that was registered in Nicole's name. They were almost ready to call the search off when an overzealous cop who had been part of the surveillance team recalled seeing Kevin running in and out of the storage unit in the apartment building behind the laundry mat. Acting on a hunch, they broke the lock off the storage unit with a crowbar and bingo, a cache of weapons were inside hangin' on every wall. Rifles, shotguns and pistols of all kinds. They even found a handheld battering device with their own OPD logo on it that was given to Cuzzo Kev by Nicole as a joke.

Cuzzo Kev was taken to North County Jail's processing unit and booked on possession of cocaine for sale, manufacturing of cocaine base, and a weight clause for having over a hundred forty-eight grams of the drug. Multiple gun charges and enhancements were tacked on later. His bail was set at the ridiculous amount of one-and-a-half million dollars. He retained the Coopers Law Office in Berkeley, California to represent him on the matters. The top dog Colin at the agency came to his rescue and got his bail reduced to seven hundred and fifty grand, all of which he paid in full, courtesy of his grandmother who signed the check to get him out. Cuzzo Kev was out on bail in less than seventy-two hours.

His candy green El Camino had been impounded during the raid along with a twenty-two foot Reinill fishing boat that he had just recently bought. None of the other vehicles were in his name and could not be touched. The Elko and the boat were being held at the police impound .

It was business as usual for Cuzzo. He switched his program up and started delegating responsibilities to a couple of his underlings. He waived time at every court date which allowed him time to get his affairs in order. In the meantime, his Mec-line kept him in it with an unlimited supply of the product.

Mexican Mike was one of many of a black oriented generation of Hispanics that was a major kilo dealer in the community. His lines stretched all the way back to Mexico's inlands and his prices were unmatched. He was getting cocaine shipped in by the truckloads. Literally.

Cuzzo Kev made a few adjustments in his life. His family was growing and him and his wife had just welcomed a new addition to their family unit. He traded in his wife's Infiniti and replaced it with a Deluxe Edition GMC Tahoe. He added another race car to his repertoire, a '70 SS Chevrolet. One of his hobbies became going to the Benicia Auction and purchasing cars to sell and strategically place around the neighborhood. He used these cars to store dope in and to make deliveries. This would throw the police off the scent to a certain degree. He sold his beloved motorcycle, the GSXR 1100.

In a sick twist of fate, Cuzzo was on his way to load up on kilos one day at one of Mexican Mike's stash houses in East Oakland on 65th Avenue. He pulled up to the location in his K5 Blazer unaware that the place was already being surveilled by the authorities. He entered the house to pick up his order and exited with a duffle bag fulla work. The police waited until he got in his truck and started to drive off before they pounced.

Based on the fact that Cuzzo was already out on bail, he decided to hit the gas and give them a run for their money. He raced around the block and then entered the nearby Lockwood Gardens housing projects at a high rate of speed. While he was driving with one hand, he reached over and unzipped the duffle bag and started frisbeeing kilo after kilo out the driver's side window as he passed groups of people hanging outside. Once he got rid of them all, he hit a couple more blocks then pulled over and surrendered. His high speed routine almost worked if not for the fact that one of the officers got out of his vehicle and chased one of the people down that had picked up one of the bricks and attempted to flee with it. The officer retrieved the kilo and logged it into evidence as Cuzzo Kev was once again booked into custody for possession of cocaine weight of a thousand grams. With the help of Beverly Nelson Bail Bonds, he was able to secure another six figure bond and got released in about four days pending a court date.

The Cooper attorneys managed to keep Cuzzo out of jail for about another six months until they came to a plea agreement with the county district attorney in which he would serve six years with half time eligibility on both cases run concurrent. The gun charges would be dismissed due to illegal search and seizure laws. Cuzzo bit and turned himself in to start his sentence in early 1999.

After serving his time in a fire camp, he was released after thirty months of incarceration. His wife Nicole maintained all of his belongings and kept his household intact during his absence. He managed to land a job in Emeryville at Home Depot to satisfy his parole conditions.

As soon as he got out, he started selling off his old toys and began replacing them with new ones. All of his race cars went first, the SS, the Maro, the Nova, then the K5. He was unable to retrieve his Elko and boat from the OPD because they played tricks with the paperwork at the impound not allowing him to meet the time constraints to obtain his property.

As they welcomed their third child into the world, Nicole decided to quit her job at the Oakland Police Department to avoid the scrutiny that she was constantly receiving by her coworkers on a day to day basis.

After about a year of being out of fire camp, Cuzzo Kev started restructuring his drug network once again. The early 2000s had kicked in and the status quo for a drug lord had diminished greatly. The competition was slim, and numerous D-boys had been killed off or were still in prison.

Before anybody knew it, Cuzzo Kev was up to his old tricks again. Only this time he decided to be a little bit wiser and camouflage his activities behind the guise of another legitimate business separate from the entity his grandmother had built. He started his own contracting business specializing in kitchens and bathrooms. While working at Home Depot, he had accumulated all the tools needed to set this new venture into motion.

He prospected and became a member of a newly formed black biker club, Wiseguys MC, eventually rising thru the ranks and taking on the role of vice president. Cuzzo purchased and built several bikes during his tenure with the club, an anniversary edition Road King, a custom Screaming Eagle, a Road Glide, a Street Glide, and another Road Glide that he repossessed from a cash delinquent club member.

Eventually, Kevin and his wife Nicole called it quits. The split was amicable and they remained the best of friends. With his newfound freedom, Cuzzo took to bachelorhood as if he had a new lease on life. He relocated to a freshly developed community in Tracy, California called Mountain House, moving into a brand new sprawling five bedroom art deco home.

Then he began amping his car game up once again, purchasing a brand new Dodge Magnum, a 645 BMW, a Transformer Camaro, a classic Buick Grand National, a lifted Ford F-250 King ranch truck, a Dodge Ram truck to pull his new boat, a twenty-eight foot cruiser with a sleep cabin, a 550SE Mercedes Benz with a panoramic roof. His multiple garages were a grown man's virtual toy box secured by dual double-reinforced metal doors. He purchased four custom painted Sea-Doo jet skis to take on the water when he pulled his boat out. All of the cars in his collection were customized from the inside out with sound systems, interior, and paint, perched nicely on seven thousand dollar Forgiato and Assanti rims.

His drug network was functioning like a well-oiled machine. He had learned to separate himself from the process over the years and began delegating duties to different members of his circle who did all the driving, collecting, and distributing between Fresno, California all the way up to Reno, Nevada. Cuzzo Kev became a behemoth in the cocaine trade in Northern California.

He started a club promotion business that he used to plan events for the biker circuit, Kambrand Entertainment. His parties were breakaway hits in cities like Fresno, California; Galveston, Texas; Phoenix, Arizona; Vegas, Reno and the Bay Area. He would book rappers and singers and fly them in to perform at the out of town biker functions. On a trip to Haiti to do relief work for Sean Penn's organization, Cuzzo Kev was faced with the grim reality of what poverty really was. He spent weeks on the storm ravaged island doing framework for the new structures that would replace the old. When he returned, he got baptized and became a Christian.

During his travels, he took boat cruises along the entire Eastern Seaboard from Miami to New York. His money was now longer than the Brooklyn Bridge and his operation spanned to cities in the south and on the East Coast via FedEx overnight shipping.

He set up a new headquarters in East Oakland on the corner of 50th and International Boulevard, buying up two apartment buildings and a commercial building that he ran his contracting business out of. The medical marijuana movement was catching fire and he built, designed and operated an indoor growing warehouse that produced hundreds of pounds of high grade sativa annually to be shipped outta town every ninety days.

His illustrious career would come to an astonishing halt, however. In 2013 he was set up by a federal informant in a Sacramento grocery store parking lot while delivering two kilos and carrying a loaded pistol in the truck with him. The rat was a Sacramento native that he met on the black biker circuit. Cuzzo Kev would lawyer up (as usual), and received an eight-year sentence. He is presently in a federal camp serving out his time.

One of his most famous sayings while he was at the top of his game was *Its the price of the toys that separates the men from the boys.* Cuzzo Kev was one of the longest standing drug lords in Oakland's dope game, and definitely The Man with his Rolex Daytona on his wrist while he was pounding gears on his many Harleys down the Foothill Strip. He will be in his early fifties when he is released.

CHAPTER 15 -- BLACK POOH

Hoover Elementary was located in Ghost Town USA. The newly designed school took up an entire city block starting on Market Street and ending on West Street. The outer streets that enveloped this massive campus were 33rd Street and Brockhurst. Directly across from the school's playground was a corner house that was the childhood home of Demetrius, Black Pooh of the well-known Dark Dude Entertainment.

He, like many children in the ghetto, was raised by his grandma along with his favorite cousin Crystal, who he called Crittal because he couldn't pronounce her name. As a snotty nosed little boy, he used to walk around his granny's house in his diapers dragging his Winnie the Pooh stuffed animal by the tail. This earned him the name Pooh, which eventually turned into Black Pooh due to his dark complexion.

Black Pooh was a skinny little hardheaded boy that didn't leave his grandmother's front yard. All of his friends had to play with him right there where his family could see them out of the picture window in the living room. Him and his buddies used to have water balloon fights and play cops and robbers after school and on the weekends.

He had two half brothers on his father's side who were both older than him. They both resided with their mothers in other parts of West Oakland. Their nicknames were June Bug and Paps. June Bug was a part of the infamous Larry-P's Acorn Mob. His other brother Paps was a lieutenant in the Hollyrock Gang that ran Ghost Town. Paps would later go on to be a backup dancer for MC Hammer, another Ghost Town native.

Black Pooh was a watcher. Even though he was kept on a short leash by his granny, that didn't mean he wasn't paying attention to all the activities that were going on around his neighborhood.

The block he grew up on was also home to three of Ghost Town's worst band of brothers, the Palmers. All they did on a daily basis was patrol the neighborhood and look for people to beat up, stab or beat with sticks. These three brothers were treacherous.

One of the neighborhood's most shining stars was Green-Eyed Clarence who grew up on 34th Street a block away. By the time Clarence was in the eighth grade, he was flying around the

199

neighborhood in drop Mustangs and Benzes with his long silky perm whipped, wearing rings on every finger. Green-Eyed Clarence was not just Black Pooh's role model, he was a role model for every kid that lived in the Ghost Town area.

June Bug and Paps used to come by and snatch their little brother up and let him tag along when he got old enough to leave his front yard. When he was with June Bug, he was exposed to some of the grimiest of project niggas that West Oakland had to offer. When he was with Paps, he was surrounded by some of the slickest and the flyest of dope dealers and celebrities that were a combination of Hollyrock's crew and MC Hammer's entourage. This opened up Pooh's eyes to both sides of the kaleidoscope as far as the game was concerned.

By the time Pooh was twelve years old, he had several options to come off the porch and participate in the street game. The apartments a block away on Brockhurst and West was boomin' with dope traffic, so he decided to start there.

The beauty of him grindin' on Brockhurst and West was that he didn't have to hook up with any of the major movements that was basically running shit in the Ghost, those being the Hollyrock Gang, D-Folks and Dee Dee's Crew, and Clarence and Beav's click. Brockhurst was a freelance spot with ten or fifteen miscellaneous hustlas, all taking turns serving knocks. There were plenty of customers to go around and everybody had their own special times that they would come out and bleed the block. Black Pooh had the natural advantage of living just a block away. He could tiptoe out of his granny's back door and serve knocks at all hours of the day and night.

Black Pooh had sprouted up to a spry six feet tall and accumulated thousands of dollars on Brockhurst and West. He flipped his first car at fourteen before he even knew how to drive. He had three grinders working for him and was copping a quarter pound a day and running it off rock for rock. He was nice from the shoulders and could whup anybody his age as well as a few grown niggas that made the mistake of taking him lightly. They would run up on him and find out the hard way that they couldn't fight.

Since Black Pooh couldn't drive, he enlisted one of his older patnas to get behind the wheel of his '73 Cutlass and chauffer him around the Town while he was sitting on the passenger seat with a straw hat on and a cigar in his mouth. His patna, Pretty Boy Troy, was already eighteen and was originally from the B-Town. He migrated to West

Oakland to grind for his cousin Green-Eyed Clarence on 34th and Market. He took a liking to Black Pooh and seen the potential in the young up and coming hustla, so he took him under his wing and became his big brother and his mentor. Together they would beat the streets up and bubble like no other. Pretty Boy Troy was a half breed black and Italian mix. Like most Berkeley niggas, he was as slick as they come, well dressed and full of game. His cousins Clarence, Mario and Beav were all ballers, but Troy was too fast to sit up under them and live off their crumbs. He was a jack of all trades. He specialized in the dope game but used his good looks to woo the ladies into writing bad checks from here to Saskatchewan. This was a trade he picked up from his uncle Frank the Bank, who just so happened to be the fraud minister in the entire Bay Area.

Black Pooh was indoctrinated into a whole new world of opportunities when he started hanging out with Troy. Pretty Boy was a crook to the core and could steal a car in less than sixty seconds. When time permitted, he also showed Pooh how to pull the ski mask down and carjack and rob dope dealers in his spare time. This was one of his side hustles that turned out to be very lucrative. These two polar opposites came together like butt cheeks and started getting money from every direction. The two of them would rob and burglarize a dope dealer's spot and be right up under their noses the next day and the D-boys in the neighborhood would be none the wiser.

Black Pooh and Pretty Boy Troy eventually set up shop on 34th inside of one of Troy's sugar momma's houses. Troy knocked the old school bitch off specifically for that reason, to sell crack out of her house twenty-four hours a day, seven days a week. Occasionally he would have to take one for the team and blow the old raggedy ass bitch's back out. That was a small price to pay for the thousands of dollars they was getting out of the joint in dope money.

Pretty Boy Troy came across a shaved key that he gave a dope fiend a kibble of crack for. This key fit any late model Chevy from '65 to '75. At night Troy and Pooh used to scour the North Oakland Bushrod area and scout around for any unattended D-boy cars on Zeniths and Vogues. They would peel them, strip them, and leave them sitting on milk crates down in Dogtown.

At sixteen years of age, Black Pooh went and flipped his first European car, a British Sterling. He took it to Blanca's House of Candy and had it sprayed candy gold tapioca pudding. While he was at it, he had his '73 Cutlass painted candy apple red. Pretty Boy Troy had his '72 Cutlass sprayed cobalt blue with twelve inch white racing stripes on the trunk and the hood.

The day Black Pooh got his candy apple Cutlass out of the paint shop, he decided to paint the town. He slid up 73rd and started cutting the wheel at every stop light. Profiling. His music was pounding and he was feeling like a million bucks. As he got to Bancroft and 73rd, a wacked out Mexican in a truck full of landscaping equipment ran the light and tore the whole front end off his shit. The amigo told Pooh in Spanish, "No problemo, yo le hablo a mi hermano." ("No problem, I call my brother.") Then he ran to the nearest phone booth. When his brother arrived, he spoke perfect English. He was the kilo man. He gave Pooh his number and it was on from that day forward. Not only did he have Black Pooh's car repainted, but he blessed him with all the dope he needed.

Pretty Boy Troy had a line on a lick and sicced one of his square bitches on a baller boy out of Richmond. The plan was for her to get him inside of his safehouse and leave the door open so Black Pooh and Troy could come in and make him open the safe. The night it all went down, they pulled up outside of the spot and parked down the street waiting for the mark and the chick to pull up. When they finally did, Troy and Pooh got real low in the car seats. The broad got out first, the nigga got out and they went up the stairs and entered the spot. Troy and Black Pooh waited patiently for fifteen minutes before pulling their masks down and creeping inside the house.

When they came through the door it was pitch black. They upped their weapons and started following the muffled moaning sounds coming out of one of the bedrooms down the hallway. When they opened the door the nigga had the bitch bent over the dresser in the corner ramming a bunch of dick in her from the back. Troy hit the lights and told the nigga to lay down on the ground.

He did as he was told and Black Pooh put his gun in his pocket and grabbed a pillowcase off of a pillow on the bed. Then they started rummaging through the closet and dumping everything of value inside of it. Troy told him to go hit the other rooms and he went down the hallway. As he came through the door of another room he seen something make a fast move in his peripheral. He reached for his pistol and grazed the trigger as he pulled it out of his pocket. It went off and the bullet entered the upper front portion of his leg near his groin. He had shot his self in the leg. The person in the room took off running past him out of the room and ran out the front door to call the police. Pretty Boy Troy and the chick that set up the lic came running in the room and helped him out the house to the getaway car. By the time they started it up and made it out of the parking stall, a SWAT team surrounded them. Pretty Boy Troy did an evasive maneuver and jumped the car on the sidewalk, then rolled out of the car while it was still in gear and took off running. Black Pooh and the female were apprehended and taken into custody for home invasion. Troy got away.

At eighteen years of age, Black Pooh was headed to prison. He was facing twenty-five to life for the home invasion robbery, but was offered a plea deal since it was his first time ever getting into any trouble. The judge felt sorry for him based on the fact that he had shot himself in the process of the crime. He took the deal and was sentenced to five years with eighty-five percent in the state prison. He was sent to Vacaville's Reception Center to start off his time. He served a total of four years and spent the majority of his time in the jailhouse library studying business books.

Black Pooh returned to the streets in 1995 with a brand new game plan. While he was gone, Pretty Boy Troy had stepped his game up and invested in a Night Club called Freaky Mondays. The Club was located on Broadway and 34th Street inside of a commercial building. Troy's gimmick was that he let the first fifty ladies thru the door for free on Monday nights. It worked like a charm. The inner portion of the club was set up nicely with a VIP section upstairs with velvet lounge chairs and booths. Black Pooh was welcomed home by Troy with a stripper party and free bottles of champagne.

Pooh and Troy sat down the next day and discussed the new business possibilities. Troy let him know that he had all kinds of irons in the fire. Literally. The whole premise of his business plan was based on insurance fraud. First chance he got, he was gonna burn the club down and collect on the insurance policy he had taken out on the property.

Black Pooh really liked the idea of owning a club. His only problem was that he was a convicted felon and couldn't acquire a liquor license. He solved this problem when he heard about a rich nigga from the Murder Dubs named Mannie Bo that was subleasing clubs and doing promotions, the most recent being a club on Fruitvale and Foothill called Twerk City. Black Pooh ran into Mannie Bo in the traffic and picked his brain about how he was doing his thang. Mannie Bo was a gangsta, a playa, and a business man all in one. He didn't waste no time givin' Black Pooh the 411 on how to do his thang. Competition or no competition. Black Pooh took some of his money that he had left over from before he left and went down to the city hall and applied for a business license. The name of his business would be called Dark Dude Entertainment.

His brother Paps still had connections from his days of dancing for MC Hammer. Black Pooh, now going by the name of Dark Dude, utilized some of his brother's contacts to start booking rap artists and R&B singers to perform at his venues.

As scheduled, Freaky Mondays mysteriously burned down in the dead of the night. Dark Dude Entertainment was off and running and posters and flyers were popping up all over the Town with his logo and information about his upcoming club promotions.

Pretty Boy Troy and Dark Dude were still in cahoots and started opening up dope houses all over their old neighborhood in West Oakland. With the money that Troy received from the payout of the blaze, he invested directly back into the dope game.

This all occurred at a pivotal period in West Oakland's climate. A group of rogue officers known as The Riders were found liable in one of the country's largest corruption scandals. The Oakland Police Department had to pay out millions of dollars to several litigants that filed claims against them stating that they had been beaten, robbed, harassed and set up by the officers who planted dope and guns on them.

The majority of the individuals that got paid were all from the Ghost Town area and some of them were heavily addicted to crack cocaine. Dark Dude and Pretty Boy Troy were in the right place at the right time and would reap the benefits of selling dope to these million dollar dope fiends, one of whom bought himself a Rolls Royce and rode around all day smoking crack with a car full of toss-ups, getting his dick sucked and having the dope fiend bitches blow smoke on his nutsack while he was driving. Him as well as several other crack monsters made Dark Dude rich.

Dark Dude got real cozy with a chick named Quana. She was a balla nigga named A-Zone's little sister. They had another sister named Chrissy who was the youngest. Chrissy was a wild little thick ass brown skinned bitch who liked to fight. All she fucked with was straight gangstas. Chrissy's nigga at the time was an ugly ass nigga named Cell Soldier from Mead Street. Cell Soldier and Dark Dude used to chop it up on occasion when they were both over at they chicks house trying to get they dicks wet. Cell Soldier was looking for a solid ass line on the white and Dark Dude was looking for some muscle to act as an enforcer in him and Troy's organization as well as a bouncer at his venues. Cell Soldier thought it was an offer he couldn't pass up and jumped on board as head of security for Dark Dude Entertainment.

Pretty Boy Troy ended up catching some cases that would finally land him in the penitentiary. This left a void in the organization that only Cell Soldier could fill. He had already proved his worthiness by opening up two five-thousand-dollar-a-day rock spots in West Oakland for Dark Dude, one on 21st and Myrtle and one on Mead Street. Seeing the potential in the young hyena, Dark gave him the reins to all the dope spots and put him in charge of distribution and payroll to all the workers. This allowed Dark Dude the freedom to focus on his entertainment company.

Cell Soldier went and purchased a fire engine red Chevrolet Suburban and put six fifteen inch Zeus Colossus speakers in the back. You could hear him for blocks coming down the street to check his money at his spots. When he wasn't in the Suburban, he would be in his hi-performance Chevy Nova on Corvette Rallies doing donuts on Market Street with a AP-9 machine pistol on his lap.

Dark Dude, who was playing out of a kitty of millions by this time, went and flipped a Callaway Corvette that used to be a national pace car for the Daytona 500. He took it to Mike at Supercars and had him redo it from top to bottom. When it came out the shop, it was candy brandy wine burgundy with a felt top on three piece offset rims. He bought his grandmother a Fleetwood Brougham to go grocery shopping, and he bought his favorite cousin Crittal a Dodge Stratus to take her kids back and forth to school.

His club promotion business was booming. He had Sweet Jimmies on Fridays and Saturdays, the Iamba Room on Mondays, On Broadway on Wednesdays, and the Moose Lodge on special occasions. He would bring artists like Suga Free, the Lost Boyz, Petey Pablo, Slum Village, Mary J. Blige and Jodeci to these clubs.

Two of his best friends from middle school got signed to Master P's No Limit label, Billy Bavgate and Crooked Eye. The name of their group was Steady Mobb'n. Both of them were from Ghost Town and looked up to Dark Dude. They would hit him up whenever they were back in Town and come out and make special appearances at his functions.

Dark Dude gave a yacht party for his birthday one year and invited everybody out to come celebrate with him. It was a black tie affair and the boat left Jack London Square at eight p.m. and cruised up and down the Bay until two in the morning. Steady Mobb'n, Mystikal and Goapele performed on the luxury vessel while everybody looked on and got jiggy with it in the night air. A couple of Richmond niggas had got on the boat and got drunk and started running off at the mouth. While the boat was anchored under the Bay Bridge, a fight broke out and both of the Richmond niggas got threw off the side of the boat head first.

Dark Dude's functions became notorious around the entire Bay Area for being action packed. He started venturing into San Francisco and subleasing Space 550, the Mission Rock, and the Sound Factory. The entertainment money started rolling in almost as fast as the dope money.

Dark Dude Entertainment became the number one club promoter in Northern California. He would make occasional cameo appearances at his functions with his signature kangol hat and his four gold teeth shining, smiling from ear to ear.

Miss Burrell, the Ghost Town Queen, passed away. Her annual Ghost Town block parties could no longer take place without her there to make them happen, so Dark Dude stepped up to the plate and carried on the tradition. He changed the location to MLK's 34th Street Park. Resident celebrities like Bavgate, Lil Holly and Pooh Sauce always performed along with the No Limit Family. On Thanksgiving he gave a turkey giveaway picnic at Lake Temescal every year. He gave back like he had seen Mother Mary Wright do every year in West Oakland.

One of Dark Dude's cousins moved to Denver, Colorado and invited him up one year. When he got off the plane in the Mile High City, he was already feeling the environment. Prior to him going up there, he wasn't aware that the city had such a massive black population. Once he seen that, he figured this would be prime territory to bring some entertainment to the nightlife up there, Bay Area style.

The gang bangers in the Denver area started coming to his venues and getting familiar with his name and brand. A couple of them had the streets on lock with the coke game, but they were paying much higher prices than he was in Oakland. Once he realized that they were paying twenty-five grand a kilo, he knew that he could flood the market. Based on the fact that he was buying twenty to thirty kilos at twelve and a half per pickup, he could mark them up significantly and still sell them at a thousand dollars cheaper than the local dealers.

He started off by Fed Ex-ing them to abandoned houses using the overnight delivery method. He would seal them in catsup cans and box them up. As soon as he dropped them off, he would board a plane and beat the delivery truck to the location. This worked for months, then eventually got too risky so he decided to incorporate his shipments into his entertainment itinerary. He would pack all the drugs into the DJ's equipment speakers and load them on the tour buses. Then he would follow behind the bus with a female of his liking and sometimes her baby in the back in the car seat, looking like a typical family on a road trip.

When he came back to the Town, he was in a whole different tax bracket. It was evident by the cars he drove, the jewelry he wore, and the moves he made. He would park his Bounder Tour Bus on West Street behind Hoover Elementary and hold court right there like the godfather. If one of the neighborhood families were behind on their bills, they would come get on the bus and tell him their dilemma. He would reach in his briefcase and pull out a stack of money and solve their problem on the spot. The school kids loved it when they seen the tour bus outside of the school because after school let out he would stand outside of the bus and give them two dollar bills and silver dollars to buy ice cream and candy with from Mary's store.

On one of his trips to Hollywood during All-star Weekend, a smoke gray 600 Mercedes Benz caught his eye in the window of a luxury car showroom. Nobody in the Town had the 600 yet and he knew this car was a must have. When he entered the dealership office, the sales people swarmed him immediately, thinking he was a NBA player. He explained to them that he was in the entertainment business and was interested in the 600 in the window. They allowed him to test drive the vehicle, and when he returned he was sold. He charged the down payment to his American Express Black Card and made arrangements for them to ship the car to Oakland.

The car was shipped to Mike Fajita's Supercars in Berkeley, California. Once there, he had it custom fitted with TV screens in the dash, the rearview mirror, the headrests, the side mirrors, and the license plate, ten TVs total. Then he had them remove all the decals on the car so it would be impossible for an onlooker to decipher what model vehicle it was. The vehicle came with twenty-two inch factory rims and looked like a spaceship when it passed by.

When Dark Dude pulled it out of the shop, the first place he went was to West Oakland to show the youngsters in his neighborhood what the turf was worth. They all crowded around and asked him if they could drive his new machine. He took them inside Hoover Elementary's playground and let each one of them get behind the wheel and drive in circles in the hundred-and-fifty thousand dollar car. Then he pulled out a knot full of hundreds and gave each one of them a C-note to stay out of trouble with. When he drove off, he was bumpin' the Gap Band's *Outstanding* and bobbin' his head to the beat.

Every morning Dark Dude would wake the West up in his 600 and hit all the backstreets at eight in the morning while the kids was headed to school and their folks was headed to work. He would throw flyers to his next entertainment venue out the car's sunroof at every intersection. This was how he promoted his clubs, along with radio commercials.

When night fell, he would turn on all his TV screens and play Billy Bavgate's latest video, *I'm Rich Bitch*, and slide through downtown Oakland's Jack London Square passing by all the clubs. Then he would hit the east and shut the sideshow down. Nobody in Oakland could light a match to his 600 Benz. Even Bill Haney had to tip his hat to him when he slid up next to him at a light in his sky blue Bentley GT Coupe.

One of Dark Dude's safehouses got infiltrated in Squarefield, California while he was out of town. This was one of his tuck spots that he kept with a super bad North Oakland chick. He let her occupy the condo with her two kids rent free. Her husband, Norm, was in the penitentiary for life on a murder and, as far as Dark Dude was concerned, he wasn't no threat. Until a total of five kilos came up missing out of the spot. The only logical explanation was that the broad had ran her mouth to her hubby and he had sent some of his goons to grab the dope.

Cell Soldier was still in town, so he was dispatched to the spot to get to the bottom of the problem. When Cell Soldier got there, the beautiful young lady swore up and down she didn't know what happened. Cell Soldier used advanced forms of mob tactics to get her to tell the truth. She was hardnosed and stuck to her mud before she went flying out of the two story plate glass window duct-taped to a chair.

Fortunately, she landed in some sticker bushes below and survived. The drugs were never located.

Approximately a year later, Cell Soldier ended up in Solano State Prison on some drug and gun charges. The exact same institution the chick's husband, Norm, had been in for years serving out his life sentence. Norm had became a high rankin' member of a Bay Area prison gang called the K-Mob. One Saturday in the visiting room of the prison, Cell Soldier was in there visiting with his woman and the chick he tossed out the window was there visiting Norm. She recognized Cell Soldier and pointed him out to Norm as the one who had sent her flying out the window of the spot. Norm was furious and told her he would handle it after the visit was over.

Norm returned back to the yard and rounded up his regime and held a cipher on the yard to discuss the situation to be handled. A few of the individuals in his regime were from West Oakland and knew who Dark Dude and Cell Soldier was and how much money and power they had. They advised their commander against making the move against Cell Soldier, especially since it concerned a bitch on the streets, wife or no wife. Norm was adamant about handling it and went and got his kisu (knife), then went to Cell Soldier's building and had somebody send him outside. When Cell Soldier came outside, he took one look at Norm and told him that Dark Dude was the one who brought his wife up here to visit him in the first place, so if he tried anything, he would never see his wife or kids again. Norm was stunned. He spun around on his heels and went straight to his building and got on the phone. When Dark Dude answered, he was speechless. From that day on, he put a hands off policy on Cell Soldier. Cell Soldier did the rest of his time worry free, laughing at Norm every time he seen him.

When he was released, Dark Dude blessed him with a bag full of kilos and a bag full of money. Cell Soldier bought a house in Las Vegas and started a trucking business. He retired from the game at an early age and married his neighborhood sweetheart, a preacher's daughter.

One of Dark Dude's trusted aides got carjacked at a Giant Burgers stand while driving in his custom Callaway Corvette. The car was tracked down to 63rd Street. The street was ran by a notorious hit man by the name of G-Lloyd. Some of the younger cats on his team were known for carjacking and robbin' dope dealers for a living. So Dark Dude had his brothers Paps and June Bug holla at G-Lloyd to get the vehicle back. Dark Dude wasn't the type to involve the police in street shit so he sent a message to G-Lloyd that he would be willing to sneeze out a few gee's to get the car back. G-Lloyd told him to shoot it and the car would be parked at the Alaska Gas station on San Pablo in the morning. Dark sent Paps with a grocery bag filled to the brim with twenty-five grand in one dollar bills to give to G-Lloyd. This was his way of letting him know how small the situation was to him. His car was returned on schedule to the location.

Dark Dude's operation hit a bump in the road when Paps and Quana's brother A-Zone got snatched up by the Feds in a drug ring that involved several Mexicans, Rick the Ruler from the Dubs, Mack Lou from Apgar and some Richmond niggas from Easter Hill housing projects. This sting put a dent in Dark Dude's program temporarily until an old school North Oakland kingpin got out of the pen. When Joe Blow touched down, he started dumping bricks on Dark like never before.

Dark still had his Denver operation in full swing. Early one morning, a young man was stopped by TSA at Denver International Airport. His luggage was flagged by the drug sniffing K-9s. The authorities escorted him to the holding area while they did an extensive search of his belongings. Twenty-five keys of pure cocaine was discovered inside of wax candles. He was taken into custody immediately and the DEA was notified. The young man was a part of Dark Dude's Denver distribution ring. He didn't waste no time cutting a deal with the Feds and revealing the source of the narcotics. The Feds bilked him for all they could and prepared for the takedown of the entertainment CEO and drug lord known as Dark Dude.

As Dark Dude's tour bus exited the freeway in Denver a week later, it was surrounded by an army of U.S. Marshals. They exited their SUVs in full regalia and had their AR-15s at the ready. Dark Dude and his entire entourage were taken into custody. Word on the streets of Oakland was that Dark Dude had gotten snatched up and was facing a life sentence. He was charged with multi-state distribution of multiple pounds and kilos of cocaine. The truth of the matter was that Dark Dude had became a multi-millionaire by moving thousands of kilos out of state for several years, all camouflaged under the guise of his entertainment business.

A dark cloud loomed over West Oakland in his absence. It was said that after months of fighting his case he had received life in prison.

However, Dark Dude could not be directly linked to the shipment and the government's case was purely circumstantial based on the young man who actually got caught with the drugs word alone. When the tour bus was pulled over it was squeaky clean. The Feds couldn't even find a doobie of weed because the drug lord didn't smoke or allow his crew members to use any type of drugs around him.

Dark Dude received five years for his troubles and was released to the federal halfway house on Macarthur Boulevard in Oakland in 2004. He worked at Bring 'em Back Bill's auto detail shop until he was released from the halfway house completely. A hooker by the name of Bambi chose up on him and gave him hundreds of thousands of dollars upon his return back to the community. Dark Dude reinvented himself and founded a black biker club known as the Untouchables. He opened up a clubhouse in the Lower Bottoms on 7th street next to the BART Station and put together a custom candy green Harley Davidson Road Glide with gold rims. He purchased a 2005 Dodge Charger to tool around in and took over a club near Lake Merritt called the Serenader until it was closed down.

Dark Dude was one of the most business-minded drug lords in Oakland's lineage of kingpins.

CHAPTER 16 - MAJOR PLAYERS

The Definition of a drug lord was defined by the fact that a leader of an organized crime faction was the mastermind behind a network of dealers, enforcers, soldiers, and hit men, with ties to cocaine, heroin and marijuana producing countries, amassing millions of dollars. In Oakland, California these individuals were and still are black folks, starting with the Late Great Big Fee, who set the bar very high for those that came after him. His legacy was never based on how he bought his dope or who he bought it from, but how he sold it. The methods he used in 69th Village and 65th Village have never been duplicated anywhere else in the United States except for New York. Big Fee was the most powerful and most sophisticated drug lord in California history.

The succession of drug lords that came after him controlled the Oakland landscape with force, mayhem, terror and flamboyance, leaving a trail of bloodshed that would bypass the Afghanistan war as far as bodies being left behind. Most of these young men were millionaires by the time they were in their teens, shaping the destinies of the grown men and children that they employed in their drug gangs.

Before the Mexicans were even in the equation as drug smugglers, the drug lords of Oakland had direct lines to Afghanistan and the original Columbian cartels via Pablo Escobar, the Ochoa Family and the Black Widow, Griselda Blanco herself.

During the 1970s, 80s, 90s, and early 2000s, thousands of young men and women participated in the drug trade in the Town, some as dealers, others as users. Families were destroyed and prisons were filled with the risk takers that chose drug dealing as their primary source of income.

The status quo of a drug lord began to diminish as the years went by. Next came the kingpins, the ballers, and the major factors who would carry on the trade into the new millennium. As technology progressed and several snitches started rolling over to save their own hides, the Feds and the local police started to make more headway when it came to capturing these drug dealers. By cutting off the heads, the bodies would follow. Many of these legendary figures' careers were short-lived. They came and went like shooting stars over the dark Oakland skyline.

One of the most memorable was Fat Bruce, also known as Bruce from Tha Deuce. Fat Bruce was a schoolhouse bully that looked like a redheaded stepchild. He grew up on 72nd Avenue below East 14th Street and went to Lockwood Elementary and Havenscourt Junior High with all the kids from 69th and 65th Village. Due to the fact that he grew up so close to these projects, he was considered one of them and they wouldn't jump him during fights. By him being a chubby little kid, he would beat up and bully the smaller kids. When he got in his teens, he started smashin' for his rations on 7-1's bammer block, an age old weed spot that relied on all the traffic from the Coliseum, the Arena and the BART Station.

As he got older and transitioned into the coke game, he started copping from the almighty Mob prodigy Lil D. When Lil D fell to the Feds in 1988, Fat Bruce inherited some of his clientele as well as some of his jewelry, including his blue face Rolex, that Fat Bruce wore religiously. He started his own record label and produced hits for the first rapper to ever come up out of the Village, MC Pooh, aka Pooh Man. Pooh Man was famous for songs like *Fucking wit Dank* and *They Call Him Lex*, which was an ode to Big Bruce for wearing the diamond studded Rolex watch everywhere he went.

Fat Bruce's rising star would be shot down on his father's front porch on 72nd late one night. He would be hosed down with bullets while trying to make it up the stairs to flee his attackers. His assassination remains unsolved to this day.

His funeral was held at Oakland's most famous mortuary and funeral parlor, CP Bannon. All of his whips were lined up in front of the funeral to follow him to his final resting place; his turquoise drop Corvette, his candy burgundy 325i drop Beamer, his candy Seville, his K5 Chevy, and his Monte Carlo Goose. The females had to be pulled from his casket kicking and screaming, some even going as far as clipping locks of his orange tinted perm out of his hair for souvenirs.

In 1986, a New York Rapper by the name of Rick the Ruler had a hit song *Children's Story* that could be heard coming out of the trunks of every old school Chevy that passed by. This song would also become the prelude for a lone young hustla from the 23rd Avenue area also named Rick. This young man defied all the laws of gravity in the area and stood on the corner of 23rd and East 24th for 365 days straight until he had enough money to buy his own self a kilo. This was unheard of at the time because of the mass destruction that P-Dub was putting down around that area if someone didn't grind for him. A person was guaranteed an instant casket when they violated his code known as Hook up or Book Up.

Rick became known in Oakland as Rick the Ruler and started juggling weight all over the Town. Being the smart young man that he was, he relocated to a neighborhood nearby in the 30's and set up his headquarters on School Street and Plietner. With the help of one of his best friends Ed he got rich without ever having to hook up with any other crews.

He survived an assassination attempt on one of his friends while he was sitting in the passenger seat of a car in Funktown wearing a bulletproof vest. He was hit several times as he bounced out the car and ran away, shooting a 9 millimeter over his shoulder. His friend Bones wasn't so lucky.

Rick the Ruler holds the distinction for gracing the streets of Oakland with the cleanest drop top 5.0 ever known to man, a lime green candy '85 Ford 5.0 GT sitting on gold Daytons and Vogues.

In the early 2000s, Rick the Ruler would have to surrender himself to the Feds to serve out a seven year sentence related to a multi-count indictment that was handed down to him and several others linked together in a drug ring that was connected to the Mexican Cartel. He was given a going away party at the Serenader Club in Oakland's Lake Merritt District by Indian Tone and several others. Once he was released, he would go underground and maintain a low profile.

During the early 80s, Oakland, California was ran by African American mayors and Assemblymen and women. The political landscape was saturated with black folks. Police chiefs, school superintendents and city planners were all people of color. One of the city's most prominent mayors had a son named Stevie. Stevie used his father's connections to create a pipeline of cocaine, guns and heroin through the Port Of Oakland, the world's largest containerized port and fourth busiest in the United States. He used his father's many properties to store the dope and to distribute to his network of cells around the Town. He also bought elaborate mansions for himself in the Piedmont Hills enclave and in Lafayette, California.

When the DEA finally got tired of hearing his name ringing in the underworld, they launched an investigation into his activities and found out the mayor's son was in deeper than they thought. They followed him on luncheons with known Mafia types in a San Francisco restaurant owned by Mayor Alioto, who just by chance happened to be

Italian. Stevie knew he was being followed and would hold up the menu when he talked so they couldn't read his lips.

They finally moved in to apprehend him in a pre-dawn raid on his Piedmont mansion. No drugs were found but the Feds did locate a million dollars and a money counter inside the trunk of his girlfriend's 450 SE drop top Benz in the circular driveway. Stevie was arrested and held until his father Lionel stepped up to the plate and claimed responsibility for the money. He said it was the proceeds from the sale of one of his many properties. Stevie was released and fell off the radar.

E. Spence was another major factor that rose up out of the East Oakland neighborhood called Maxwell Park. He was a chubby little mamma's boy that got whatever he wanted as a child from beach cruiser bikes to Honda Spree mopeds when they came out.

He started his hustling career on Congress Avenue grindin' for an independent baller named Dre-Cleve. Dre was a rich young nigga that had whips lined all the way up and down his momma's driveway on Congress; a coke white Falcon on Trues and Vogues, two drop Stangs, a drop '72 Cutlass, a Suzuki Samarai truck, and a Drop ZR1 candy gold Corvette.

E. Spence and his best friend Tione hooked up with Dre and started selling rocks in front of E. Spence's apartment building. In thirty days straight they both had earned enough money to flip vehicles. E. Spence flipped a white '71 Cougnut and Tione flipped a '70 Chevy Nova.

Dre-Cleve caught a case and had to go lay down for a couple of years. He gave E. Spence the sack and a drop '71 Mustang on Star Wires and Vogues. The Mustang was the cleanest thang in the area, white with a lavender purple top. This car put E. Spence on the map in Maxwell Park.

He started posting up on 50th and Melrose with the rapper DruDown. Melrose was a hundred thousand dollar spot that different D-boys took turns gettin' knocks on. The police couldn't capture none of the block monstas because the backyards would go on for miles once one of them hit a fence.

When Dre-Cleve got out of the pen, he took E. Spence under his wing one more time and sewed the whole neighborhood up. He brought his cousin Green Eyed Keefe into the fold from North Oakland's Bushrod. Keefe was a killa. He laced E. Spence up on the murder game and created a monsta.

One day while E. Spence was on the turf, another crew of hittas from the bottom of 5-0 came thru Melrose buckin' at some other niggas and E caught a slug in the ass and lived. He promised himself from that day on that if it was any gunplay involved, he was gonna be the one behind the trigger.

Eventually, he started selling weight and got a line through some major Mec's in Jingletown, Fat Tone and Gordo. They started dumping the bricks on him like 90 goin' north. As it would turn out, the student E started to outshine the teacher, Dre. They still remained a team but now E. Spence was the man.

A few niggas tried to infiltrate the 50's and 48th, but got knocked down instantly. E. Spence was a beast behind that chopper and knew all the cuts. He would lie in the bushes for hours doing his homework on his victims, then pop out of nowhere and end their career forever. He caught his first hot one when one of the Mec's he was copping from came up slumped over the steering wheel of his Chevy. E. Spence got snatched up and sat in the Santa Rita County Jail for sixteen months fighting it with a paid attorney. The case was kicked out for a lack of evidence in a 995 hearing and he was back on the streets.

Behind his back all of his patnas referred to him as the Bone Collector, because of all the bodies he was known for having. Every time a new face popped up trying to get money, they would end up stankin courtesy of E. Spence the Bone Collector. It wasn't no secret that he was the biggest fish in the 50's pond.

He rewarded his mother with a child care center on Foothill Boulevard and Cole Street across from Fairfax Liquors and Motors. The owner of the liquor store and the luxury car dealer smelled money and took the Bone Collector under his wing and started laundering money for him and getting him any car he wanted off the lot. His sky blue ZR1 on gold BBS rims could be seen sitting in the backstreets of Maxwell Park, while he was riding on his bright yellow and white Harley Davidson through the East Oakland streets.

One night, Dre-Cleve got into a dispute with some Seminary niggas at the Vintage Inn. When he got outside, one of the cats pulled out a Mac 10. Dre-Cleve fired on the nigga and snatched it out his hand and popped him in his leg as he was running away. Later that night, Dre and the Bone Collector jumped in one of their under cars and slid down Seminary whoppin' at a crowd of niggas in front of the Vintage Inn with the same chopper he took from them. At least eight people got hit but lived. Witnesses identified both of the barefaced gunmen and they were snatched up by homicide days later and charged with seven attempted murders.

They both lawyered up instantly and fought the cases for months tooth and nail. Finally, they just paid the victims' family members not to come to court and testify. During the court dates, Dre and E would be the only ones there. After about a year, the judge finally kicked the cases out and they were free to go.

In 2005, a month after the Bone Collector had been released, he was shot in the head at point blank range while sitting in the passenger seat of his girlfriend's car waiting for her to come out of the liquor store on 50th and Bancroft Avenue. He lay in the hospital for a week until his mother finally decided to pull the plug on the life support. He is now at rest in Evergreen's Cemetery Lawn overlooking the Foothill Strip. Rest in peace E. Spence.

After the first and second generation of the Acorn Mob fizzled out, a new generation would emerge. The leader and the torch bearer of this new movement would turn out to be a jailhouse rapper that went by the acronym of MAC, which, according to the graffiti in the Santa Rita bullpens, stood for Machine guns, Artillery, and Choppers. As his notoriety would progress and he would prove to be a headbusta and a wig splitta that controlled the minds of all the remaining youths in the Cornfields, he would be called several different things such as the Elohim, or the Baldhead Scientist. MAC was a bloodthirsty strategist in the game of funkin' and ushered in a group of young killas that went by the name of the Gas Team, which was the parent crew to the Acorn Hard Hittas, the Acorn Spot Smashers, and the Baby Gas Team. Their epicenter was the Acorn hi-rizes and their influence reached all the way to Sacramento's G-Parkway and Detroit's Eight Mile Road.

MAC released a double disc music CD called the Belushi Mix, an ode to the Acorn tradition of snorting powder coke and heroin at the same time. He was featured on several nationally televised documentaries on the Discovery Channel and DVD, *The Gangs of Oakland PT. II, and HOOD 2 HOOD PT II*. These programs as well as his music CDs would fall into the hands of the OPD and they would wrap MAC up in one of the Town's biggest stings dubbed Operation Nutcracker. He would go on to receive forty-seven years to life along with his crimee Elijah for his murderous reign of terror in the Oakland streets. The Acorns have a MAC Day every year at Lowell Park in his absence. *Free the Elohim* had been the rallying cry heard throughout

West Oakland by his loyal followers.

There are too many major factors to chronicle that have came and went in the Town. These were the ones that left the biggest impact, negative or otherwise, in our illustrious town's history.

WAR

Life is like war when ya Black and ya poor
with rats and roaches crawling all over
and luck ain't involved when the world's on your shoulders.
Black women populate the earth, our sisters
see young Black men hunted from childbirth
cursed like the Pharaohs
The Big Fees, the Little Darryls
living life under a microscope
where there is life, there is hope (Stephen Hawking)
Our coping strategies consist of dope
sales or use, it's still abuse
it's still a noose, life's still reduced.
I digress, I am a Revolutionary
Police brutality's incendiary..boom
The Town
Home of Oscar Grant before he was gunned down
Fruitvale Station
slavery, segregation
wasn't all that abolished
or did we take two steps forward
then ten steps backward? Acknowledged
Queens protect Kings in freedom and exile
Dear brothers and sisters
You can't make a pet out of a reptile

CORNERSTONE

Red Walker told me personally
it started in Harbor Homes
Therefore, this huslin' and gangsta shit
is part of my chromosomes
It's also the cornerstone
of my whole life story
Allow me to introduce you
to the Fame and Glory
My life started poorly
in the streets of West Oakland
and shortly thereafter
my sister started smokin'
I was heartbroken
seeing Sis out there trippin'
Right about this same time
Green-eyed Clarence started flippin'
All I seen outside my window
was Cougars and Drop Stangs
and I was so hungry
you could probably see my fangs
That's when I decided
to hang with Grady and Charlie Rock
Sheila E wrote a song
She called us Hollyrock

ABOUT THE AUTHOR

Titus Lee Barnes is a 47-year-old Oakland, California native. He was raised during the 1970s, '80s, and '90s when crack was king and there were literally teenage millionaires on the blocks. At the age of twelve, he came off the porch to participate in a life of crime. By the age of fourteen, he was a member of a notorious drug organization in West Oakland. His street career would span three decades.

He has now put the game behind him and embarked on a career as an author. His motto is, Each one, Teach one. This is the first of his many planned novels. Stay tuned because the lessons of one are many.

CONTACT

Comments are welcome and will receive responses.

Facebook: Titus Lee Barnes

Instagram: titusleebarnes

Email: barnestlee@gmail.com

U.S. Mail:
  Julian Barnes AP9368
  Titus Lee Barnes
    PO Box 92
  Chowchilla, CA 93610

In Loving Memory
of
Felix Wayne Mitchell
1954 - 1986